IN STATU NASCENDI

JOURNAL OF POLITICAL PHILOSOPHY AND INTERNATIONAL RELATIONS

Vol. 1, No. 1 (2018)

IN STATU NASCENDI—
Journal of Political Philosophy and International Relations

In Statu Nascendi *is a new peer-reviewed journal that aspires to be a world-class scholarly platform encompassing original academic research dedicated to the circle of Political Philosophy, Cultural Studies, Theory of International Relations, Foreign Policy, and the political Decision-making process. The journal investigates specific issues through a socio-cultural, philosophical, and anthropological approach to raise a new type of civic awareness about the complexity of contemporary crisis, instability, and warfare situations, where the "stage-of-becoming" plays a vital role.*

In Statu Nascendi welcomes all types of partnership and collaboration for fostering a knowledge-based society, organizing events and framing new projects. If you are an academic institution, research institute and investigation team or group, a non-profit organization, research center, research funder and you are willing to become a long-term partner for *In Statu Nascendi*'s activities, please fill in the form, and we will get back to you as soon as we can.

For further information, please visit:
http://www.instatunascendi.com

Alternatively, you can visit our old website:
https://irinstatunascendi.wixsite.com/journal

Please send all articles, reviews, polemics, reports, and inquiries to:
irinstatunascendi@yahoo.com

Editor in chief
Piotr Pietrzak

Editorial Board & International Advisory Committee
Sophie Grace Chappell
Koumparoudis Evangelos
Maryia Lappo
Sami Mehmeti
Stavros Panayiotou
Piotr Pietrzak
Ivan Solakov
Ivan Simić
Hristiyana Stoyanova
Francesco Trupia
Nieves Turégano
Krzysztof Żegota

Proofreading:
Matthew Gill

Any views expressed in this publication are the views of the authors and are not necessarily shared by the editorial board of this journal. In Statu Nascendi *is committed to freedom, liberty, and pluralism of opinions and endeavors to contribute to unconstrained public discourse and debate on relevant social, political, and philosophical matters.*

Bibliographic information published by the Deutsche Nationalbibliothek
The Deutsche Nationalbibliothek lists this publication in the Deutsche Nationalbibliografie; detailed bibliographic data are available on the Internet at http://dnb.dnb.de.

Bibliografische Information der Deutschen Nationalbibliothek
Die Deutsche Nationalbibliothek verzeichnet diese Publikation in der Deutschen Nationalbibliografie; detaillierte bibliografische Daten sind im Internet über http://dnb.d-nb.de abrufbar.

In Statu Nascendi—Journal of Political Philosophy and International Relations
Vol. 1, No. 1 (2018)

Stuttgart: *ibidem*-Verlag / *ibidem* Press

Erscheinungsweise: halbjährlich / Frequency: biannual

ISSN 2568-7638

ISBN-13: 978-3-8382-1229-6

Ordering Information:
PRINT: Subscription (two copies per year): € 72.00 / year (+ S&H: € 4.00 / year within Germany, € 7.00 / year international). The subscription can be canceled at any time.

Single copy or back issue: € 44.00 / copy (+ S&H: € 2.00 within Germany, € 3.50 international).

E-BOOK: Individual copy or back issue: € 28.99 / copy.

For further information please visit www.ibidem.eu

© *ibidem*-Verlag / *ibidem* Press
Stuttgart, Germany 2018

Alle Rechte vorbehalten
Das Werk einschließlich aller seiner Teile ist urheberrechtlich geschützt. Jede Verwertung außerhalb der engen Grenzen des Urheberrechtsgesetzes ist ohne Zustimmung des Verlages unzulässig und strafbar. Dies gilt insbesondere für Vervielfältigungen, Übersetzungen, Mikroverfilmungen und elektronische Speicherformen sowie die Einspeicherung und Verarbeitung in elektronischen Systemen.

All rights reserved

No part of this publication may be reproduced, stored in or introduced into a retrieval system, or transmitted, in any form, or by any means (electronical, mechanical, photocopying, recording or otherwise) without the prior written permission of the publisher.
Any person who performs any unauthorized act in relation to this publication may be liable to criminal prosecution and civil claims for damages.

Printed in the EU

In statu nascendi (Latin)

In the process of creation, emerging, becoming

Table of Contents

Editorial IX

PART I:
PHILOSOPHY & THEORY OF INTERNATIONAL RELATIONS 1

John de Geus
Corporate Instrumentalization of Deliberative Democracy
in Global Governance 3

Sophie Grace Chappell
Being Transgender and Transgender Being 19

Stavros Panagiotou
A Comparative Study between Levinas and Kierkegaard on
Subjectivity and the Self 31

Maryia Lappo
Historical Truth, Fiction, and Ideology in the Novel "Каласы пад
сярпом тваім" by Uładzimir Karatkievič 45

BOOK REVIEWS

Piotr Pietrzak on Immanuel Kant's Categorical Imperative and his
"Perpetual Peace: A Philosophical Sketch" (1795) 55

Piotr Pietrzak on György Lukács: "The young Hegel: Studies in the
Relations between Dialectics and Economics" 63

Piotr Pietrzak on 'Disenchantment and Re-enchantment': Chapter 3,
The 'death of God' and the Crisis of Philosophy. Neascu, Michaela.
(2010) 'Hans J. Morgenthau's Theory of International Relation:
Disenchantment and Re-Enchantment 77

PART II:
POLITICS & INTERNATIONAL RELATIONS 83

Krzysztof Żęgota
The Kaliningrad Oblast' of the Russian Federation:
A Geopolitical Challenge for the Baltic Sea Region 85

Piotr Pietrzak
The Kremlin's Reaction to the St. Petersburg Metro Attacks
seen through the Prism of Russian Intervention in Syria 101

Piotr Pietrzak & Francesco Trupia
**Interview with Francesco Trupia
on the Nagorno-Karabakh Conflict** 117

Christina Korkontzelou, Evangelos Koumparoudis
**Was it Greece's Lost Decade (2007–2017) or just a Culmination of the
Process that has led Athens to the Brink of Economic Collapse?** 129

Stavros Panagiotou
**(Neo-)Liberalism and the Unresolved Political Problem in Cyprus:
A Philosophical Perspective** 155

Piotr Pietrzak
**Donald Trump's visit to Saudi Arabia, Saudi-Iranian Relations,
and the Future of the Iranian Nuclear Deal** 173

Hristiyana Stoyanova
The United Kingdom on the Verge of a "Constitutional Crisis" 187

BOOK REVIEWS

Piotr Pietrzak on Charles P. Webel, (2004) "Terror, Terrorism,
and the Human Condition", New York: Palgrave Macmillan......... 207

Piotr Pietrzak on Edward Luttwak on the 2016 Turkish
Coup d'État Attempt: Insights and Recommendations....................215

Call for Papers 225

Biographic Notes 227

What we stand for in fourteen different languages 231

Coming up next on In Statu Nascendi 235

Editorial

What first made you want to create a new journal? Aren't there enough new journals on the market already? What is your primary motivation? These are just a few of many similar questions that I have been recently asked, and I do agree with you completely; we owe you a proper explanation, and we do have every intention of responding to these questions with an answerable courage. Before we do so, let us first try to unravel even more critical mystery on why we chose such a distinguished name in the first place: what do we mean by "in statu nascendi"? I expect that since you have bought the first volume, you already know that depending on the translation, this Latin phrase can be understood as either in the process of creation or in the state of being born. The state of nascendi also relates to the process of disambiguation, commonly associated with the procedure of removal of ambiguity or, in another word, a clarification of even the most complicated matters at hand, liberating the hidden meaning into the hands of the curious audience. That is precisely what we stand for, by choosing such a remarkable name, we have made sure to seriously acknowledge that we are fully committed to meeting the expectations of reshuffling the stagnant market of ideas, leading the social science discourse into new, uncharted territories where the leading ideas and conventional paradigms will be challenged; and no one, no longer will dare to take them for granted.

For sure, there are many new academic journals on the publishing market at the moment. Most of them are created by people who came together because they are motivated by the notion of launching an alternative, pluralistic, and more accessible environment for the promotion of knowledge. We share this passion. Yet, the origin of the other initiatives in the field may come down to the impatience of a younger generation of academics who feel that their freedom of expression is being stifled by the monopoly of more reputable journals, as more established members of academic community tend to be quite sluggish about decisions as to whether the work of their younger colleagues should get published. Indeed, we understand that some of the traditional journals have been quite slow to open up to new ideas, to fresher perspectives and more diverse paradigms and for these reasons, one may anticipate the need for reorganizing the publishing market, but we refuse to merely self-publish and separate ourselves from this tradition. As much as we refuse to take part in the 'publish or perish' culture that diminishes academic creativity and vigour to the status of quantified metrics, impact factor, popularity that tries to assign an alphanumeric value to knowledge, we seek to replicate the best practices available in the publishing market and we endeavour to supplement and embrace all of the positives of traditional publishing, but in the meantime we intend to be more original, more diverse, more transparent, and more inclusive than any academic journal currently available on the market.

At In Statu Nascendi we are anything but dogmatic; as a matter of fact we have every intention to build this journal as a place where you can share the fruits of your work in very diverse social science areas and themes relating to the mission of our journal, but we also take pride in bringing to the fore new approaches, new dimensions, and unusual paradigms; that is why we are open to discussing matters that are related, but not confined, to foreign affairs, foreign policy, international relations theory, political theory; political philosophy, cultural studies, foreign policy, decision-making process, modern decision-making process; conflict resolution strategies, contemporary conflicts and many other aspects of the social sciences. In the future, we will supplement these discussions with matters related to the economy, sociology, and culture. Meanwhile, we do realize that we live in a globalized knowledge-based environment that does not settle for anything less than relevant, readily available information, which means that even a slight procrastination can turn our commentary into an old piece of proverbial yesterday's news. That is why we intend to be quite swift with our decisions; instead of waiting for weeks or months, we will provide you with a quick decision as to whether we are interested or not. There is a high demand for relevant analysis and verifiable information in contemporary society, and we have every intention to meet this requirement.

We aspire to turn this initiative into a world-class scholarly first point of reference in the field of social science. Therefore, we understand that there is no cutting corners in excellence and that the process of legitimizing our credentials cannot happen overnight; having said that we need to emphasize the fact that we are committed to offering something more attractive to the academic community. It is not only the end product but also an explanation as to how we got there which very often lies hidden in the process of creation, and we intend to uncover it. As much as at times we will be forced to reject certain individual manuscripts, our road towards fulfilling our high standards and high aspirations will not be marked by the loss of the sight of the human story in the process. This initiative is being built upon the belief that all voices matter when it comes to shaping the debate around the topics that will contribute to raising a new type of civic awareness about the complexity of the contemporary world, crisis, instability, and warfare situations, where the stage of becoming plays a vital role in explaining the complexity of our existence on this planet. That is why we understand that there are a lot of hurdles ahead of young researchers at the moment, and some of our colleagues just don't know how to keep up with a continually changing publishing environment. That is exactly where In Statu Nascendi is determined to step in, because we believe that by sharing our expertise and experience with those who need it the most, we will stimulate academic discourse, attract more participants into the process of credible scholarly publishing and transform this initiative into an easily approachable platform for various academics and political commentators from multiple backgrounds and stages of professional development.

We plan to trigger a debate on the topics that interest you, endeavor to review every single article that will be submitted to our journal, provide everyone with a clear feedback, and a proper guidance can enhance their work in the long run. We are established by the people and for the people, and we understand the longstanding rule **una validiores sumus et in omnia parati** that translates to together we are stronger and ready for anything. As a matter of fact it would never have materialized without the enthusiasm, hard work and professionalism of: **Ilona Ivova Anachkova, Victoria Angelova, Delyana Boyadzhieva-Pietrzak, Prof. Sophie Grace Chappell, Prof. Maria Dimitrova, Dalia Elbanna, Christina Korkontzelou, Maren Krebs, Maryia Lappo, Vaska Solakova, Hristiyana Stoyanova, Nieves Turégano, Viktoriya Wieczorek, Serap Yilmaz, Omar Ibrahim Al-Ali, Koumparoudis Evangelos, Bruno Fox, PhD John de Geus, Prof. Marcin Grabowski, PhD Błażej Grygo, Sébastien Joannès, Erkin Koray, PhD Sami Mehmeti, Stavros Panagiotou, Francesco Trupia, Ivan Solakov, PhD Ivan Simić, PhD Krzysztof Żęgota** and our proofreader **Matthew Gill,** one of the most reliable, hard-working and fearless groups of individuals I have ever had the privilege of working with, future leaders in their respective fields, who have seriously contributed to the quality of the discourse in this volume. For these reasons, on behalf of the editorial board, I would like to take this opportunity to thank them for submitting their work to the first ever issue of our newly established journal. We were humbled by your enthusiastic response to this initiative, as it has already exceeded our wildest expectations. For these reasons, we have extended offers of cooperation to them, and they have enthusiastically answered our call to join our efforts. Last but not least, I would like to add to this list: **Valerie Lange, Christian Schön, Florian Bölter** and all of the people from

***ibidem*-**Verlag responsible for printing this issue, who have helped us to reach out to our readers.

We are committed to keeping our readers updated about all of our initiatives, and publishing the next volume of this journal by the beginning of the spring of 2019. That is why we encourage our prospective authors to take part in our great adventure and submit their proposals by the end of the summer of 2018. We are open to various forms of academic discussion: scholarly articles, book reviews, interviews, political commentary, comments, polemics, etc. So please don't hesitate and email us with your proposals, I promise that we will get back to you within a reasonable amount of time.

Thank you for purchasing this volume. We hope that you enjoy it.

Yours sincerely,

Piotr Pietrzak
Editor-in-chief
In Statu Nascendi
Journal of Political Philosophy and International Relations
pietrzak@alumni.manchester.ac.uk
pietrzak_IR@hotmail.com

PART I:
PHILOSOPHY & THEORY OF INTERNATIONAL RELATIONS

John de Geus

Corporate Instrumentalization of Deliberative Democracy in Global Governance

Abstract: *In recent decades, processes of multistakeholder deliberation based on Habermas' concept of deliberative democracy have increasingly been implemented by corporations as part of their efforts to address the negative social and environmental impacts of their activities. These efforts to engage in corporate self-regulation have led to the development of multistakeholder initiatives (MSIs), which constitute governance institutions largely outside the scope of the traditional nation state. The deliberation employed by MSIs ostensibly aspires to consist in an inclusive ideal discourse not subject to power or domination in which the participants are committed to the consideration of all available evidence and alternative conceptual schemes. This article seeks to clarify the role of corporations in multistakeholder deliberation as a form of governance. An examination of existing research focusing primarily on MSIs involving small, local stakeholders as well as corporations demonstrates that the processes of deliberation fall short of the criteria for Habermasian ideal discourse. Problematic aspects of the implementation of multistakeholder deliberation include the reinforcement of local power asymmetries, lack of access to discourse, exclusion from discourse and the hegemony of corporations through mutual accommodation. Rather than seeking to engage in a discourse free from domination, corporations actively seek to dominate by maintaining power asymmetries and excluding other stakeholders from discourse. Moreover, within MSIs the processes of communicative rationality themselves are increasingly instrumentalized. Corporations' strict adherence to instrumental economic rationality furthermore prevents the consideration of alternative ideas. Corporate self-regulation through processes of multistakeholder deliberation, ostensibly meant to mitigate the negative social and environmental impact of corporate activities, thus instead appears to support the continued hegemony and exterritoriality of multinational corporations while strengthening the existing economic order.*

Keywords: Jürgen Habermas, corporate exterritoriality, Multistakeholder Initiatives, globalization, global governance, deliberative democracy, marginalization, hegemony

Introduction

The nation state is increasingly deprived of its traditional bases of sovereign power, as economic processes, modes of communication, culture, and risk all become more globalized (Habermas, 2001). The power of the nation state is thereby diminishing in relation to the power of multinational corporations (Bauman, Globalization: The Human Consequences, 1998; Palazzo & Scherer, 2006; van Tulder, 2011). In such a globalized world, multinational corporations are confronted with a multiplicity of often contradictory moral and legal demands. Issues of corporate responsibility demonstrate a higher degree of complexity at the international level in comparison with similar questions at the national level (van Tulder & van der Zwart, 2006, p. 284). In order to deal with this complex mix of societal demands, multinational corporations are replacing the more traditional approach of implicit compliance regarding consensual societal norms with explicit participation in public processes of deliberation and justification, as embodied in multistakeholder initiatives (MSIs). In doing so, corporations take on a political role as they engage in a form of global governance through voluntary self-regulation. While some scholars have hailed this as a positive development, others are more critical, asserting that these processes of multistakeholder deliberation are in fact utilized to strengthen the hegemony of multinational corporations and maintain the existing economic order, while removing matters of governance from the sphere of the nation state.

This article seeks to clarify the role of corporations in multistakeholder deliberation as a form of governance, in particular where existing research identifies potential problems with regard to the manner in which corporations engage in this form of deliberative democracy. This article first presents the notion of multinational corporations as exterritorial actors in a globalized world in which the power of the nation state is diminishing. It then discusses the political role of corporations as agents of a new form of global governance through self-regulation which largely bypasses the nation state, with a focus on multistakeholder initiatives as instruments of governance employing a form of deliberative democracy that reflects the ideas of Jürgen Habermas. This article then goes on to present Habermas' theory of deliberative democracy, intended to be a means for preventing the colonization of the Habermasian 'lifeworld' by the instrumental rationality of the 'system'. Next, this article provides an overview of existing research on the role of corporations in multistakeholder deliberation, with a focus on problematic aspects that stand in opposition to Habermas' criteria for ideal discourse. Finally, the role of corporations in multistakeholder deliberation as a form of governance is discussed, as well as the broader implications thereof.

Corporate Exterritoriality and the Decline of the Nation State

Because they operate on a global playing field, multinational corporations can choose from various legal systems (Roach, 2005; Scherer & Palazzo, 2007; Scherer & Palazzo, 2011; Scherer, Palazzo, & Baumann, 2006). They are able to move production sites and financial investments to wherever the local laws are the most hospitable, to take advantage of local systems that are not well-adapted to the provision of corporate regulation and even to play legal systems against each other. When selecting a physical location, such as a production site, they can select the combination of labor regulations, social regulations and environmental regulations that is most suitable to their economic criteria (Roach, 2005; Scherer & Palazzo, 2007; Scherer & Palazzo, 2011; Scherer, Palazzo, & Baumann, 2006). National governments, in turn, are keen to attract capital with low taxes, few rules (deregulation) and a flexible labor market (Bauman, 2000, p. 150). This dynamic thereby pressures developing countries into a 'race to the bottom' by investing in those countries that offer the most favorable conditions in terms of low tax rates and low levels of environmental regulation and restrictions on workers' rights (Crane & Matten, 2010, p. 18). The competing attempts by national governments to attract and/or retain corporations by offering subsidies, favorable tax conditions, investments and cutbacks on regulations can potentially lead to a downward spiral in social and environmental conditions at the level of global governance (Roach, 2005; Scherer & Smid, 2000).

As multinational corporations increasingly operate beyond the reach of individual nation states, the nation states themselves are increasingly unable to provide public goods and regulate business activities (Beck, 2000, p. 14; Habermas, 2001, p. 68–80; Scherer & Palazzo, 2011). Capital and global finance take advantage of a proliferation of weak nation states that only have enough power to maintain sufficient order needed for the conduct of business, but do not have the power to limit the free movement of capital (Bauman, 1998, p. 65–69).

The Rise of Governance by Corporations

While governance at the national level consists in the nation state's monopoly on the use of force, together with its capacity to enforce regulations within its territory, governance at the global level relies on voluntary contributions and mechanisms of enforcement that are either weak or non-existent (Scherer

& Palazzo, 2011). Global governance, which can be viewed as the process of defining and implementing global rules and providing global public goods, is a polycentric and multilateral process to which governments, international institutions, civil society groups and business firms contribute knowledge and resources (Detomasi, 2007; Scherer & Palazzo, 2011).

Rendtorff (2010) asserts that, in their effort to be seen as legitimate by society, corporations have become private political actors. Corporations are therefore not just economic agents, but also take a political stance and participate in policy-making (ibid., p. 23). In recent decades multinational corporations have thereby started to perform activities that were traditionally viewed as being the role of governments (Matten & Crane, 2005; Scherer & Palazzo, 2011). These corporate activities contribute to global regulation and the provision of public goods (Scherer & Palazzo, 2011). Corporations are active in the areas of public health, social security, education and human rights protection, particularly in countries with failed state agencies (ibid.). Also, some corporations engage in environmental protection (Marcus & Fremeth, 2009) and some work to promote societal peace and stability (Fort & Schipani, 2004). Additionally, some engage with social issues such as homelessness, illiteracy, and malnutrition (Margolis & Walsh, 2003). Finally, multinational corporations define ethics codes and engage in self-regulation where there are global gaps in legal regulation and moral orientation (Scherer & Smid, 2000). As part of their efforts to engage in what is often referred to as 'corporate social responsibility', 'corporate citizenship' and/or 'corporate sustainability', corporations thus assume social and political responsibilities that extend well beyond existing national regulatory requirements. Some scholars assert that such attempts at private governance have produced meaningful cooperation to solve global problems (Haas, 2015).

The cumulative efforts of corporations to engage in self-regulation have led to the emergence of governance institutions and procedures which are mostly outside the scope of the nation state (Matten & Crane, 2005; Palazzo & Scherer, 2006; Scherer & Palazzo, 2007; Scherer & Palazzo, 2011; Scherer, Rasche, Palazzo, & Spicer, 2016; Ronit & Schneider, 1999). Such transnational governance institutions are increasingly taking the form of multistakeholder initiatives (henceforth referred to as MSIs), which seek to address social and/or environmental issues through soft law regulation (Baumann-Pauly, Nolan, van Heerden, & Samway, 2016; Cheyns & Riisgaard, Introduction to the symposium: The exercise of power through multistakeholder initiatives for sustainable agriculture and its inclusion and exclusion outcomes, 2014; Mena & Palazzo, 2012; Rasche, 2012).

Ostensibly to develop solutions to the negative social and environmental consequences of globalized corporate business activities, MSIs engage in processes of multistakeholder deliberation involving corporations, NGOs and other stakeholder groups (Mena & Palazzo, 2012). A number of scholars argue that MSIs can be seen as manifestations of a type of corporate social responsibility that is inherently political, whereby multinational corporations engage in a form of deliberative democracy developed by philosopher Jürgen Habermas (Palazzo & Scherer, 2006; Scherer & Palazzo, 2007; Scherer & Palazzo, 2011; Scherer, Rasche, Palazzo, & Spicer, 2016). An inventory compiled in 2012 lists a total of 37 separate MSIs active in areas of regulation such as sustainable forest management, fair working conditions, sustainability reporting, mining, fair trade, finance, human rights, and supply chains in agricultural production (Mena & Palazzo, 2012). Many of these MSIs affect small stakeholders at the local level. Examples of MSIs include the Forest Stewardship Council (FSC), the Global Initiative on Fiscal Transparency (GIFT), the Marine Stewardship Council (MSC), the Extractive Industries Transparency Initiative (EITI), the Roundtable on Sustainable Palm Oil (RSPO), the United Nations Global Compact (UNGC) and the Global Reporting Initiative (GRI).

Habermas: Deliberative Democracy and the Colonization Thesis

As a second-generation member of the Frankfurt School, Habermas develops his concept of deliberative democracy as a means for progressing towards the goal pursued by Critical Theory, which he considers to be "a form of life free from unnecessary domination in all its forms" (McCarthy, 1984, p. 7). Habermas' concept of deliberative democracy builds on his theories of communicative rationality and discourse ethics, and entails popular participation in a discourse that is not subject to power or domination. Such an 'ideal discourse' is unequivocally committed to the consideration of all available evidence and, if necessary, alternative conceptual schemes (West, 2010, p. 81–82). Moral claims are only valid if there is a rational and unconstrained consensus among all the participants, who are thereby, subject only to the "unforced force of the better argument" (Habermas, 1996, p. 306). Consensus is always provisional, as new evidence, new ideas and new participants may enter the discourse (West, 2010, p. 82).

Deliberative democracy assumes that legitimate political decisions are based on public deliberation. According to Habermas, legitimacy is derived from the "institutionalization of those discursive processes of opinion and will-formation in which the sovereignty of the people assumes a binding character" (Habermas, 1996, p. 104). Political legitimacy is based on three aspects: "a general analysis of the institutional design of discursive arenas, the procedural design of public will formation and the analysis of those discourses that develop within those arenas of will-formation and are synthesized into 'bundles of topically specified public opinions', echoing the problems of citizens" (ibid., p. 360). Civil society organizations are key actors in this process (ibid., p. 367). Such a shift of political decision-making from political institutions to actors in civil society has been described as "subpolitics" (Beck, 1992, p. 223) and "globalization from below" (Beck, 2000, p. 68).

With his concept of deliberative democracy, Habermas seeks to further the goal of Critical Theory and counteract the increasing dominance of bureaucratic power and money in modern society. In Habermas' view, the Enlightenment has maintained an undue focus on instrumental rationality, or 'purposive-rational action', which simply works to "realize defined goals under given conditions" and includes instrumental action, or labor, and strategic action, which is calculative in nature and does not question the validity of the values that underpin it (Habermas, 1972, p. 314, as cited in West, p. 73). Purposive-rational action thus concerns itself with instrumental control over objects and people, and the Enlightenment's excessive focus on it has contributed to an oppressive social reality consisting in various forms of domination. In contrast, communicative action arises from human intersubjectivity and "provides a pragmatic context for the interpretation and validation of moral norms" (West, 2010, p. 74). This context forms the basis for the development of a communicative rationality which can counterbalance the prevailing instrumental rationality with the "discursive validation of norms governing relations between subjects" (ibid.).

The juxtaposition of instrumental rationality and communicative rationality is one of purposive-rational action, acting through a 'system' of (bureaucratic) power and money, versus communicative action, consisting in a 'lifeworld' of meaning and culture expressing norms and values (Finlayson, 2005, p. 56–61). Public will-formation, embodied in a thriving public sphere situated in the lifeworld, is essential for two reasons: first, to allow alternative views and their associated ethics to be debated, and second, to ensure that these alternative views and their associated ethics actively guide the application of instrumental rationality (Edward & Willmott, 2011). Habermasian deliberative democracy is thus designed to facilitate public will-formation through ideal discourse, as a means for ensuring the robustness of the lifeworld and counterbalancing the economic instrumentality of the system.

Habermas asserts that in modern societies, the lifeworld is being 'colonized' by the system as systemic mechanisms increasingly suppress forms of social integration (Habermas, 1985, p. 196). Supposedly universal values are thereby supplanted by technocratic consciousness (West, 2010, p. 79). This concern is echoed by Flyvbjerg (1992), who asserts that 'value rationality,' defined as the ability to collectively pose, answer and act upon value-rational questions such as 'Where are we going?', 'Who gains, who loses?', 'Is it desirable?' and 'What should be done?', has increasingly become dominated by instrumental rationality, resulting in a "civilization of means without ends" (ibid.). Flyvbjerg posits that in today's globalized world, value rationality is nevertheless needed more than ever before, as the future of life on earth has become contingent upon man's own actions (ibid.).

Corporations and the Implementation of Deliberative Democracy in MSIs

This section examines existing research in order to identify problematic aspects of the implementation of deliberative democracy by corporations in settings of multistakeholder deliberation. In particular, this section focuses on aspects that stand in opposition to Habermas' criteria for ideal discourse. The bulk of the existing research focuses on MSIs in which the processes of deliberation involve and/or affect small, local stakeholders such as farmers and indigenous tribes. Potentially problematic aspects concerning the implementation of multistakeholder deliberation include the reinforcement of local power asymmetries, marginalization of small stakeholders, exclusion from discourse and the hegemony of corporations through mutual accommodation.

Reinforcement of Local Power Asymmetries

In their analysis of multistakeholder initiatives for sustainable agriculture, Cheyns and Riisgaard (2014) assert that MSI standards, which are usually presented as being neutral and objective, are necessarily implemented in contexts of local political and economic power asymmetries. When these contexts are ignored, MSI regulation tends to reinforce these inequalities. For example, in an examination of the Roundtable for Sustainable Palm Oil (RSPO), which concerns itself with land conflicts in Indonesia related to palm oil production, Köhne (2014) finds that local power inequalities and related access to resources to a significant extent determine the possibilities that stakeholders have to use the rules of the RSPO to their advantage. Corporations, which occupy a position of power, enjoy direct influence within the

RSPO and are able to leverage its procedures to strengthen their negotiating position in the numerous land conflicts with rural communities. Meanwhile, the local farmers who constitute these communities are only able to access the RSPO and its procedures indirectly by engaging in an elaborate collaboration with local and international NGOs and are thereby hindered in their attempts to seek justice in the land conflicts (ibid.). While the RSPO's procedures ostensibly constitute a fair and ethical discourse which results in a technical, apolitical consensus, the consensus reached often continues to obscure the existing power asymmetries and the accompanying structural inequalities within the RSPO (Cheyns & Riisgaard, Introduction to the symposium: The exercise of power through multi-stakeholder initiatives for sustainable agriculture and its inclusion and exclusion outcomes, 2014).

When local power asymmetries are reflected within the structure of the MSI, the processes of deliberation are not free from domination and therefore do not approach Habermas' ideal form of deliberative democracy. The focus on economic solutions within the MSI thereby limits the ability of small stakeholders to address structural inequalities within the MSI. One can posit that any 'consensus' reached within such an MSI will tend to favor economic solutions that benefit the participating corporations and serve to maintain their privileged access to resources while limiting that access for others. Furthermore, their direct access to the MSI gives corporations an advantage in land conflicts with local stakeholders. The existence of the MSI and MSI standards, therefore, may not be effective at deterring corporations from appropriating land and initiating new land conflicts.

Marginalization of Small Stakeholders

The Forest Stewardship Council (FSC), a certification scheme for sustainable forestry, has been presented as an exemplary MSI engaging in an effective, pragmatic application of Habermasian deliberative democracy (Scherer & Palazzo, 2007; Scherer & Palazzo, 2011). However, some argue that the FSC employs a superficial, instrumental rationality that does not seek to promote conditions for ethical discourse in the manner intended by Habermas (Edward & Willmott, 2011). This critical view asserts that the FSC's processes and procedures of multistakeholder deliberation, in fact, reflect "…a triumph of system <…> over the lifeworld" (ibid.). The instrumental rationality employed by the FSC privileges stakeholders such as certification bodies and commercial clients while simultaneously marginalizing small local stakeholders, such as NGOs, timber industry workers and (indigenous) communities, which simply do not have the resources to access the FSC's increasingly complex processes and procedures (Moog, Spicer, & Böhm, 2015).

Additionally, the FSC's standards have weakened over time in response to pressure from neoliberal market forces, prompting some civil society organizations to cease their involvement in the MSI out of concern for their reputation (Edward & Willmott, 2011; Moog, Spicer, & Böhm, 2015). Moog et al. (2015) go on to posit that the existence of MSIs like the FSC may bolster the overall hegemony of neoliberal governmentality and concomitant privatization of regulatory authority, legitimizing the withdrawal of nation states from responsibility for global environmental issues.

As local stakeholders suffer from de facto exclusion from discourse due to lack of resources, privileged commercial stakeholders are able to dominate deliberation and standard-setting within the FSC. As the FSC's instrumental rationality does not appear to provide adequate space for deliberation about values, it seems unlikely that the instrumental rationality itself will be questioned.

Practices of Exclusion from Discourse

On the basis of a case study on deliberation about the construction of a waste-producing pulp mill in Chile, Ehrnström-Fuentes (2016) argues that in processes of multistakeholder deliberation, that which is generally perceived as legitimate by corporations is based on the assumption that the 'modernity' emerging from Europe through globalization is superior and should be universally applied. However, compared to corporations, local stakeholders often have a very different worldview originating from a different 'social imaginary' (Castoriadis, 1987). The modern perspective considers such local worldviews to be unreasonable and thus illegitimate, and therefore systematically excludes them from deliberation (Ehrnström-Fuentes, 2016). In this manner, corporations can conveniently ignore local stakeholders whose radically differing social imaginaries would make consensus impossible. Corporations can nevertheless continue to claim that their actions are legitimate since they are engaging in supposedly apolitical multistakeholder deliberation.

Local stakeholders can thus be excluded from discourse a priori for merely having a worldview that differs the mainstream economic worldview held by corporations. These local stakeholders are labeled as being unreasonable, in a manner that reflects Foucault's concept of the 'division of madness'. In this method of exclusion, an individual is declared to be mad, and the spoken words of that individual are henceforth simply ignored as nonsense, thus excluding the individual from discourse (Foucault, 1996, p. 340–341).

Other research focusing specifically on MSIs that govern sustainable agriculture finds that these MSIs generally employ technical legal and statistical language which is considered to be the only legitimate form of knowledge within the MSI (Cheyns & Riisgaard, Introduction to the symposium: The exercise of power through multi-stakeholder initiatives for sustainable agriculture and its inclusion and exclusion outcomes, 2014). Local stakeholders, such as workers and farmers, and local communities in general, nevertheless present their views using other forms of knowledge, such as personal testimonies and local features that act as physical markers. Such non-technical input by local stakeholders is immediately dismissed as illegitimate (Cheyns, 2014; Nelson & Tallontire, 2014; Selfa, Bain, & Moreno, 2014; Silva-Castañeda, 2015). This a priori dismissal of alternative forms of knowledge prevents any attempt to critically discuss which forms of knowledge should actually be considered legitimate within the MSI, thus permanently preventing any attempt at deliberation that does not employ the 'proper' technical language (Nelson & Tallontire, 2014; Silva-Castañeda, 2015). Sustainability standards resulting from such limited deliberation support solutions with optimum economic effects, which take the form of intensive agro-industrial production. Alternative solutions which are unlikely to maximize economic returns, such as alternative small-scale production and diversified production, and the possibilities for local farmers to engage in such alternative forms of production, are excluded from consideration and therefore not supported by the MSI's standards (Cheyns, 2011; Nelson & Tallontire, 2014).

In this example, one can posit that knowledge must meet specific criteria set by modern disciplines such as law and economics, since only statements that conform to the specific technical legal and statistical language employed by these disciplines are considered to be legitimate. This reflects Foucault's notion of the 'will to truth' as a system of exclusion, which argues that disciplines constitute systems of control in the production of discourse and exclude those viewpoints that do not meet their conditions (Foucault, 1996, p. 347–349). In this Foucauldian perspective, power and knowledge are interrelated concepts and discourse, as a means of creating and spreading knowledge, has the potential to affect power relations. Actors work to maintain existing power relations by controlling and organizing discourse through rules of exclusion, thereby limiting the proliferation of a great variety of discourse (Foucault, 1996, p. 340–350). Either by dismissing stakeholders outright by labelling them unreasonable or even mad, or by dismissing their statements for not conforming to specific forms of technical language, corporations thus exert power to maintain their dominant position within the processes of multistakeholder deliberation. This is far removed from Habermas' notion of an ideal discourse that is not subject to power or domination, committed to the consideration of all available evidence and open to alternative conceptual schemes.

Hegemony of Corporations through Mutual Accommodation
Based on their longitudinal study of the development of standards for sustainable coffee, Levy, Reinecke, & Manning (2016) find that processes of multistakeholder deliberation can be subject to strategically motivated political dynamics between participating corporations and civil society organizations, whereby the corporations are dominant actors because they have greater resources. These processes attain a state of hegemonic stability in which the dominant actors are accommodated economically, politically and ideologically by subordinate actors. New participants in a particular discourse may initially engage in a disruptive dynamic as they seek to unbalance the hegemonic stability, which is then followed by an accommodative dynamic in which all participants in the discourse make strategic concessions. This accommodative dynamic leads to a convergence in positions in a manner similar to Gramsci's process of 'passive revolution' (Gramsci, 2007, p. 252). Nevertheless, despite the concessions made by all participants in discourse, the eventual state reached by this process of disruption and mutual accommodation continues to privilege the corporations as dominant actors, and the situation of hegemonic stability remains unchanged. The democratic appearance of multistakeholder negotiations is thus upheld while the existing power inequalities are maintained (Levy, Reinecke, & Manning, 2016).

As both dominant and subordinate actors engage in strategic action during the deliberation process, the consensus reached is constrained by each actor's attempt to gain and/or maintain power and influence. Consensus is thus not based solely on the 'unforced force of the better argument.' Furthermore, subordinate actors such as civil society organizations accommodate the hegemony of corporations, which in turn follow the rules of capitalist economics. Since corporations, as dominant actors, and hegemons, to a large extent, determine what is possible within the processes of multistakeholder deliberation, subordinate actors have little choice but to follow the same capitalist economic logic.

Discussion

As a Critical Theorist, Habermas develops his ideas with the utopian goal of eradicating all forms of unnecessary domination and halting the colonization of the lifeworld, where moral norms arise from human intersubjectivity, by the economic instrumentality of the system. Deliberative democracy must then take the form of an ideal discourse that is not subject to power or domination, is committed to the consideration of all available evidence and remains open to alternative conceptual schemes. Although an ideal discourse can never be fully attained in practice, assertions by some scholars that multistakeholder deliberation, as a form of 'political corporate social responsibility', engages specifically in *Habermasian* deliberative democracy (Scherer & Palazzo, 2007; Scherer & Palazzo, 2011; Scherer, Rasche, Palazzo, & Spicer, 2016), nevertheless imply that the stakeholders involved in processes of deliberation make every effort to conform to these criteria.

The existing research examined in this article provides evidence of processes of multistakeholder deliberation that fall significantly short of the Habermasian ideal. Large corporate stakeholders generally enjoy a dominant position which they actively strive to maintain, either by excluding other stakeholders from discourse or by accommodating them so long as they remain subordinate. Rather than seeking to engage in a discourse free from domination, corporations actively seek to dominate. Moreover, by requiring the use of technical (legal, statistical, economic) language, a subtle 'rule of exclusion,' large stakeholders can work to limit the variety of discourse. Rather than demonstrating a commitment to consider all available evidence, they can then instead ignore any non-technical evidence which other stakeholders attempt to introduce into deliberation. Additionally, adherence to a primarily instrumental economic rationality precludes any consideration of alternative rationalities and non-economic conceptual schemes, as well as deliberation about values. Where corporations are dominant, smaller stakeholders have little choice but to follow the same economic logic.

One can conclude that the processes of multistakeholder deliberation examined in this article represent an economically instrumentalized version of deliberative democracy that appears to consist primarily in instrumental and strategic action, which together comprise the 'purposive-rational action' of the system and not the 'communicative action' of the lifeworld. Taken together, this appears to represent a further colonization of the lifeworld by the system, which runs contrary to what Habermas aims to achieve with his concept of deliberative democracy. Since MSIs represent a form of global governance, one can argue that this contributes to the global spread of an economically oriented technocratic consciousness at the cost of global social integration and universal values. Additionally, nation states may be tempted to withdraw from their responsibility to engage with social and environmental issues as corporations are increasingly seen to be assuming responsibility by engaging in self-regulation through MSIs. Such a dynamic would appear to support the continued hegemony and exterritoriality of multinational corporations while strengthening the existing economic order.

Bibliography

Bauman, Z. (1998). *Globalization: The Human Consequences.* Cambridge: Polity Press.

Bauman, Z. (2000). *Liquid Modernity.* Cambridge: Polity.

Baumann-Pauly, D., Nolan, J., van Heerden, A., & Samway, M. (2016). Industry-specific multi-stakeholder initiatives that govern human rights standards: Legitimacy assessments of the Fair Labor Association and the Global Network Initiative. *Journal of Business Ethics*, 1–17.

Beck, U. (1992). *Risk Society: Towards a New Modernity.* London: Sage.

Beck, U. (2000). *What is Globalization?* Cambridge: Polity Press.

Castoriadis, C. (1987). *The Imaginary Institution of Society.* Cambridge: Polity Press.

Cheyns, E. (2011). Multi-stakeholder initiatives for sustainable agriculture: Limits of the 'inclusiveness' paradigm. In S. Ponte, P. Gibbon, & J. Vestergaard (Eds.), *Governing through Standards: Origins, Drivers and Limitations* (p. 318–354). London: Palgrave.

Cheyns, E. (2014). Making "minority voices" heard in transnational roundtables: The role of local NGOs in reintroducing justice and attachments. *Agriculture and Human Values, 31*(3), 439–453.

Cheyns, E., & Riisgaard, L. (2014). Introduction to the symposium: The exercise of power through multi-stakeholder initiatives for sustainable agriculture and its inclusion and exclusion outcomes. *Agriculture and Human Values, 31*, 409–423.

Crane, A., & Matten, D. (2010). *Business Ethics: Managing Corporate Citizenship and Sustainability in the Age of Globalization* (3rd ed.). Oxford: Oxford University Press.

Detomasi, D. A. (2007). The multinational corporation and global governance: Modelling global public policy networks. *Journal of Business Ethics, 71*(3), 321–334.

Edward, P., & Willmott, H. C. (2011, August). Political corporate social responsibility: Between deliberation and radicalism. *SSRN Electronic Journal.*

Ehrnström-Fuentes, M. (2016). Delinking legitimacies: A pluriversal perspective on political CSR. *Journal of Management Studies, 53*(3), 433–462.

Finlayson, J. G. (2005). *Habermas: A Very Short Introduction*. Oxford: Oxford University Press.

Flyvbjerg, B. (1992). Aristotle, Foucault and progressive phronesis: Outline of an applied ethics for sustainable development. *Planning Theory, 7*(8), 489–507.

Fort, T. L., & Schipani, C. A. (2004). *The Role of Business in Fostering Peaceful Societies*. Cambridge: Cambridge University Press.

Foucault, M. (1996). The Discourse on Language. In R. Kearney, & M. Rainwater (Eds.), *The Continental Philosophy Reader* (p. 339–360). London and New York: Routledge.

Gramsci, A. (2007). *Prison Notebooks* (Vol. 3). (J. A. Buttigieg, Ed.) New York: Columbia University Press.

Haas, P. M. (2015). Post hegemonic global governance. *Japanese Journal of Political Science, 16*(3), 434–441.

Habermas, J. (1972). *Knowledge and Human Interests*. (J. J. Shapiro, Trans.) London: Heinemann.

Habermas, J. (1985). *The Theory of Communicative Action, Volume 2: Lifeworld and System: A Critique of Functionalist Reason*. (T. McCarthy, Trans.) Boston: Beacon Press.

Habermas, J. (1996). *Between Facts and Norms: Contributions to a Discourse Theory of Law and Democracy*. (W. Rehg, Trans.) Cambridge, MA: MIT Press.

Habermas, J. (2001). *The Postnational Constellation: Political Essays*. (M. Pensky, Ed., & M. Pensky, Trans.) Cambridge, Massachusetts: The MIT Press.

Köhne, M. (2014). Multi-stakeholder initiative governance as assemblage: Roundtable on Sustainable Palm Oil as a political resource in land conflicts related to oil palm plantations. *Agriculture and Human Values, 31*(3), 469–480.

Levy, D., Reinecke, J., & Manning, S. (2016). The political dynamics of sustainable coffee: Contested value regimes and the transformation of sustainability. *Journal of Management Studies, 53*(3), 364–401.

Marcus, A. A., & Fremeth, A. R. (2009). Strategic direction and management. In R. Staib (Ed.), *Business Management and Environmental Stewardship: Environmental Thinking as a Prelude to Management Action* (p. 38–55). Basingstoke: Palgrave Macmillan.

Margolis, J. D., & Walsh, J. P. (2003). Misery loves companies: Rethinking social initiatives by business. *Administrative Science Quarterly, 48*(2), 268–305.

Matten, D., & Crane, A. (2005). Corporate citizenship: Toward an extended theoretical conceptualization. *The Academy of Management Review, 30*(1), 166–179.

McCarthy, T. (1984). *The Critical Theory of Jürgen Habermas.* Cambridge: Polity.

Mena, S., & Palazzo, G. (2012). Input and output legitimacy of multi-stakeholder initiatives. *Business Ethics Quarterly, 22*(3), 527–556.

Moog, S., Spicer, A., & Böhm, S. (2015). The politics of multi-stakeholder initiatives: The crisis of the Forest Stewardship Council. *Journal of Business Ethics, 128*(3), 469–493.

Nelson, V., & Tallontire, A. (2014). Battlefields of ideas: Changing narratives and power dynamics in private standards in global agricultural value chains. *Agriculture and Human Values, 31*(3), 481–497.

Palazzo, G., & Scherer, A. G. (2006). Corporate legitimacy as deliberation: A communicative framework. *Journal of Business Ethics, 66*, 71–88.

Rasche, A. (2012). Global policies and local practice: Loose and tight couplings in multi-stakeholder Initiatives. *Business Ethics Quarterly, 22*(4), 679–708.

Rendtorff, J. D. (2010). Philosophy of management: Concepts of management from the perspectives of systems theory, phenomenological hermeneutics, corporate religion, and existentialism. In P. Koslowski (Ed.), *Elements of a Philosophy of Management and Organization* (p. 19–44). Berlin: Springer.

Roach, B. (2005). A primer on multinational corporations. In A. D. Chandler, & B. Mazlish (Eds.), *Leviathans: Multinational corporations and the new global history* (p. 19–44). Cambridge: Cambridge University Press.

Ronit, K., & Schneider, V. (1999). Global governance through private organizations. *Governance: An International Journal of Policy and Administration, 12*, 243–266.

Scherer, A. G., & Palazzo, G. (2007). Towards a political conception of corporate social responsibility: Business and society seen from a Habermasian perspective. *Academy of Management Review, 32*(4), 1096–1120.

Scherer, A. G., & Palazzo, G. (2011). The new political role of business in a globalized world: A review of a new perspective on CSR and its implications for the firm, governance, and democracy. *Journal of Management Studies, 48*(4), 899–931.

Scherer, A. G., & Smid, M. (2000). The downward spiral and the US model business principles-Why MNEs should take responsibility for the improvement of world-wide social and environmental conditions. *Management International Review*, 351–371.

Scherer, A. G., Palazzo, G., & Baumann, D. (2006). Global rules and private actors: Toward a new role of the transnational corporation in global governance. *Business Ethics Quarterly, 16*(4), 505–532.

Scherer, A. G., Rasche, A., Palazzo, G., & Spicer, A. (2016, May). Managing for political corporate social responsibility: New challenges and directions for PCSR 2.0. *Journal of Management Studies, 53*(3), 273–298.

Selfa, T., Bain, C., & Moreno, R. (2014). Depoliticizing land and water "grabs" in Colombia: the limits of Bonsucro certification for enhancing sustainable biofuel practices. *Agriculture and Human Values, 31*(3), 455–468.

Silva-Castañeda, L. (2015). What kind of space? Multi-stakeholder initiatives and the protection of land rights. *International Journal of Sociology of Agriculture & Food, 22*(2), 67–83.

van Tulder, R. (2011). With Great Power Comes Great Responsibility. *With Great Power Comes Great Responsibility: Fourth Max Havelaar Lecture* (p. 17–58). Rotterdam: Max Havelaar Lecture Series.

van Tulder, R., & van der Zwart, A. (2006). *International Business-Society Management.* Abingdon: Routledge.

West, D. (2010). *Continental Philosophy: An Introduction* (2nd ed.). Cambridge: Polity Press.

Sophie Grace Chappell

Being Transgender and Transgender Being

It starts in Eden where everything starts, in the unconsciously-known of early childhood. It starts out as the snake hidden in the garden; the thing about yourself that you know and don't know, can't avoid but can't admit, can't ever say but can't honestly gainsay either.

Self-knowledge is extremely hard when there is something about yourself that no one around you wants you to know, and that you yourself are trying as hard as you can not to know. You do not want to know it, simply because it is so wrong: so strange, so unexpected, so contrary to everything that you've been taught and told ever since you had ears at all. Above all (and the younger you are the more this matters), it's so deeply embarrassing.

But there, inescapably, it is. You have the body of a male; you want to have the body of a female. You want to be female, and you want everything that goes with being female.

You want to be a woman: is it that it, though? Do you want to be a woman, or do you just ("just"?) want to dress as a woman? Is it about your sex—femaleness, the actual physical body? Or is it about your gender—femininity, the social role? Do you want to dress and present feminine as a means to the end of being female (or getting as close to it as you can)? Or do you want to be female as a means to the end of dressing and presenting as feminine (again, as far as possible)?

In everything I say here, I can only speak authoritatively for one transgender person: myself. But for me, it was, and is, both changing gender as a means to changing sex, and changing sex as a means to changing gender. I wanted to be feminine in order to be female, and I wanted to be female in order to be feminine. It ran in both directions. It still does.

And is it nature or nurture? What trauma or hormone triggered it? Was it the wrong mix in the chemical brew of the womb, or was it too many Saturday mornings spent covertly reading Ballet Shoes instead of Biggles? Was it in my parents or in my DNA? I find these questions as unanswerable as "Who started it?" about the Eden narrative.

What made me transgender? What made you cisgender?

When I was small, I had magical beliefs about clothing. The more emphatically "feminine" it was—by which I meant: the pinker, the frillier, the prettier, the girlier—the more power I believed it would have to make me female. Putting it on was, in all sorts of senses, magical. Like Frodo putting on a Ring of Power, I became my invisible self, the me that no one could ever be allowed to see. Dressing feminine defined me, I then believed, as feminine. After all, I thought, that was how it worked for my sister: didn't my parents define her as a girl by the way they dressed her? But there wasn't the slightest hope that my parents would ever do the same for me. (I knew this. I'd asked.) So, I thought, I'd better try to do it for myself. It wasn't like I had any other magic wand to wave.

Secret time spent dressed feminine was time off from public being masculine. And that was always a huge relief. Dressing masculine was a weariness to the spirit: it made me feel tired, ugly, constrained, trapped, suffocated, awkward, wrong. It still does. But dressing feminine was, simply, a delight: it brought a sense of serene, calm, happy, relaxed, floating-away euphoria that nothing else gave me, a simple and straightforward innocent childlike joy; just a sense of rightness. It still does.

Except dressing feminine didn't just do that—as any avid reader of Tolkien might have predicted. (And I was an avid reader of Tolkien. Given the uncanny fit between his myth and my own phenomenology, I have sometimes wondered what he had in his closet.) Being transgender may be euphoria, but it is also, as they say, dysphoria. Rings of Power are addictive, Tolkien taught me, and the addiction is evil and destructive. The more you give in to it, the more it turns you into—something different. But not into a beautiful girl. Into an evil spirit either squalidly pathetic or satanically terrifying or both: into Gollum, or a ring-wraith. I could get very afraid about where all this was going, what I was doing to myself, where it might be heading if I let it… and I so wanted to let it.

For most people, the teenage years are probably the high season for guilt, and they certainly were for me. But I felt guilty long before I hit adolescence because everyone and everything around me was telling me that little boys were simply not supposed to be the way I knew quite well I was: the way I kept finding I simply couldn't help being. So I felt guilt, and I felt just plain puzzlement. Why could girls wear boring old clingy dull-colored trousers if they liked, when boys couldn't wear pretty floaty primary-color skirts and dresses if they liked? Why could a girl put on my soldier outfit to play in, and get chuckles and smiles of approval and pats on the head, whereas if I put on her ballet tutu to play in, it was like I'd been caught trying to blow up Westminster Abbey?

A girl who wants to be a boy is a tomboy, I read in The Famous Five. Right, I said when I first read that, all excited ("Perhaps after all people do have words for what I'm like," I was thinking)—so what is the word for a boy who wants to be a girl?

My peers at school answered that for me, bluntly and in chorus and repeatedly, for the next fourteen years. (They didn't know about me, of course, not officially; for a start, I didn't have the words to tell them, even if I'd been kamikaze enough to want them to know—I didn't even learn the word "transgender" till I was 36. Yet their trans-radars were in full working order. They both knew and didn't know; just like me.) What the kids at school told me was that the word I was looking for was sissy, or queer, or mincing lisping nancy-boy, or poof, or bender, or fairy, or pansy, or big girl's blouse, or plenty of other things. OK, I thought, so they do have words for what I'm like. And they have hand-gestures and tones of voice and funny walks and mime-routines as well. And every single one of them is charged with hatred and contempt.

I would say school was consistently awful, except that it wasn't; it got worse as I went up the years. It was the kind of school where everyone randomly gives unthinking abuse to everyone else, all the time (that is to say: a 1970s north of England boys' school). And I was the kind of child who showed it when I was hurt. And the more you show them you're hurt, the more abuse they give you. "Don't react," my parents told me, "don't react." Right; but don't react? When everyone around you all day every day is telling you the worst and most negative things about your own body and appearance that you can think of? When your entire outer world is insisting on how male and how ugly you are, when inside—so far down inside you can barely even say it yourself—all you want to be is beautiful and feminine?

Children and parents naturally stop their physical contact, the hugs and kisses and the sitting on the knee, as the children grow. The more that reassurance was withdrawn, the more I was reassured every day by my classmates at school that I was ugly, lumpen, awkward, physically contemptible, ridiculous to look at.

I'm a Christian, and always have been, and I took it that the forces of good and evil were at war not only, self-evidently, around me, but also within. When I wasn't praying with all my heart, last thing at night, that I would wake up the next morning and find I'd been turned into a girl, I was praying with all my heart, last thing at night, that I would wake up the next morning and

—In Statu Nascendi 1:1 (2018)—

find that the side of me that wanted to be a girl had just disappeared. I was a city divided against myself, and in the civil war within me, a lot of the time, I didn't even know which side I was on, or which side of myself loathed the other more.

Mind you; I didn't think it was bad to be transgender only for religious reasons. Everything I knew seemed to enforce that message for every other kind of reason too. I wanted a family, for instance, I wanted a wife, I wanted children; so how could I also want to be a woman myself? And alongside hopes and desires that simply went in contradictory directions to my transgender hopes and desires and guilt whether religious or cultural, the self-loathing I've just talked about is always within easy reach. But I did naturally see the turmoil within me—rather grandiosely, to be sure—as one small part of a universal Manichaean cosmological conflict. This was my bit-to-do in the wider battle in the cosmic war. This was my cross to bear or the thorn in my side. The thing of darkness that I'd do anything not to acknowledge mine was—being transgender. It was a horcrux, an evil alien implant, a Trojan virus within me that I just couldn't seem to delete, so had to build firewalls and quarantines around.

As a teenager I found myself in a weekly cycle, from school to the weekend to Evensong and back to school. Even now the Anglican liturgy of Evensong has associations for me that I can barely stand. The past week of failure, derision, and confusion; the long grey miserable afternoon/evening of dark and dismal Pennine rain; the cold mostly-empty church and the doleful slow liturgy with all its talk of sin and darkness and inner desperation; the insupportable weight of repressed, redirected, curdled or soured emotions that it seemed to carry; my own awful dull dread of school again in the morning and the start of another week just the same as the last; and the whole of my being crying out to God for rescue like a drifting ship lost and alone on a stormy dark sea in a night that is empty of landmarks.

How long wilt thou forget me, O Lord? for ever? how long wilt thou hide thy face from me?

How long shall I take counsel in my soul, having sorrow in my heart daily? how long shall mine enemy be exalted over me?

You can't be transgender and not know that there is a crack in everything. Because what you experience every single day is that there's a crack in you. There's a gap between your body and your mind, between your sense of yourself and what you see when you look in the mirror, between what you dream of being every night and what you've got to be every day. And that gap, so far as I can make out, simply isn't there for cisgendered people. They too may suffer from physical self-loathing; but by definition, it won't be for quite this reason. They may have serious problems with their body-image: there can be a gap between the shape they are and the shape they want to be. But they experience no gap between being the gender they are and being the gender they want to be. Often they have difficulty even imagining what it might be like to feel such a gap.

In this sense it is not wrong, it seems to me, to think of being transgender as a kind of body dysmorphia. I don't mean that that's the only way to think about being transgender. There are as many ways of being transgender as there are transgender people, so there are lots of ways to think about it. Nor, despite the bitter old joke that goes "Q. What's the difference between a transvestite and a transsexual? A. A divorce and about five years", is there any such thing as the one transgender journey. Despite a surprising willingness among some trans people to prescribe to other trans people the one correct way for their individual lives to unfold, there's no one place that everyone on the transgender spectrum is bound to end up "if they're doing it right".

Still, at least some of the time, at least for me, dysmorphia is exactly it. And I know other transwomen who've found the same. It distresses you to have the body you've got; you long with all your soul to have a different one—a female one. And you don't just want to be a woman; you want to be a beautiful woman, too. And seeing how far you're always going to be from that can leave you feeling absolutely desolate: drained and self-loathing and close to despair. The word "dysmorphia" fits. (The punning suggestion of "addiction that makes you feel like shit" is spot on as well, unfortunately.)

One common response to this distress is to run away from it, as far and as fast as you can. Plenty of transwomen get into body-building or join the Territorial Army or a rugby team. (A male one.) "If I have to have a male body, I'm going to have the best one I possibly can": I understand that urge; indeed for many years I lived on it. I equally understand how following through on the urge to repress can turn transgender people suicidal, as it regularly does. (It didn't do that to me, or not often, or not quite.) And I understand, too, the opposite urge, to use surgery as your magic wand to get you medically across to the other side of the great gender divide. But that isn't always a happy piece of magic either. It seems it works out sometimes, and that, obviously, is great. But it also seems that some can have the surgery and still not feel like they've crossed over or made peace with themselves. And that can be a terrible experience.

—In Statu Nascendi 1:1 (2018)—

For the first 33 years of my life, my own approach, on the whole, was to hide. Well, anyone who meets me today can see that that has changed. How did it change? To report my own experience properly I have to talk about it in distinctively Christian terms; I recognize that other people might put it in other terms, or might never have felt guilty, the lucky sods, about being transgender in the first place. So my own way of putting it would be this: it was a matter of grace. Over about a month in April to May 1998, I was shown with unmistakable clarity and force that God's love and mercy are not merely great but infinite, and that their reach very easily goes far enough to reach even to me. God loves me—the message of these peak experiences was—just as I am. God made me this way, and God made no mistake. God wants me to be this way. So, Sophie/Tim, or whatever your name is, you think you're the worst of sinners? But this isn't evil at all; not even a bit. Evil is running off with the pension fund, beating people up for being different from you, treating your employees (or your boss) like dirt, cruelty to animals, casual pollution. Evil is flying a passenger jet into the Twin Towers or invading Iraq. Evil is every act of unkindness or arrogance or obstinacy or rudeness or self-absorption you've ever done. But being transgender? No. That's just a way of being gendered. And there is no more an evil way of being gendered than there is an evil flavor of ice cream.

Hiding the fact that you're transgender is hard. I know this: I hid it from absolutely everybody for 34 years, and from nearly everybody for 50 years. It's hard in lots of ways. It gave me, for one thing, more or less permanent impostor syndrome; the whole time I was just waiting to be found out, denounced, and disgraced, and mostly I myself felt that, when that inevitably happened, it would serve me bloody well right. (This mindset still comes naturally to me even now.) For another thing, almost always I felt that I was being dishonest and two-faced and deceptive with everybody around me. This is both exhausting and profoundly dispiriting. (And sometimes it was true; sometimes I was dishonest and two-faced and deceptive.)

What's hardest of all is that, so long as you hide it, there is one thing you can never know, which is how people would react if they knew. You're bound to suspect that your family and friends if they really knew all about you, couldn't possibly go on loving you. (That's the problem of other minds, right there; and I've already talked about my own experience of the problem of evil, of akrasia, and of limitless Cartesian skepticism. Being transgender is endlessly philosophically educational.)

But—thank goodness—my suspicions about how others would react were all, or nearly all, completely wrong. I recognize that not all transgender people are as lucky as I've consistently been since I came out in December 2014 and that there are all too many tragedies out there. But what I have found is that my wife and my children, and nearly all my family and friends, do still love me despite the surprising fact that I'm transgender. (And some of them were very surprised indeed.) To them, as to anyone who sees me from the "outside", it's likely to seem that things have got weird; there have been bumps in the road since I came out. Whereas to me, that's exactly where the weirdness stopped and where the road smoothed out. Psychologically and personally, even morally, the difficult thing for me was being transgender in secret. After that, being openly transgender is dead easy. Or at least, relatively easy.

So much for the autobiography. What does it mean for the politics? On the basis of my own experience of being transgender, what do I want to say about transgender being in society?

Well, the first thing I want to say is simply that being transgender typically involves a lot of plain distress. If you're lucky, you can end up a happy transgender person; I have myself been very, very lucky in that way. But it doesn't happen easily, and there are plenty of pitfalls along the road, and it never becomes completely easy. On the basis of my own experience, the first thing I feel for anyone else who's transgender is that my heart goes out them. To be transgender is to be wounded; being transgender hurts.

Secondly, their pain, and the alienation that often accompanies it, can lead transgender people into unfortunate responses. One is seediness or sleaze. That was one standard way of representing transgender in the 1970s and 80s: as a kind of Rocky Horror/Kenny Everett/drag-queen kinkiness. Nothing wrong with kinkiness in its place. But its place is between consenting adults in the bedroom. (Or maybe the cinema.) The kinky has no place as a representation of what it is to be transgender. A lot of the time, being transgender has very little directly to do with sexuality at all; it's about as louche and dark and pervy as *The Sound of Music*. (How do I solve a problem like not being Maria?) But when the whole of society is busy telling you that you're a filthy unnatural, disgusting pervert who needs either to disappear completely, or at the very least to slink off into some murky disreputable corner, then it's quite easy to respond, even if you don't exactly mean to, by internalising that categorisation and behaving accordingly. I think this is changing now, thank goodness. I think it's now become possible to express transgender as I want to express it, which is as an exuberant celebration of a perfectly innocent freedom; a gigantic Yes to life, really. But my goodness, it's taken long enough.

—In Statu Nascendi 1:1 (2018)—

Another unfortunate response is anger. No one can listen to recent debates between feminism and transgender without catching a whiff of cordite. There is a huge amount of anger on both sides, and on both sides, it seems, it's for the same sort of reasons. It's partly lashing out in pain. And it's partly that one historically oppressed group hopes for the support of another—and finds them not supportive at all, but treacherous. Some feminists see transgender people as treacherous because they often seem to buy, perhaps for suspected fetishistic reasons, into an ideologically constructed version of femininity which is just another part of patriarchy's intricate system of systems of oppression. And some transgender people see feminists as treacherous because they say things like "You can't make yourself into a fucking woman by cutting your bloody bits off". (Excuse my Australian accent.) The feminists in these debates insist that there's more to being a woman than any socially constructed version of what it is to be a woman. And they're right. And the transgender debaters retort that when the feminists deny the right of transwomen to call themselves women at all, they're being essentialist. And they're right too.

For my part, to be honest, I buy the essentialism. Or sort of. Please don't burn me at the stake if you think this is all wrong. I'm not that well-read—to put it mildly—in feminism or gender studies or queer theory. It's just my view, based on my own experience and not much else; if you want to persuade me of a different view, I'm happy to listen. But to put it at its crudest: I think sex is nature, gender is nurture. On the one hand, there is the body you were given by biology, which usually (not always) takes a fairly definite male or female shape. That fixes your sex. And there is the feminine or the masculine that you were brought up as and/or that you choose to identify as. And that's your gender.

This is too crude because there are plenty of other factors in the mix too. The most obvious one is hormones, which as we're increasingly realizing, do a very great deal of work indeed in making people "feel masculine" or "feel feminine". But what I'm saying in my telegraphic way is this: there is a side of being male or female that is a matter of choice, and there is a side that isn't.

So the unrestricted voluntarism of some trans activists—their idea that gender or sex is purely a matter of choice—seems unwarranted to me. Sure, whether you present as masculine or feminine, or neither, or a bit of both, is a matter of choice. But your gender or sex can't be simply a matter of choice. If it was, wouldn't being transgender be easy? I can tell you this for sure: if I could become completely and unequivocally a woman just by choosing to, just like that, right now, then you wouldn't have time to blink. I'd do it like a shot, and poof—all my troubles (or at least all my gender troubles) would be over in a flash. But no transgender person's gender troubles are ever over in a moment. Ergo, pure voluntarism has got to be wrong.

But the unrestricted essentialism of some feminists—their idea that your gender or sex can't be a matter of choice at all: if you ask me, that's not true either. In fact, it's false for the same reason as unrestricted voluntarism is false. My natal sex isn't a matter of choice for me, but my gender presentation is.

So here's the upshot of my little bit of naïve gender theory. If feminists of the school of dear old sweary Germaine want to insist that women are one thing and transwomen are another, then I think that they're just right about at least many transwomen. They're probably not right about all transwomen. Some of us really do make the journey all the way, and become pretty well completely indistinguishable from natal women, at both the gender and sex levels, in every respect except history and internal anatomy. But they're certainly right about, for example, me. I'm not a ciswoman. I might wish I was, but I don't claim that I am. I'm a transwoman, and that's not the same thing.

The thing is, I don't think I should have to claim to be a ciswoman to be treated, as a transwoman, with full respect by society at large, and as an ally by feminists. I hope for the full respect of society because I think there's room on the gender spectrum for more than two binary positions. (There's room, too, for a choice not to place yourself anywhere on that spectrum: being non-gender-defining is another thing again.) In politics, though I'd also describe myself as a socialist, I'm basically a soppy old John Stuart Mill liberal: I am a feminist, and I am a trans activist, because and insofar as feminism and trans activism are corollaries of Millian liberalism. So naturally, I think that people should be allowed to try what Mill in *On Liberty* calls "experiments in living" that aren't either traditionally male, or traditionally female, or even traditionally transgender. I suppose an experiment in living is what I'm doing in my own life. Call me naively optimistic, but it's a free country still, just about, and I don't expect to be out-grouped for living as I do, either by people on the "right", or by people on the "left".

The future of feminism, then? As you'd expect from a soppy old liberal like me, the future I hope for is one of entirely platitudinous and straightforward liberal niceness. For me it's all about boring platitudes and truisms like these:

—live and let live

—In Statu Nascendi 1:1 (2018)—

—play nicely
—love is all you need
—do as you would be done by
—maximal freedom for each consistent with maximal freedom for all
—don't forbid or condemn anything at all unless you really, really need to
—mutual tolerance and respect wherever humanly possible.

And more specifically, as these platitudes apply to the case in hand:
—a rainbow rather than a bipolarity
—a deeper acceptance of gender diversity, including the kinds of diversity that go way beyond the gender binary
—a wider understanding that there are lots of different ways of being either masculine or feminine (or neither) and indeed lots of different ways of being transgender too
—an understanding that playing and exploring and experimenting with the typology and imaginary of gender as our society has variously constructed it can be just that—play, exploration, experimentation—and doesn't have to be the reinforcement of any oppressive stereotypes at all.

It goes without saying, mind you that any such happily liberal future is as threatened today as is the liberal democracy that has given us all, cis or trans, these freedoms that we now live by. We need to keep up our guard, and we need to stand up for our rights. And above all, we need not to tell ourselves that all the major battles are already won. When I look around the world scene at the moment, I'm afraid I suspect that some of the biggest battles that we liberals are going to have to face are only just beginning. And this is not just to or for feminists only, or transgender people only. My cry to everyone, for everyone's sake, is: to the barricades[1].

Further Reading

Morris, Jan, *Conundrum*, New York, NYRB Classics, 2006.
Morris, Jan, *Conundrum*, Penguin Books Australia Ltd, 1987.
Morris, Jan, *Conundrum*, Harcourt Brace Jovanovich, 1974.

---

[1] For kindness, support, friendship, forgiveness, love, and their encouragement to me in thinking through all this personal stuff and in working out how, if at all, to go public about it, I am grateful to many people, including Claudia Richardson, Miriam Chappell, Imogen Chappell, Thalia Chappell, and Roisin Chappell, Philip and Cherry Chappell, Frances Moody, everybody at All Souls' Episcopalian Church Invergowrie, the members of the Philosophy Department at the Open University, the members of the Mind Association Executive Committee, and all my lovely friends.

Chappell, Timothy, *Knowing What To Do: Imagination, Virtue, and Platonism in Ethics* (2014).

Chappell, Timothy, *Ethics, and Experience: Life Beyond Moral Theory* (2009).

Chappell, Timothy, *The Inescapable Self: an Introduction to Western Philosophy since Descartes* (2005).

Chappell, Sophie Grace, Seeds: on personal identity and the resurrection (2016–12), In *Cholbi, Michael ed. Immortality and the Philosophy of Death* (p. 85–98).

Chappell, Sophie Grace, How Encounters with Values Generate Moral Demandingness (2015-09-23), In: van Ackeren, Marcel, and Kuehler, Michael eds. *The Limits of Obligation: Moral Demandingness and Ought Implies Can. Routledge Studies in Ethics and Moral Theory* (p. 84–99).

Chappell, Timothy, Augustine's ethics (2014), In Stump, Eleonore, and Meconi, David eds. *The Cambridge Companion to Augustine* (2nd ed). Cambridge Companions (p. 189–207).

Chappell, Timothy, Virtue ethics and rules (2013-11-28), In: van Hooft, Stan ed. *Handbook of Virtue Ethics.*

Stavros Panagiotou

A Comparative Study between Levinas and Kierkegaard on Subjectivity and the Self[1]

Abstract: *In this essay, I argue that the (subjective) self-merits an ethical and not an ontological task, comparing the ethical (to some extent) with the existential. Levinas and Kierkegaard share similar theological perspectives in their philosophical aspects to explore their arguments on subjectivity but with different philosophical methods. Levinas really believes in God but in Judaism God is a Transcendence unknowable for us. We, as finite beings, cannot name, understand or communicate directly with God, but we can know Him indirectly via negationis and via emanentiae. We can communicate with Him indirectly by the face of the Other and not by attributing secular characteristics to Him. The Other human is not a God but His only trace. According to Levinas, we are not in a position to say "truth" about transcendence that is infinity, because we are finite beings and Transcendence does not dwell in immanence. The most critical issue of Levinas' philosophy is not his faith but his ethics as first philosophy to discuss the problem of the (subjective) self. Otherwise, there is a danger of losing ourselves in psychology instead of finding what a Self is in philosophy. Kierkegaard emphasizes the infinite qualitative difference between God and human beings. As a result, this philosopher rules out a direct knowledge of God. When Kierkegaard stresses subjectivity, it is to challenge the arrogant claims of speculative knowledge and aesthetic consumption. He not only involves but also requires an assertion of identity between the transcendent and the immanent.*

Keywords: Transcendence; immanence; subjectivity; ethics; existentialism; otherness;

---

[1] As is widely known, subjectivity and the Self are philosophically divided into two different categories from extremely different lines of thought. Even though they both examine the notion and characteristics of human beings (as humans and not beings), they explore different perspectives analyzing philosophical terminology with their own specific optical angle. For instance, philosophical lines of thought such as existentialism (Kierkegaard, Sartre, Nietzsche), ontology (Husserl, Heidegger), and ethics (Levinas), explore the issue of subjectivity in great separation from the notion of the Self. However, in this essay I explore arguments regarding both terms introductorily since I intend to expand the study of subjectivity in depth after the completion of my PhD thesis (forthcoming).

Introduction

If there is an opportunity to explore the debate of subjectivity and the Self from a solid standpoint, it can only be achieved through existential philosophy and ethics which defend that personhood belongs to the metaphysics of existence and ethics rather than to the ontological essence of Being. Before starting a discussion about the notion of the self and subjectivity in the works of Levinas and Kierkegaard, it would be worthwhile to clarify the basis of the bulk of this essay. It is prudent from the beginning to unequivocally declare that ethicists (Levinas) and existentialists (Kierkegaard) define human nature not by its predestined essence—ontologically—but mainly by its actions—praxis (Dimitrova 2006: I.1, p. 15). Thus, this essay explores mostly theses dealing with metaphysical, ethical and existential perspectives rather than ontology and epistemology[2]. What matters is not being qua Being but man as human. It is, therefore, an urgent need to ask questions using the interrogative word 'why' rather than 'how' and the term 'ought to be' rather than 'is.' For Levinas, as M. Dimitrova correctly points out, "Heidegger's wisdom is not an original or primordial truth. It deduces the personal from the ontological while the personal is ethical" (ibid., 16).

In this essay, I argue that the (subjective) self-merits an ethical and not an ontological task, comparing the ethical (to some extent) with the existential. Levinas, despite his great interest in Heideggerian ontology during his early time in France, later on, realizes that his phenomenology needs further elaboration to fabricate a more ethical phenomenology exploring humans and not ontological beings qua beings. Levinas expresses his critique of Heidegger by claiming that the latter provides a quasi-phenomenological idea of the truth of beings qua disclosure (Tsakiri, 2009, p. 65) and unconcealment. Concerning Heidegger's latter term as well as clearing in *Being and Time*, Levinas contends that "the idea that a transcendence of the transcendent depends on its extreme humility enables us to glimpse a kind of truth which does not take the form of unconcealment. The humility of a persecuted truth is so profound that it will not even venture to present itself in the Heideggerian clearing" (ibid.). Levinas' alterity seems to transcend beyond and above any Husserlian epistemological preoccupations and any Heideggerian ontological preoccupations. Levinas' insistence on alterity

---

[2] For instance, Heideggerian methodology of being-in-the-world impacts the majority of the ontological standpoint of self-rejecting subjectivity and activism giving priority to fundamental ontology of Beings.

surfaces even before he raises ethics to first philosophy. Levinas, as Bernet points out, "had already exhibited in his first writings on time a particular attention to the question of alterity. In his question of the other (aliud) at the heart of the sameness of my experience of time, it is already the other person (alter) that Levinas is aiming at" (Bernet, 2004, p. 86–87). Bernet similarly underlines a quite crucial fact on Levinas' subjectivity and time which is contrasted to Husserlian epistemology and Heideggerian fundamental ontology: "he attempts to establish that the past itself, in its most original sense, is not my past but the other's past. The important analyses of the 'trace' and the 'immemorial' do nothing else than establish the idea of a past which has never been present" (ibid., p. 89).

Comparison Between Levinas and Kierkegaard

Levinas and Kierkegaard—though from remarkably different philosophical backgrounds—contend that personhood passes through total otherness. Both give priority to subjectivity rather than objectivity; the other has the character of the subject rather than an object. Both link the ethical and the religious and set them off as a region of self-transcending subjectivity thoroughly different from violent objectivity (Westphal, 1992, p. 242). Levinas and Kierkegaard speak about the person underlining the signification of the other (human and divine), presenting their arguments by insisting on the relationship between (a) the I with the Thou and (b) the I with the divine other. However, below I argue in more detail that Levinas prefers the interconnection between the 'other and me' rather the Buberian I-Thou relation. In contrast, Kierkegaard (being Protestant) develops his existential theory concerning the concept of the self and subjectivity from a more Christian standpoint.

For Levinas, the human other is logically prior, while for Kierkegaard the divine other is logically prior. Regardless of the disagreement, the critical point is that Levinas seeks to mitigate the antithesis of the philosophical and the religious with the help of the ethical. His philosophy can be defined as a form of ethical metaphysics (Whyschogrod, 1974). Levinas, comparing human subjectivity with ethics, claims that "my ethical relation of love for the other stems from the fact that the self cannot survive by itself alone, cannot find meaning within its own being-in-the-world, within the ontology of sameness" (Levinas, 1969, p. 60). Despite his divine-command ethics[3], Levinas

---

[3] For further analysis of the definition of divine command ethics and theory, see a work by M. J. Harris, Divine Command Ethics, London-New York: Taylor and Francis, 2004; T.

contends that 'the face to face' encounter with the human other is before any discourse with the divine other. Levinas, as I have mentioned above, transforms the Buberian I–Thou relation, since the 'me' matters, providing a different view concerning the human-divine issues indirectly and asymmetrically:

"The invisible[4] but personal God is not approached outside of all human presence. Rather, to encounter the Other first as the orphan, the stranger, the poor, in short as the neighbor in the pentateuchal, is to prohibit the metaphysical relation with God from being accomplished in the ignorance of men and things. The dimension of the divine opens forth from the human face. God rises to his supreme and ultimate presence as correlative to the justice rendered unto men. There can be no 'knowledge' of God separated from the relationship with men. The Other is the very locus of metaphysical truth and is indispensable for my relation with God" (Westphal, 1992, p. 250).

Similarly, Kierkegaard promotes the importance of love by saying:

"A human being's love is grounded in God's love...if God were not love, then there would be not a man's love...a man's love mysteriously begins in God's love" (Kierkegaard, 1946, p. 27).

Kierkegaard also in his *Works of Love* gives us a profound reading of the Kantian claim, "religion is (subjectivity regarded[5]) the recognition of all duties as divine commands" and that "religion without ethics is empty, while ethics without religion is blind" (Kant, 1960, p. 142). Kierkegaard has a dialectical concept of the self as essentially relational (Westphal, 1987, p. 29–33). The self, according to his famous definition, is "a relation that relates to itself and in relating itself to itself to another" (ibid., p. 13–14). Thus, we need "the perpetual particularity of Levinas and the commanded universality of

---

Chappell, "The Goods and the Persons They Are Goods For", Philosophical News, 5 (2012), 1–7 and idem. Chappell T., "Knowledge of Persons", European Journal of Philosophy of Religion, 5. 4 (2013), p. 27–8: VIII.

[4] This term has crucial significance in order to clearly understand Levinas' view concerning the human-divine relation. The divine, let's say God, is not incompatible with humanity; for Levinas God might exist. There is no evidence that Levinas argues for the inexistence of God. However, Levinas insists that humans (and not beings) as mortal and finite entities cannot merit direct and reciprocal relation with God; tete-a-tete communication through contemplation and prayer is thoroughly rejected in Levinas' thought. Below, we observe that Kierkegaard has a different observation concerning the divine-human debate and subjectivity.

[5] According to Kierkegaard subjectivity is transcendent directly by only integrating ethics with religion and faith (using personal pronoun in the nominative case: as I). According to Levinas subjectivity is transcendent indirectly and through the responsibility of the other person not through faith (using personal pronoun in the accusative case: as me.

Kierkegaard in tandem. Only through their union does the Other get welcomed" (Westphal, 1992, p. 258).

In a similar sense, Bonhoeffer states that "there was a clear connection between love for the other and affirming the dignity of the personhood of the other" (Spezio, 2013, p. 435). The concept of the self is then integrated with morality, and a specific morality, which is, according to Levinas, not only a branch of philosophy but 'first philosophy' (Levinas 1969: 304), which can only be understood in terms of persons-in-relation, ultimately with the divine, but not separate from the community. In a similar tone, L. Zagzebski tries to define the concept of the person, claiming that "those who have a deep and sympathetic understanding of another person do not see him or her as an impersonal he or she, but as you" (Zagzebski, 2004, p. 374). However, according to Levinas, a sympathetic understanding of another person is indeed personal by, being asymmetrical and responsive to the other as me and not I.

Thus, inter-human love relations as construed by Levinas and Kierkegaard are closely linked with religious (divine) ethics, as regards the notion of the self and the concept of the person. In parallel, Levinas and Kierkegaard also agree that "the true lover will rather sacrifice him or herself for the benefit of the beloved than sacrifice the beloved for the lover's interests" (Welz, 2008, p. 239). But this argument needs further analysis. The initiated point of understanding the self and its notion towards subjectivity and to the response of other humans needs to be clarified; justice and individual characteristics of man do not "result from …any ontological game" (as Heidegger claims); rather justice appears as a principle from 'beyond' invoked by generosity, goodness, and charity. These motives are understandable in their authenticity only as proximity, love, and responsibility for others (Dimitrova 2006: I.1, p. 28). The Self, therefore, goes beyond totality through his responsibility to the present (Drossev, 2012, p. 65).

Also, it is worth citing Levinas to explore a bit more the importance of the second-personal in ethics to show how important the definition of the self might be. Levinas (and Darwall) tends to underline that the significant characteristic of persons is that they are not only deliberated about; they are also deliberators (Chappell, 2012, p. 2). It is necessary to treat other human beings as equal interlocutors even if they are skilled or full interlocutors. What matters is to encounter something that deserves to be addressed as you. Also, Chappell's thought also favors (together with the argument of equal deliberators) Levinas' Divine Command Ethics (DCE), that is, "the person above all to whom I have to justify myself second-personally is God. Ethics is a matter of divine commands because ethics is a second personal affair, and relative to every person. God is super-eminently second-personal" (ibid., p. 6). Thus, we can infer that if we take ourselves as co-deliberators and the second-personal as necessary for personhood, then we could easily compare this fact with the theological phrase 'loving my neighbor as myself' (ibid., p. 7), building bridges for a future reconciliation between (a part of) philosophy and theology.

Despite the partial truth of the above Buberian statement that Chappell follows, it needs a further unpacking to understand Levinas' thought about the relation between human and divine and 'me' (not I) and others from an ethical rather than ontological standpoint. M. Dimitrova comprehensively sketches the Levinasian ethical overview (and purview) against the Heideggerian fundamental ontology of what it is to be a person, its attributes as well as its connection with other humans and the divine.

For Levinas, if everything human is reduced to ontology, to be a man is to be in service of Being. And to be a part of Being's adventure is to obey something like the "faceless" fate. Fundamental ontology is a philosophy of power supporting obedience to the Neutral. Levinas thinks that the humanness of homo humanus constitutes itself first of all in the face-to-face relationship with the Other as a real and quite tangible person. The whole Self as me is in service not to the system of Being (available only through mineness), but in service to concrete, here and now an existing neighbor, whereby the conatus essendi of mine-ness is surmounted. Most often Levinas' philosophy is considered to be devoted to the problem of the Other or the otherness of the Other. But in fact, Levinas' thought is concerned not with the Other as such but with my relation to him or her. The main issue is my responsibility for the Other, and it can be extended to the substitution of the Other by me, wherein I am transformed into a hostage of the Other. The focus of Levinas' philosophy is the moral subject: the "I" in the accusative case, that is, "me," who has no chance to hide behind a mask of a Third one" (Dimitrova, 2006, p. 17).

The afore-mentioned fragment on How to think Humanitas of Homo Humanus, is an implication of the Levinasian line of thought contrasting not only ontological perspectives of the self but also Christian perspectives concerning the relation of humans to each other and divinity. Levinas, like Sartre, contends that 'me' encounters the Other by inventing or constituting her. However, Levinas goes a step forward, alleging that I do not encounter the Other merely as Thou but as a face which is asymmetrical and non-reciprocal to 'me', because contrarily to Kierkegaard, if I expect the other to be merely a Thou it would have been only an empirical event without transcendence, facing only the immanence. But for Levinas Transcendence of the Alter Ego is very crucial for subjectivity. As M. Dimitrova points out, "I am summoned to enter into a relation with the other in his or her dimension of Transcendence" (ibid., p. 18).

The human-divine relation, therefore, is a trivial and hard issue to get involved in. However, Levinas stresses that God cannot directly be known and understood by humans. God's attributes (if we may say that God has understandable attributes for human beings) cannot be explained or disrobed by finite thinkers. As M. Dimitrova correctly mentions, "God is Transcendence and Transcendence cannot be possessed" (ibid., p. 23). Anthropomorphism has trapped people especially in modern Western societies; that is they mistakenly, according to Levinas, transmit God from Exteriority to Interiority, from 'outside to inside,' from Transcendence to Immanence. M. Dimitrova objects to Western culture alleging that it falsely creates a secular/cosmic onto-theo-logical God (ibid.). In parallel, she explains that the human-divine relation still stands in a mistakable strand as modernity promotes the medieval Christian tradition "endowing man with being a co-creator of the Creation" (ibid.).

For Levinas, in parallel, what matters most is a responsibility to the Other. Our finitude transcends into infinity by showing our responsibility to the other face-to-face. In contrast to Heidegger, Levinas does not underline only the care of myself but also for the other's being, not ontologically but ethically. In this sense, responsibility must sustain Otherness in a fantastic way where the response to the other must be asymmetrical and indirect (ibid., p. 19). However, the primary understanding of Levinas' thought is not the otherness of the other par excellence but rather 'me' as a moral subject. It is me and not I that matters in a non-reciprocal condition.

"The Word, the conversation according to Levinas' model, cannot be adequately understood as a reciprocal relation between equal partners, i.e., dialogue (as it is for Buber, for example). The conversation is not a partnership since the Other is in a position of superiority: he or she questions me. But this does not mean that I am in a position of inferiority. I am the Single One who is responsible for responding, for giving to another because he or she is one in need. As a moral subject, I am called to pay attention to the Other and thus feel chosen, unique, and irreplaceable. I can't avoid the responsibility because my failure to respond is already a kind of response". (M. Dimitrova, 2006, p. 26).

Levinas' subjectivity consists in several neologisms and newness. It is suggested here that despite its great influence from Husserl and Heidegger, whose works were presented to the French people and scrutinized by Levinas, the latter's purpose was to expand an innovation across continental philosophy: "he seeks a meaning beyond the esse of being, meaning that no longer states itself in terms of Being and is prior to Being" (ibid., 25). For Levinas, subjectivity depends on the face of the other, but through indirect ethics. If the human face is taken either as too sublime or too real, he loses its bewilderment and thus he is unable to present its self through the other. Thus if we consider ethics phenomenologically, by approaching the other in such a way ethics turns into moralism, and this would be a fatal mistake, according to Levinas. 'Similar to Merleau-Ponty that ontology can approach Being only regarding an indirect ontology, we can assume that [Levinas'] ethics can approach the other only regarding an indirect ethics" (Waldenfels, 2004, p. 64). Subjectivity, according to Levinas, can only be understood via negationis and via eminentiae. Similar to apophatic theology, it is meaningless and awry to intend to designate human attributes to God. We are living in the face of the other, seeking or fleeing it, running the risk of losing our face; it is a continuous attempt of hunting traces that we will never find; our selves can only be identified, ethically speaking, when the common face turns into the uncommon, into the unfamiliar, even into the uncanny (ibid., p. 65). There is not me (and not I) without the response of the other. 'Whether he regards me or not, he considers me. This is the question of the meaning of being: not the ontology of the understanding of that extraordinary verb, but the ethics of its justice" (R. Kearney and M. Rainwater [eds.], 2005, p. 134).

Levinas underlines that in contrast to fundamental ontology, (moral) subjectivity is devoted to the Other sustaining other's presence but "the excess over the presence is the life of the infinite" where the moral subject is even responsible for the responsibility of the other (ibid., 27). Kierkegaard, on the other hand, presents some similarities regarding subjectivity with Levinas, though he apparently stresses his view antithetical to Levinas that human beings can reach God's commandments and essence directly with reciprocity and contemplation and that there is a symmetrical relation between individuals and the divine[6]. Kierkegaard as a Protestant promotes a 'leap of faith' (Tsakiri, 2009, p. 58) in his writings, something that is rejected by both

---

[6] See a brief implication in favor of this thesis in M. Dimitrova, "Levinas: How to think Humanitas of Homo Humanus", *Sofia Philosophical Review*, I.1 (2006), 29, n. 10.

Heidegger and Levinas. However, he agrees with the latter that it is subjectivity and not objectivity that matters most.

Kierkegaard in parallel lays down the example of God's command to Abraham and its 'monstrous paradox': the natural emotional ties of parental love and the basic moral principles of any conceivable human society. However, despite the strength of the absurd, faith begins precisely where thinking leaves off. We must believe, according to Kierkegaard, even though faith violates human rationality, nature, and morality. "It is the absurdity of religion which proves its unique value, its irreducibility" (West, 1996, p. 125). It is also worth noting that Kierkegaard, though he insists on Christian faith and religious principles, is vehemently against what he calls, 'Objective Christianity,' which falsely provides biased historical evidence by establishing the Church's dogmata. Faith, he asserts, is a necessary and sufficient condition of subjectivity, emphasizing his existential exploration by providing examples from the Old Testament such as Job and Abraham to support his arguments for the 'leap of faith.' As V. Tsakiri states, "Abraham's exercise of freedom converges with the leap of faith which for Kierkegaard always happens within the realm of the finite but opens up human singularity towards the infinity" (Tsakiri, 2009, p. 60).

Further Debate on the Singularity and the 'Single One' in both Kierkegaard and Levinas'

Concerning singularity and the 'Single One,' we need to be quite careful not to misunderstand Kierkegaard's singularity with Levinas' uniqueness. The latter contends that singularity of the moral subject depends on asymmetrical, indirect and non-reciprocal attributes while the former defends—through faith, repetition (Kierkegaard, 1983, p. 46), secrecy, silence and absurdity—the direct, immediate and reciprocal relation to God. The leap of faith, therefore, moved by the virtue of the absurd, converts finitude into infinity and a return to the finite yet again. And this is because God allows it to be done "since for God everything is possible, everything also becomes possible in the finite world by virtue of the absurd" (Tsakiri, 2009, p. 60).

Kierkegaard provides an entirely different perspective concerning the notion of faith and its relation to reason. He claims that idea has nothing to do with faith that subsequently has nothing to do with rational reason. He not only puts a huge gap between them but also creates a separate existential framework in which faith surpasses human understanding. In this way, he renews the theological tradition of fideism for which religious belief is diminished rather than strengthened by its reduction to merely a human reason. Kierkegaard develops a more radical version of fideism which asserts that religious faith not only does not require the support of reason but is fundamentally at odds with it.

Kierkegaard rejects both objective knowledge and contemplative theory as making no useful contribution to understanding human life. Religion and faith cannot be reduced to theory. There can be no rationally moral system of religion. The truths of religion according to Kierkegaard belong to the sphere of subjective existence and thus cannot be maintained by theoretical knowledge. In this respect, existence can only be understood subjectively or from within. Also, Kierkegaard gives priority to ambivalence, dread, and responsibility which play a crucial role to achieve freedom (West, 1996, p. 121–124). Human beings are, according to Kierkegaard, a mixture of the animal and the divine; a synthesis of the finite and the infinite, the temporal and the eternal, of freedom and necessity (ibid., p. 122).

Kierkegaard compares freedom with a contemporary mass society where people despair obeying rules and living in the 'mediocre and the average' (ibid.). By raising the issue of despair, Kierkegaard leads human beings to rethink their destiny to return to religious faith (as a Protestant). "Only a self which comes to a self-conscious decision to accept God overcomes despair…only religion answers to the fully self-conscious individuality of authentic existence" (ibid., p. 124). Summing up Kierkegaard's existential subjectivity of religious faith we may imply that, through his inward renewal of faith, Kierkegaard also sheds an additional light on the subjective existential truth of the human condition.

Several continental and analytical thinkers express their great interest in exploring philosophical accounts to construe sound and valid propositions on subjectivity and the conception of the Self as well as to compare (if it is possible) Levinas' phenomenology and metaphysical ethics with Kierkegaardian Christian existentialism. Taking into consideration the aforementioned discussion about Levinas' and Kierkegaard's views on subjectivity and the Self I argue in the next paragraphs that although they both object to fundamental ontology (mainly derived from Heidegger's Dasein) and give priority to subjectivity and metaphysics ethics, they consider the concept of the Self from different philosophical angles.

For example, if we want to note some similarities between Levinas and Kierkegaard, we may underline the fact that they both consider the duty of love and sacrifice, which are characteristics of the Self, as subject to individual experience rather than claiming objective validity and universality (Tsakiri, 2009, p. 61). However, the two thinkers explore their views from different standpoints. For instance, Levinas, on the one hand, believes that the ethical individualizes us treating everyone as a unique individual, a Self. On the other hand, Kierkegaard seeks to generalize the subject by trying to provide theological perspectives to ethics called second ethics or Christian ethics (ibid., p. 61–62). Another similarity is that, according to V. Tsakiri, "it seems plausible to suggest that they both delineate a transcendent state-of-affairs, irreducible to universality and the totalizing powers of reason" (ibid., p. 62). However, one of the most important discrepancies between the two thinkers which emerges from a reverse (theological) point of the above similarity is that Kierkegaard, on the one hand, claims that "the love of one's neighbor is mediated by the love of God, whereas for Levinas the love of God is reached through the path that opens up as consequence of the love of one's neighbor" (Westphal, 2008, p. 70–71). Another crucial difference between the two thinkers concerning the theological/ethical issue of the Self and its relation to divinity and the other is that for Levinas "a face is of itself a visitation and a transcendence. To be in the image of God does not mean to be an icon of God but to find oneself in his trace. Subsequently, to go toward Him is not to follow this trace, which is not a sign; it is to go toward the Others who stand in the trace of illiety" (Tsakiri, 2009, p. 66).

Although Levinas agrees with Kierkegaard concerning the pitfalls and awry points in totalitarian ontology, he expresses a kind of skepticism (even suspicion) of the Protestant element in Kierkegaard's thought (Tsakiri, 2009, p. 62). This might seem logical and quite expected since Kierkegaard openly accepted the 'Protestant label.' However, Levinas, despite his sharp criticism of Kierkegaard's allegation of adopting God directly attributing theological historicism, supports Kierkegaard's theological view that "the Kierkegaardian God is revealed only by being persecuted and unrecognized, reveals only in the measure that he is hunted. God (remaining with the contrite and humble on the margin, a 'persecuted truth') is not only a religious consolation but the original form of transcendence" (ibid., 65). The objection Levinas raises on this matter, however, is that Kierkegaard mistakenly insists too much on human directness to God; that is, "it does not open us out to others but to God in isolation" (ibid., p. 65).

Summary

To sum up this brief discussion concerning the comparison between Levinas and Kierkegaard on subjectivity and the Self, we can infer that for Levinas' ethics the point of departure in order to conceive the Self and its relation to divinity and the Others is that "my Self, becoming 'me', can be elevated inspired, to fly beyond his attachment to the totality of worldly interests. For Levinas, this happens only when the Self is not merely for-itself, but for-the-Other" (Dimitrova, 2009, p. 51). Concluding, several continental thinkers present the issue of subjectivity and the Self as an eternal combat between ontology and ethical transcendence. Levinas, however, seems to overcome the primacy of ontology by offering an ethical reconciliation of the ontological I with the Other (Drossev, 2012, p. 56). As D. Drossev points out "the I of Levinas enters into a heteronymous relationship with the Other and the I who has met the Other passes grammatically and ethically from the imperative to the accusative case, thus the I becomes 'me.' The activity of the Other is through the I towards the accusative, towards the 'me.' That is how the active approach to the philosophy of Levinas is preserved" (ibid., p. 61). And as T. Chappell remarks "selfhood is not something I achieve on my own; it is a gift, the gift to me (and not I) of others" (Chappell, 2013, p. 3–28). T. Chappell also supports Levinas who "speaks of the individual soul as living in the Other" (ibid.). Finally, it is important to point out that for Levinas, "ethics is first philosophy where it is understood as a radically asymmetrical relation of infinite responsibility to the other person" (Critchley et al., 2002, p. 6).

Bibliography

Barber M.D., "Autonomy, Reciprocity, and Responsibility: Darwall and Levinas on the Second Person", International Journal of Philosophical Studies, 16.5 (2008), p. 629–644.

Bernet R., "Levinas's critique on Husserl", in The Cambridge Companion to Levinas, (eds.) S. Critchley and R. Bernasconi, Cambridge: Cambridge University Press, 2004, p. 82–99.

Chappell T., "The Goods and the Persons They Are Goods For", Philosophical News, 5 (2012), p. 1–7.

Chappell T., "Knowledge of Persons", European Journal of Philosophy of Religion, 5. 4 (2013), p. 3–28.

Critchley S., "Introduction", in The Cambridge Companion to Levinas, S. Critchley and R. Bernasconi (eds.), Cambridge: Cambridge University Press, 2004, p. 1–32.

Darwall S., The Second Person Standpoint: Morality, Respect, and Accountability, Harvard: Harvard University Press, 2006.

Dimitrova M., "Levinas: How to Think Humanitas of Homo Humanus?", Sofia Philosophical Review, I. 1., (2006), p. 15–29.

Dimitrova M., "Levinas' Outrageousness as a Grotesque: in Response to Jacob Rogozinski", Sofia Philosophical Review, III.2 (2009), p. 50–57.

Drossev D., "The Grotesque 'I' Before the Face of the Other: The Eschatology of the Grotesque", Sofia Philosophical Review, VI.2 (2012), p. 56–65

Harris M. J., Divine Command Ethics, London-New York: Taylor and Francis, 2004.

Heidegger M., Being and Time, J. Macquarrie and E. Robinson (tr.), Oxford: Blackwell, 1967.

Kant I., Religion within the limits of reason alone, tr. Th.M. Green and H.H. Hudson, New York: Harper and Row, 1960.

Kearney R. and Rainwater M. (eds.), The Continental Philosophy Reader, London and New York: Routledge, 2005.

Kierkegaard S., Works of Love, tr. H. and F. Hong, New York: Harper and Row, 1964.

Levinas E., Totality and Infinity, tr. A.L. Pittsburg, PA Duquesne University Press, 1969.

Levinas E., Otherwise Than Being, or, Beyond Essence, Pittsburg: Duquesne University Press, 2009.

Spezio M.L., "Social Neuroscience and Theistic Evolution: Intersubjectivity, Love, and the Social Sphere", Zygon, 48 (2013), p. 428–438.

Tsakiri V., "The "persecuted" Other: Levinas' perception of Kierkegaard", Sofia Philosophical Review, III. 2, (2009), p. 58–68.

Waldenfels B., "Levinas and the Face of the Other", in The Cambridge Companion to Levinas, (eds.) S. Critchley and R. Bernasconi, Cambridge: Cambridge University Press, 2004, p. 63–81.

Welz C., "Love as Gift and Self-Sacrifice", NSZTh, 50 (2008), p. 238–266.

West D., An Introduction to Continental Philosophy, Cambridge: Polity Press, 1996 (repr. 1997).

Westphal M., Levinas and Kierkegaard in Dialogue, Bloomington: Indiana University Press, 2008.

Westphal M., "Levinas, Kierkegaard and the Theological Task", Modern Theology, 8.3 (1992), p. 241–261.

Westphal M., Kierkegaard's Critique of Reason and Society, Macon, GA, Mercer University Press, 1987.

Wyschogrod E., Emmanuel Levinas: The Problem of Ethical Metaphysics, New York: Fordham University Press, 2000.

Zagzebski L.T., Divine Motivation Theory, Cambridge: Cambridge University Press, 2004.

Maryia Lappo

Historical Truth, Fiction, and Ideology in the Novel "Каласы пад сярпом тваім" by Uładzimir Karatkievič

Abstract: *The article aims to analyze the correspondence between historical truth and fiction in the historical novel "Каласы пад сярпом тваім" by Belarusian author Uładzimir Karatkievič. During the discussion of the novel at the meeting of the Writers' Union Secretariat, the author was often accused of distortion of the historical truth—but what was exactly meant by this? The first part of the article is devoted to the works of Benedetto Croce, Robin Collingwood, Paul Ricoeur, who regard history as "something middle" between fiction and science. The notion "truth" applied to history is different from the "truth" in natural sciences. "Historical truth" combines the factual information and the author's ideological position. Political ideology defines the main characteristics of the writer's sociocultural convictions. In the last part of the article, the discussion of the novel is analyzed in detail. It turns out that most accusations of distortions of historical truth are connected not with the writer's falsification of the historical facts, but with the writer's ideological position, although in both cases the discussion is about "historical truth".*

Keywords: philosophy of history, historical novel, narrative, ideology, national identity, Belarusian literature

Introduction

The novel "**Каласы пад сярпом тваім**" (1965, 1968), written by Uładzimir Karatkievič, was the first well-known and significant historical novel in Belarusian literature. It described Belarusians as a unique social group with their national self-awareness. This book strongly influenced the formation of Belarusian national identity: many readers admit that after reading this novel they became interested in Belarusian culture and history. However, it must be pointed out that the novel had many publishing difficulties: it was written for eight years, and then it was left lying in the publishing house for two years. The reviewers asked to change the novel's conception according to the socialistic ideology—to present peasants as main characters and to emphasize the emancipative nature of the peasant revolution. These changes did not correspond to the author's idea and to the historical facts to which the writer responded. To defend his position, Karatkievič wrote an appeal to the Writer's Union of the BSSR, and they organized a meeting of the Writer's Union Secretariat where the main problems of the novel were discussed.

During the critical discussion of the novel, the question about the correspondence between historical truth and reality was raised several times. This article aims to clarify what the notion of "historical truth" means and what kinds of problems were discussed during the meeting when the critics and reviewers talked about "the historical truth" in Karatkievič's novel. These notions are subsequently explored in the chapter called "Multiplicity of "historical truths": the problem of the inconsistency of different "historical truths". In the section "History as narrative and product of imagination", I review the philosophical theories that question history as an academic discipline with a set of the axiomatic statements. The following sections are mainly devoted to the analysis of the novel itself.

The Multiplicity of Historical "Truths"

The novel "Каласы пад сярпом тваім" "constructed" Belarusian national myth to a certain extent—however, it does not mean that Uładzimir Karatkievič "invented" a new past for Belarusians. Before writing the novel, the author carefully studied the archives and collected necessary materials for about twelve years. The writer defined his position concerning the correspondence between truth and fiction in the historical novel in an interview with Roza Stankievič. Answering the question "What kind of writer's features do you appreciate?" the author maintains "– Honesty! Never lie when you are writing. <…> this law is valid even in small details: do not lie, write as it is (another thing that there can be unbelievable cases). Anyway: if you don't know something, it is better not to put pen to paper"[1]. At the same time, Uładzimir Karatkievič admits that the creation of historical novels is not merely a "reconstruction of life" (which is rather the purpose of a historian), but the ability to imagine life in its entirety, which is connected with the work of creative imagination and with fiction. Therefore it is asserted that "It's clear that to write historical novels you should know the language and the way of people's lives very well; it means to know what they wore, how they

---

1   Уладзімір Караткевіч, "Любую справу рабіць хвацка", гутарыла Роза Станкевіч, Полымя, № 11, 2010, 165—169. [Uladzimir Karatkjevich, "Ljubuju spravu rabic hvacka [Any business should be done superbly]", interview by Roza Stankjevich, Polymja, № 11, 2010, 165—169].

ate, what their attitude towards this or that phenomenon was. For this, you need to scrutinize the documents and archives. But, on the other hand, the writer certainly can fantasise. For instance, I don't know what knights were talking about to each other preparing an attack on the city. This is the space for phantasy. I must fill in the book's pages with human life, with its joy and anxiety, happiness and grief"[2].

The paradox is that studying the archives and in-depth historical knowledge do not solve the problem of the "truthfulness" of the events described in the novel–and it is not because the author "over-interprets" the scenes which are absent in the historical sources, but because the historical sources break up into different views on the same events. Consequently, when the author chooses some sources and rejects the others, he becomes an adherent of a certain historical theory. It can be illustrated with the following example. One of the historical figures described in Karatkievič's novel is Kastuś Kalinoŭski–the inspirer of the anti-imperial revolt on the territory of contemporary Belarus and Poland. In the context of the novel, Kalinoŭski becomes the national hero and one of the first Belarusians who became aware of their national identity. There is also a strong group of scholars who believe that Kastuś Kalinoŭski should not be seen as a national hero. Valer Bułhakaŭ in "The history of Belarusian nationalism" says that it is incorrect to describe the 1863 revolt as a Belarussian national revolt. Bułhakaŭ assumes that it was a Polish revolt for the restoration of Reč Paspalitaja—the Commonwealth of The Kingdom of Poland and The Grand Duchy of Lithuania. The problem is that documentary information about Kastuś Kalinoŭski and his activity gives a possibility for the coexistence of completely different views on the historical events. For instance, it is a well-known fact that Kalinoŭski appealed to the peasants from the pages of the "Mužyckaja praŭda" using the Belarusian dialect. This fact is interpreted in various ways: some researchers affirm that "Mužyckaja praŭda" was the first printed Belarusian-language newspaper and by its publication Kalinoŭski sought "to awaken national consciousness" of Belarusians; others suppose that the publication of leaflets in Belarusian dialect was rather a forced measure, a strategic move that helped to add additional human resources to the anti-king revolt. We see that historical fact is just a basis for interpretations. Facts give the possibility to build

---

2   Уладзімір Караткевіч, "Кожная кніга – частка жыцця," інтэрв'ю ўзяў В. Аляшкевіч, пераклад з рускай Пятра Жаўняровіча, Интеграл, 15 красавіка 1982 [Uladzimir Karatkjevich, "Kozhnaja kniga – chastka zhyccja [Every book is a part of life]," interview by V. Aljashkjevich, translated from Russian by Pjatro Zhawnjarovich, Integral, 15 April, 1992].

different, often contradictory hypotheses and can be interpreted in completely different ways. As a result, we have several "historical truths".

History as a Narrative and a Product of Imagination

It is often said that the postmodern turn in philosophy of history and, in particular, the works of Hayden White and Frank Ankersmit, "destroyed" the view of history as a positive science with the set of factual truths. However, this tendency was evident long before Ankersmit and White—for instance, we can find it in the works of Benedetto Croce and Robin Collingwood. Croce shows, in his "Estetica" (1902), that the historian takes part in the selection and assembling of historiography's material and interferes with the historical process. According to Croce, the historian operates the synthesis of objectivity and subjectivity. He must creatively interpret his article, invoking the human experience and filling the informational blanks of his documentation, from inferences or various speculations[3]. In this respect, it is worth emphasizing the fact that since Croce, multiple scholars have come to understand that historical narratives have irreducible interpretative characteristics. For these reasons, historical narrative is a sequence of represented events, facts established and inferred, a representation which is an interpretation that is made by the re-invoking of the entire process reflected in the narrative. The validity of the story is a recurrent problem in the historiographical tradition. It has to be admitted that there is a vast difference between a writer of fiction and a historian. A writer of fiction was free to imagine anything as long as his narrative had continuity and coherence. A historian had to use his imagination within the constraints of a specific time and place, and according to existing historical evidence.

Subsequently, it is essential to emphasize the fact that the works of Robin Collingwood was inspired by the works of Benedetto Croce. His work "The Idea of History" (1946)[4] shows that the picture of the past which belongs to the historian and is the product of his imagination determines the choice of the sources used in his work. These sources are sources just because they are substantiated in such a way. Any source can be spoiled: this author is biased, that one received false information, another is a bad specialist who incorrectly read an inscription, etc. The historian who thinks critically should

---

3   Patricia Horvat, History as Art in Benedetto Croce, Academia.edu, Available at: <https://www.academia.edu/5119388/History_as_Art_in_Benedetto_Croce_-_Patricia_Horvat/>[Accessed on 10.06.2017, at 21:13].
4   Robin Collingwood, The Idea of History, (Oxford University Press, 2004), p. 510.

Historical Truth, Fiction, and Ideology in "Каласы пад сярпом тваім"

correct all similar distortions. And he is doing it only by deciding for himself if the picture of the past created by the evidence is a continuous picture with historical meaning. Subsequently, we can also draw our attention to the fact that Paul Ricoeur in his work "Time and narrative" also focusses on the "entrecroisement" of literature and history: they both use the tools of the other[5]. History uses the methods of literature to refigure and restructure time by imposing narrative contours on the non-narrative time of nature. In real time, events just happen one by one in sequence, which may seem random or determined by causal connections. This reality has nothing common with the narrative form and, consequently, narration imposes on reality a form completely alien to it. Understood in this way, a narrative looks like something that inevitably distorts reality. According to Ricoeur, being a narrative, history cannot be an academic discipline that "proclaims[s] the truth about reality". We should look on history as on a mixture of fiction and fact, or maybe even doubt the difference between fiction and non-fiction literature. Finally, it is important to point out that the mentioned-above researchers lead us to the following assertions:

- historians choose material according to their personal view, ignoring the sources that contradict this picture
- historians themselves interpret the facts and create the narrative, establishing the causal link between the events and using their imagination.

In this case, it is worth bringing to the fore the opinions of Georg Iggers and David Carr, who argue in favor of establishing a "middle" position between historical objectivism, which presents history as an intellectual discipline close to the natural sciences, and relativism, which erases the border between history and fiction. It is important to notice in this case that Carr does not agree with Paul Ricoeur, who insists that "narrative structures" are structures of the human reality because they express the specificity of the human perception of time:

"Narrative corresponds with this world because narrative structures are rooted in the human reality itself. A historian should not "inscribe" the spent time in the natural time by the act of narration, as Ricoeur says about it; spent time "is inscribed" there even before the historian starts the work. To tell stories about human past does not mean to put on these stories some alien

---

[5] Paul Ricoeur, Time and Narrative, 3 vols. trans. Kathleen Blamey and David Pellauer, (Chicago: University of Chicago Press, 1984, 1985, 1988).

structure, but it means to continue the very activity which constitutes human past"[6]. At the same time, Carr points out that history as such has much in common with literature, especially in its narrative form. Historians, as well as writers, actively use imagination. However, this does not mean that historical literature merges with fiction or that literary elements lie embedded in historical knowledge. Historians use literary methods to narrate the truth about the events that happened to people in the past.

History and Ideology

Slavoj Zizek defines ideology as our perception of the world and as meaning that we give to any phenomenon. "Ideology is not a dreamlike illusion that we build to escape insupportable reality; in its basic dimension, it is a fantasy-construction which serves as a support for our reality itself; an illusion which structures are effective, real social relations and thereby masks some insupportable, real, impossible kernel"[7]. This formulation makes ideology very close to the imagination which as well as ideology helps us to create some fundamental dimension of existence. Political ideology is the vector of this dimension that forms reality by the individual's preassigned criterion. The further we move from the ability to imagine the ability to give meaning, the more political ideology becomes outspoken. Many already "outspoken" contemporary ideologies such as feminism, ecologism, and others show us how a certain vector forms reality. Consequently, history is also transformed according to a certain direction predetermined by ideology. In one of his interviews, the German-American historian and professor Georg Iggers gives attention to the tendencies of contemporary historiography: "Women and gender history have become extremely important (…) it was the concentration of attention on the aspects that were ignored before. (…) We start to understand that men and women also have their history. I think it is a positive development (…) but, on the other hand, it often leads to the creation of the new historical myths"[8].

---

[6] David Carr, "History, Fiction and Human Time: historical Imagination and Historical responsibility," in The Ethics of History, ed. David Carr, Thomas R. Flynn & Rudolf A. Makkreel, (Northwestern University Press, 2004), p. 247–260.

[7] Slavoj Žižek, The Sublime Object of Ideology, (New York, 1989), p. 45.

[8] Георг Иггерс, "Как историки мы должны бороться против инструментализации истории," Уроки истории XX век, Обржушко, Польша, 29 мая 1993 года, Available at: <http://urokiistorii.ru/node/52051/>[Accessed on 10.06.2017, at 21:13]. [Georg Iggers, "Kak istoriki my dolzhny borot'sja protiv instrumentalizacii istorii [As historians we must fight against the instrumentalization of history]," Uroki istorii XX vek [The lessons

The recording of the discussion of the novel "Каласы пад сярпом тваім" by Uładzimir Karatkievič demonstrates that often the accusations of deviations from the "historical truth" turn out to be encounters of different ideologies and worldviews (that had different backgrounds and were based on various historical sources).

Maryna Kazłoŭskaja and Hanna Butyrčyk view the version of the national myth proposed by Uładzimir Karatkievič as an "alternative" to the dominant ideology of the 1960s and the 1970s in the BSSR[9]. In the novel, the writer showed the becoming of the "nationally conscious intellectuals", which was new to Belarusian literature. Before Karatkievič's works, literature mainly showed Belarusians as uneducated peasants or poor students who came from the peasantry. Despite the numerous accusations of the "falsity" of his historical conception, during the novel's discussion, Uładzimir Karatkievič was sure that truth was on his side: "You will not push me to a lie. It is a time to tell the most actual truth in our literature (…) This is why I insist that the revolt was launched by the nobles that were not different from raznochinstvo"[10]. "Someone from the reviewers wanted me to put in the center of the novel, not the knyaz Aleś Zahorski, but the peasant. However, it would be contrary to the historical truth. The new works of the Russian, Belarussian, Lithuanian and Polish historians—for instance, Smirnoŭ, Kisialoŭ,

---

of history The XXth century], Obrzhushko, Poland, 29 May, 1993, Available at: <http://urokiistorii.ru/ node/52051/> [Accessed on 10.06.2017, at 21:31].

[9] Ганна Бутырчык, Марына Казлоўская, "Каласы пад сярпом тваім" Уладзіміра Караткевіча як альтэрнатыўны варыянт нацыянальнага міфа", у Славянскія літаратуры ў кантэксце сусветнай: да 750–годдзя са дня нараджэння Дантэ Аліг'еры і 85-годдзя Уладзіміра Караткевіча : матэрыялы XII Міжнар. навук. канф., рэд. Г. М. Бутырчык, (Мінск: РІВШ, 2016), p. 8–22. [Ganna Butyrchyk, Maryna Kazlowskaja, "Kalasy pad sjarpom tvaim" Uladzimira Karatkjevicha jak alternatywny varyjant nacyjanal'naga mifa" ["Kalasy pad sjarpom tvaim" by Uladzimir Karatkjevich as an alternative version of the national myth], in Slavjanskija litaratury w kantekscje susvjetnaj: da 750–goddzja sa dnja naradzhennja Dante Alig'jery i 85–goddzja Uladzimira Karatkjevicha : materyjaly XII Mizhnar. navuk. kanf. [Slavic literature in the context of the world: to the 750th anniversary of the birth of Dante Alighieri and the 85th anniversary of Uladzimir Karatkjevich: materials of the XII Intern. Sciences. Conf.], ed. G. M. Butyrchyk, (Minsk: RIVSH, 2016), p. 8–22].

[10] Сяргей Шапран, "Прыміце мяне такім, які я ёсць," Дзеяслоў, № 12 (2013), accessed October 4, 2017, Available at: <https://http://dziejaslou.by/old/ www.dziejaslou.by/ inter/dzeja/dzeja.nsf/htmlpage/shap2302ec.html?OpenDocument> [Sjargjej Shapran, "Prymicje mjanje takim, jaki ja josc" [Accept me as I am], Dzjejaslow, no. 12 (2013), accessed October 4, 2017, <http://dziejaslou.by/old/www.dziejaslou.by/ inter/dzeja/dzeja.nsf/htmlpage/shap2302ec.html?OpenDocument/> [Accessed on 10.06.2017, at 21:13].

Kianievič—show us that the moving force of the revolt in Belarus was exactly the nobles"[11].

Conclusion: the Historical Truth in The Novel "Каласы Пад Сярпом Тваім"

I would like to get back to the questions placed at the beginning of the article—what the notion "historical truth" means and what critiques and reviewers talked about when analyzing the "historical truth" in the novel. Typically, when we talk about "historical truth", contrasting it with fiction, it is understood as infallible factual truth, similar to the truth in natural sciences like "The Earth is round", etc. Part of the critiques' allegations concerning "historical truth" in the novel are justified—there are allegations that the novel contradicts with the concrete historical facts. However, there are not many such allegations (Iryna Połaŭcava points out that among such deviations—Belarusian-language play in the old Vezha's theatre (which is impossible in the XIXth century when the Belarusian language was not finally formed) and the transfer of the dziadźkavańnie tradition, typical for the XVI–XVIII centuries, into the XIXth century)[12]. The other allegations about the distortion of "historical truth" turn out to be ideological—creating the novel, Uładzimir Karatkievič relied on historical sources which were ignored by Soviet power. Karatkievič's opponents relied on different sources (it happens because of the "multiplicity" of historical "truths" and narratives). It can also be said that the author presented his "personal ideology", which apparently did not coincide with the official one.

---

[11] Анатоль Верабей, "Уладзімір Караткевіч: жыццё і творчасць", (Мн.: "Беларуская навука", 2005), p. 110. [Anatol' Vjerabjej, "Uladzimir Karatkjevich: zhyccjo i tvorchasc" [Uladzimir Karatkjevich: life and creating], (Mn.: "Bjelaruskaja navuka", 2005), p. 110].

[12] Ірына Полаўцава, "Мастацкая праўда і праўда гісторыі ў рамане У. Караткевіча Каласы пад сярпом тваім", у Класіка і современность: сб. науч. тр. молодых ученых-філологов, науч. ред. Т.В.Сенькевич, (Брест: Альтернатива, 2009), p. 98–100. [Iryna Polawcava, "Mastackaja prawda i prawda gistoryi w ramanje U.Karatkjevicha "Kalasy pad sjarpom tvaim" [The artistic truth and the truth of history in the novel "Kalasy pad sjarpom tvaim" by U. Karatkjevich], in Klassika i sovremennost' : sb. nauch. tr. molodyh uchenyh-filologov [Classics and modernity: a collection of scientific works of young philologists], nauch. red. T.V.Sen'kevich, (Brest: Al'ternativa, 2009), p. 98–100].

Further Reading

Uładzimir Karatkievič, Spikes under your sickle [Kałasy pad siarpom tvaim, Каласы пад сярпом тваім (Belarusian edition 1965), (Russian edition 1974)].

Uładzimir Karatkievič, Christ landed in Grodno [Chrystos pryziamliŭsia ŭ Harodni, Хрыстос прызямліўся ў Гародні (Belarusian edition 1972), (Russian edition 1966)].

Uładzimir Karatkievič, The Dark Castle Olshansky [Čorny zamak Alšanski (Belarusian edition 1979), (Russian edition 1984)].

Uładzimir Karatkievič, King Stakh's Wild Hunt [Dzikaje palavańnie karala Stacha, Дзікае паляванне караля Стаха (Belarusian edition 1964), (Russian edition 1980), (English edition 2012)].

Uładzimir Karatkievič, The Boat of Despair [Ładździa rospačy (Belarusian edition 1978), (Russian edition 1987)].

Uładzimir Karatkievič, The Mother's Soul [Matčyna duša (Belarusian edition 1958)].

Uładzimir Karatkievič, Chazenia [(Belarusian edition 1967), (Russian edition 1969)].

Uładzimir Karatkievič, The Evening Sails [Viačernija vietrazi (Belarusian edition 1960)].

Uładzimir Karatkievič, My Iliad [Maja Ilijada (Belarusian edition 1969)].

Uładzimir Karatkievič, The Land Beneath White Wings [(Belarusian edition 1977), (English edition 1982)].

Valentīna Prokofjeva, The image of the serpent in Vladimir Korotkevich's novel 'Christ has landed in Grodno.' Comparative Studies (p. 1691–5038). 2012, Vol. 4 Issue 1.

Book Reviews

Piotr Pietrzak on Immanuel Kant's Categorical Imperative and his "Perpetual Peace: A Philosophical Sketch" (1795)

There is a strong feeling within continental philosophy suggesting that by defeating Ernst Cassirer in the debate held in Davos in 1929; Martin Heidegger sent Kantian philosophy to the dustbin of history[1]. It is argued that this controversial German philosopher managed to expose all of the dogmatism associated with Immanuel Kant, yet, despite all of the limitations related to Kantian and Neo-Kantian philosophy, this Königsbergian tradition cannot just be casually dismissed. Martin Heidegger has not discovered America by assigning more importance to his deliberations on the position of the individual in the society, and he was relating his findings to the passage that was already well-traveled by Kant. If anything, this Prussian thinker who is respected by both continental and analytical traditions should be considered as a real pioneer of modernity. Indeed, Kant succeeded in creating a philosophical system that transformed the position of individuals from obedient and clueless masses who were treated as political helots to the position of moral agents empowered by their free will and their sense of moral responsibilities towards both their fellow human beings and themselves and were given a unique chance to become increasingly aware of their political rights and obligations as citizens. To anyone who has had the pleasure of carefully studying Kantian treatises, it is more than evident that the magnitude of his philosophical insights can be compared only to grand discoveries made by Nicolaus Copernicus and Galileo Galilei in the field of astronomy. There are several reasons behind this assertion: the sophistication

---

[1] **Emanuel Levinas** who had witnessed Davos debate of 1929 later recalled that a young student could have had an impression that he was witnessing the creation and the end of the world, as the drama built into this confrontation between the two the most eminent philosophers of their time was very intense. For more information on Davos Debate, please refer to: **1.)** *Friedman, Michael, (2000). A Parting of Ways: Carnap, Cassirer, and Heidegger; Gordon, Peter, (2010).* **2.)** *Continental Divide: Heidegger, Cassirer, Davos, Hass, Andrew, (2007). The Irony of Heidegger,* ISBN 9780826497963: *Xavier University Press.* **3.)** *Heidegger, Martin, (1997). "Davos Disputation between Ernst Cassirer and Martin Heidegger" in Kant and the Problem of Metaphysics.* **4.)** *Skildelsky, Edward, (2008). Ernst Cassirer, The Last Philosopher of Culture; The Continental Philosophy Reader, Edited by Richard Kearney and Mara Rainwater.* **5.)** *West, David, (2010). Continental Philosophy, An Introduction, Cambridge: Polity Press.* **6.)** *Wrathall, Mark, (2005). How to Reach Heidegger, London: Granta Publications.*

of his methods, the complexity of his analysis, and the originality of his approach. Taken together, they can be considered as genuinely exceptional scholarly achievements, but there is something even more exceptional about Kantian philosophy, namely the fact that his ethical school at its core does not draw on the supernatural being as a reference of morality, guidance or an ultimate point of reference, but considers a reason as a sole source of morality. The question remains: how does Kant come to such a conclusion? The best way to answer it is to emphasize the fact that this philosopher is very keen to carefully investigate the relationship between morality and religion and the role of religion in the dynamics of human interactions, culture, and history. It is only after application of such complex inquiries and investigations that this philosopher would come to the conclusion that ethics can be based solely on human faculties, logic, reason, and moral intuition. Despite the fact that the Catholic Church ostracized this philosopher, treated him as a heretic and placed the work of this moral thinker on Index Librorum Prohibitorum, Kant's discoveries would prove instrumental in inspiring hundreds if not thousands to work on his secular ethical system, not in order to fight any religion or diminish a sense or value of anyone's religious feelings, but in order to prove to each and every individual (even those of us who do not believe in the almighty or hold any religious beliefs) that he can be an honest and decent man who can act in accordance with a universally acknowledged moral law. Subsequently, this deontological moral thinker advances the view that moral judgments should be based on rationality and human understanding because at the end it is the ultimate source of the general laws of nature that structure all of our experiences. In this sense, the status of a man as a moral being follows from his status as a rational being.

This notion is, consequently, dictated by the logic of the fact that rational beings can evaluate the worthiness of an individual's actions and for these reasons Kant believes that they should be allowed to decide for themselves whether to act in a given way or not, meaning that our experience of reality is not merely passive but somewhat active, as it exposes our minds to various structures that determine how we encounter the world. This philosopher has also argued that percepts without concepts are blind, which means that our reason is not only the source of morality, but it also provides us with the standard by which everyone can make moral justifications, as long as we can comprehend it. Besides, from his perspective, once an action is reasoned, rational beings should be perfectly capable of distinguishing what moral conduct accounts for, and should be able to determine if their efforts can be considered as morally permissible or impermissible. Consequently, to educate the individual to recognize their moral duties, this free thinker formulates three categorical imperatives which could be easily applied to any circumstances that would guide the behavior of individuals at large.

Accordingly, the first categorical imperative suggests acting only according to that maxim whereby you can at the same time will that it should become a universal law without contradiction. The second formulation recommends acting only in such a way that you treat humanity, whether in your person or the person of any other, never merely as a means to an end, but always at the same time as an end. The last imperative advises that every rational being must so act as if he were through his maxim always a legislating member in the universal kingdom of ends. Such a law could aspire to the **kingdom of ends** (understood as an ideal society in which people are at once both the authors and the subjects of the laws they obey) only if certain preconditions are met. According to this line of reasoning, when one tries to determine what the moral worth of any given action is, whether it is morally acceptable or deplorable, one has to first and foremost check what the intention of the person who undertakes such an act is. Interestingly, it is not a consequence of an action that makes it right or wrong but the motive of the person who acts. In this respect, this philosopher advanced the view that circumstances do not matter; even if actions take place within a particular society at a specific time, a universal set of values must apply to everyone without exception in every situation. The logic behind this rule is based on the fact that the consequence of an act of willing cannot be used to determine if the person started any given action with a good intention or not. As this philosopher explains, good consequences could arise by accident from an act that was motivated by a desire to cause harm to an innocent person, and adverse effects could result from an act that was well-motivated. Therefore, the best way to assess the worth of the motivation behind any given action is by asking whether we could turn that motive into the universally enforceable law, or not. That is why Kant suggests that principles must be valid for all rational beings in all circumstances. He further concludes that action is moral only if it is performed without ulterior motives, with no attention to consequences, and out of pure respect for morality. Such a law consequently could be recognized if it could apply to every individual in the world. In his Foundations of the Metaphysics of Morals Immanuel Kant makes it explicit that to act morally, one has to treat every individual as a moral agent. These individuals should be, subsequently, treated as ends in themselves rather than the means by which other people can achieve their ends (Kant, 1795, p. 400–489).

Furthermore, it is important to point out that it is predominantly thanks to his **"Perpetual Peace: A Philosophical Sketch"** (1795), that Kant can be seen as a precursor of a practical application of his system of secular ethics into the realm of politics. The originality of his thought in this respect shows this philosopher as less dogmatic, less formalistic and pedantic because despite being generally in favour of the principle of non-intervention in the internal arrangements of independent countries, Kant makes a suggestion that under exceptional circumstances (of scandalous internal dissension and deterioration of the situation in a given country into a civil war), other countries should be allowed to take certain action to restore the status quo; even if it would have meant a full-scale intervention in such a state. This suggestion alone, clearly shows that this philosopher was well ahead of his times. Indeed, in his "Perpetual Peace: A Philosophical Sketch" (1795) Kant brings to the fore a vision of an ideal system of international affairs based on mutual respect and fraternity where a federation of free states is composed out of a union of representative governments (republics) (Kant, 1894, p. 111–116).

The main reason behind forming such a federation is explained by Kant by the fact that it would have allowed the international community to form and become a custodian of laws governing actions and behavior between every country in the structure. Furthermore, the existence of such a body would also secure fundamental laws for world citizenship such as the right to hospitality and freedom to travel that would enhance the prospects of peace and stability. The payoff of embarking on the perpetual peace agenda would be great as once attained; the eternal peace could finally liberate the members of the international community from the unpredictability of the state of nature and constantly breaking out destructive wars waged against one another. In turn, averting the dreadful consequences of war would consequently trigger all of the benefits of peace.

The primary conditions for an everlasting peace programme to be achieved would be: abstaining from signing secret treaties (that tacitly reserve the right to wage wars) refraining from dominating other independent states, agreeing not to use national debts as a pretext to exercise any external influence on other countries, promising not to interfere with force in a constitution or in a government of independent states, and, finally, dissolving standing armies, as there would be no practical use for them, given that every member of the Federation would obey their obligations to the global community. One could argue that the author of this sketch was hopeful that attaining perpetual peace would be just a matter of time, but Kant was not delusional about how humanity would attain it. This freethinker argued that there are at least two ways for this idea to come into existence: either through peace or through war.

Despite the fact that the former alternative seemed more desirable as it entailed the notion assuming that the vast majority of countries in the world would voluntarily reject the idea of war and reach an executive decision to send war to the dustbin of history, Kant was of another opinion. This thinker, argued that the citizens of the world were likely to choose the latter option which inevitability presupposed a great war that would result in a catastrophe of such magnitude that it would leave humanity with no other choice but to agree to overcome their main differences and embark on an eternal peace agenda in order to avert the destruction of our planet. Aware of the fact that it may take us a while before we finally outlaw war as a means of attaining one's political goals and objectives, Kant makes sure to warn us that if we choose war over peace, we should restrain from permitting such acts of hostility that would make it difficult to reconcile with our former enemies after the hostilities eventually end. What this philosopher meant by that was to induce any potential aggressors to restrain from an employment of assassins, mistreatment of prisoners, breach of the terms of capitulation, inciting treason in the opponent, etc. for their own good.

It is possible that, to many contemporary political commentators and philosophers, the notion of perpetual peace sounds like a childish superstition of someone who did his best to remain blissfully unaware of the way human nature will always be constructed. This criticism turns out to be far-fetched as from the perspective of hindsight we know that the idea of ever-lasting peace has encouraged masses of philosophers, policymakers, decision-makers, global leaders and political commentators to force large chunks of this idea into reality. Despite the fact that global peace was interrupted by countless wars, conflicts, and skirmishes for the vast majority of the last 200 years, Kant's proposal of eternal peace has withstood the test of time and has played a massive role in the construction of the contemporary security system. Although there is no official United Nations record making any direct reference to the work of this philosopher, it is commonly understood that Kant has every right to consider himself to be a legitimate forefather of the idea of the contemporary global security system in its modern form. Without his work, the idea of the League of Nations would never have come into existence after the First World War, and the United Nations would never have been established in 1945 after the Second World War. In this instance, one has to draw attention to the fact that both Kant and United Nations share more things in common than is generally understood. For starters, their work is very often misused and abused by various parties that are interested in using the authority of this organization, and this philosopher to either inadvertently prove the validity of their claims or in order to attain specific tangible political goals.

In this respect, we need to emphasize the fact that Kant's work very often applies to general aspects of this philosopher's work when his scholarly contributions to the literature on the subject prove to be either vague or otherwise unspecified. Accordingly, the fifth preliminary article of the Perpetual Peace treaty (on the right to non-intervention in internal affairs of other countries) accounts for a classic example of such abuse. This short chapter of this remarkable philosophical treaty was separated into two main parts. One suggests that even if one can witness an internal dissension happening in a given country, no justification for intervention in the internal affairs of this country can be put forward, especially if the situation in this country has not come to any critical point.

Subsequently, the second part of this publication specifies that there may be certain exceptions to this rule: Kant argues here that "if a state, by internal rebellion, should fall into two parts, each of which pretended to be a separate state making a claim to the whole, it would be permissible to lend assistance to one of these parts". According to this perspective, such an intervention cannot be considered as an intrusion in the constitution of other states or infringement of the rights of their people. As we may appreciate, Immanuel Kant is making a wager in this respect. He on the verge of being stingy with the use of his words in this respect, and for this reason he leaves us wondering what he meant by this clarification. By refraining from giving us a full disclosure of what Kant actually meant by connecting these positions, he has also left us wondering what we should read as his intentions as regards the idea of humanitarian intervention in general. On one hand he presents an explicit prohibition of any attempt of interference in the internal affairs the independent countries, but on the other hand this rule is followed by the exception that diminishes its weight. Does he mean to say that states should be obliged to defend only their citizens or should they be allowed to assist other peoples from different distant countries should they face violent internal disputes? The former interpretation seems to be forbidding a humanitarian action, while the latter paves the way to an endorsement of humanitarian interventions. Altogether, we are faced with a twisted logic of catch–22 because no matter which option we choose, we open our interpretation to criticism from either group within Kantian philosophy. The best solution in such a situation would be to question Kant in person for his opinion in this respect. The problem that we are inevitably facing is the fact that the tradition in question has become pluralized and internally divided over matters that to the outside world seem of very little importance, but let us submit to any trivializations in this respect. Such criticism should not cloud our judgment; the beauty of bringing to the fore various interpretations of Kant's work presents us with a hope of elaborating the best possible juxtaposition that may be strengthened by the richness, pluralism, and intensity of this debate.

References

Archibugi, Daniele. (1995). Immanuel Kant, Cosmopolitan Law, and Peace. European Journal of International Relations, 1: 429.

Franceschet Antonio, Kant, International Law, and the problem of humanitarian intervention, Journal of International Political Theory, 6(1) 2010.

Kant, Immanuel. (1894–1920). Eternal Peace. The Advocate of Peace, Vol. 59, No. 5 (May 1897).

Kleingeld, Pauline. (2004). Approaching Perpetual Peace: Kant's Defence of a League of States and his Ideal of a World Federation. European Journal of Philosophy 12:3, p. 304–325.

Jokic Aleksandar, (2003). Humanitarian Intervention: Moral and Philosophical Issues, New York: Broadview Press.

Pape Robert A., When Duty Calls. A Pragmatic Standard of Humanitarian Intervention, International Security, Vol. 37, No. 1 (Summer 2012), p. 41–80.

Piotr Pietrzak on György Lukács: "The young Hegel: Studies in the Relations between Dialectics and Economics"
(1938; translation: London: Merlin Press, 1975, translated by Rodney Livingstone)

GYÖRGY LUKÁCS (1885–1971) is considered to be one of the most important Western thinkers, aestheticians, literary historians, critics, and political activists, and there is definitely a tangible reason behind this state of affairs, as this continental philosopher is known for developing an alternative, pre–Bolshevik interpretation of Karl Marx's theory that rejects the deterministic and scientific excesses of Stalinist dogma. Unlike the later scholars in this tradition who came to similar conclusions only from the perspective of hindsight, this Hungarian scholar acknowledged the massive distortions in the Stalinist interpretation of Marxist theory at the beginning of the 1930s, long before the full scope of Soviet atrocities were revealed to the broader public. In this respect, it is worth emphasizing the fact that Lukács' interpretations of Marxist theory also account for a softer, more genuine and much more approachable version than the ones offered by the majority of the Hungarian Communist Party members, even at the time of Imre Nagy's reforms. It is noteworthy that, while the majority of his hardliner comrades made an unfortunate choice of prioritising the Kremlin's "one and only" interpretation of Marxist theory over common sense, this philosopher resisted yielding to the central theorists' dictate, and did his best to underline the fact that socialism should have a human face, meaning that it should be of the people, by the people, for the people.

Of course, we could just dismiss this argument by pointing to the fact that this state of affairs had changed after 1956 Revolution, when his fellow Communists left Lukács no choice but to engage in various self-criticisms and self-retractions from his initial positions, and entertain various more opinionated, dogmatic and hard-nosed positions than ever before. In his defense, we need to point out that he did not engage in this activity to satisfy the official line of the Party, but in order to be allowed to return to his homeland, as he had had to seek refuge in neighboring Romania to survive the post–1956 purge in Hungary organized by the forces within the party sympathetic to the Soviet Union. Subsequently, despite the fact that this scholar was very often forced to work under duress in this troubled post–revolutionary period, Lukács managed to remain true to himself and contribute to the literature of the subject a number of hidden warnings against the tyrannical attempts of both the central planners and the capitalists decisionmakers whose dictates aimed at causing the curtailing of individual freedoms within contemporary societies, and that is something that cannot be taken back. Indeed, the best testament to the above-mentioned assertion is evidenced in his **'The History and Class Consciousness' (1923)** [(German: *Geschichte und Klassenbewußtsein: Studien über Marxistische Dialektik*), (especially in the chapter dedicated to Reification and the Consciousness of the Proletariat)], where Lukács brings to the fore of continental discussions such themes like the theory of class consciousness, the theory of reification, social alienation, objectification, and a very comprehensive analysis of the relationship between commodity fetishism and the reification of human beings. One may say that these findings were very relevant at the time and on some levels remain still applicable to the debate on the locus of the individual in contemporary society localized within the constraints of the global village. In this respect, Lukács draws our attention particularly to the centrality of commodity exchange and its fundamental importance for the functioning of socialist and capitalist societies at large to reassure us that this debate is likely to have a much more profound impact on our lives in the not so distant future.

Naturally, the weight of the Lukács insights into Marxist literature has been recognized by various members of the continental tradition, especially within the so-called Frankfurt School, and the leading members of this group, such as Theodor Adorno, Max Horkheimer, Herbert Marcuse, and Jürgen Habermas who benefited the most out of this tradition. However, it is crucial to emphasise in this case that as much as all of these members of the *Frankfurter Schule* may have drawn heavily on Lukács' interpretations of Karl Marx's philosophy, they have also benefited from his insights into Hegel's philosophy, and this scholar's explicit emphasis on the fact that Hegel's philosophy had an immense effect on the Young Marx. For these reasons, pigeonholing this Hungarian merely as a Marxist philosopher would be doing him a huge disservice as he was evidently wearing a lot of different hats during his life. What is also worth noticing in this instance is the fact that Lukács' example illustrates the fact that it could be challenging to be a leading commentator on Marx's work without being able to relate this commentary to Hegel's dialectical element in his philosophy. Otherwise, we may struggle to uncover the real complexity of the Marxist Opus Magnum as well as get a proper grasp of this thinker's early work.

For these reasons we should come to terms with the fact that Lukács should also be seen as a leading expert in Hegelian philosophy and his **'The** young Hegel' (1975) [German: *Der Junge Hegel* (1938)] testifies to the validity of this assertion because this publication offers profound insights into the two early stages in Hegel (1770–1831)'s philosophical development prior to his move to the University of Jena in 1801 at the age of thirty-one. What is especially noticeable in this instance is the fact that unlike the other commentators in this tradition who show an unhealthy tendency to over-focus their investigations of this German philosopher's thought through the prism of his later publications, Lukács categorically refuses to follow this pattern. However, it must be pointed out that this does not mean that this thinker would be necessarily more fascinated by the early stages in the formation of young Hegel's thought, but that he definitely would not want to disregard it completely simply because it dates from before Hegel's groundbreaking discoveries in Jena. Lukács in this respect is certain that the rationale of revisiting Hegel's work from the perspective of his humble beginnings can definitely open our eyes to various hidden paradigms and methods from this period, which is why Lukács is very keen to devote so much effort to investigating Hegel's philosophy through the prism of his formative period. By focusing on Hegel's early period, Lukács expects to uncover something of real value that has been hidden behind a veil of ignorance from Hegelian thinkers for a very long time, and now this is in need of exploration.

Undoubtedly, by approaching Hegel's contribution to the literature on the subject in a sequential manner, Lukács is doing Hegel the courtesy of investigating the relevance of various evolutionary developments in his thought in a chronological manner, stage by stage, in a way similar to that which Hegel developed in order to describe the different stages in the circular transformation of the Hegelian Spirit. This seems to be very important, as, from the perspective of hindsight, we already know that leaving Frankfurt in 1801 coincided with Hegel publishing his first serious philosophical book: **"The difference between Fichte's and Schelling's System of Philosophy"** (German: *Differenz des Fichteschen und Schellingschen Systems der Philosophie*); that in turn would lead him to publish his opus magnum "Phenomenology of Spirit" (1806), so if we assume that there is absolute continuity in his thought we may assert that there must have been a particular correlation between studying theology, working as a tutor for families in Bern and then Frankfurt, and at the same time developing the backbone of his incredibly sophisticated philosophical system. Lukács in this respect also makes a strong suggestion that however brilliant Hegel was, he could not develop his later system of philosophy overnight without proper preparation. By following this line of investigation, we eventually need to come to terms with the fact that his "Phenomenology of Spirit" was built in stages, possibly over decades, not months or weeks. For these reasons, by entertaining Lukács' investigations of Hegel's Tübingen (1788–93), Bern (1793–96), and Frankfurt (1797–1800) periods out of his 'Young Hegel,' we are investigating the foundation on which the Hegelian philosophy was established.

Tübingen Period (1788–1793)

There are various exciting developments in young Hegel's life that happened while he was attending a Protestant seminary associated with the University of Tübingen for five years between 1788 and 1793. It is emphasised in this respect that during this period Georg Hegel acquainted himself with most of the leading philosophical debates related to antiquity, Christianity, and the Enlightenment, Immanuel Kant, Baron de La Brède et de Montesquieu, François-Marie Arouet, known by his nom de plume Voltaire, Denis Diderot, Baron d'Holbach, Jean-Jacques Rousseau, Hugo Grotius, David Hume, Friedrich Schiller, and Benjamin Constant. On the other hand, Lukács draws our attention to the fact that what might have been even more critical in his early education than his lecturers at the Tübinger Stift was the fact that during this period young Hegel befriended fellow students poet-to-be Friedrich Hölderlin (1770–1843) and the philosopher-to-be Friedrich Wilhelm Joseph Schelling (1775–1854). Not only were these three boys at that time engaged in a number of sophisticated debates both at school and in their spare time but they also were actively involved in the proceedings of a secret society devoted to the reading of forbidden writings of ancient thinkers that were not part of the traditional curriculum, reading poetry and philosophising.

Reportedly, during some of the proceedings of this society Hölderlin, Schelling and Hegel planted a tree of liberty, danced around it and sang revolutionary songs about the French Revolution. Of course it is still too early to suggest that his time at Tübingen had given Hegel the first idea that one day he would attempt to establish an inclusive tradition that would revolutionize the way we approach contemporary philosophy, but one may definitely indulge in the speculation that being part of such a productive and challenging environment made an impact on his future.

Bern Period (1793–1796)

Having been exposed to academic rigor, discipline and the art of freethinking at Tübingen helped young Hegel to open his eyes to more sophisticated philosophical debates that would shape his future thinking in Bern, where he became a house tutor (German: *Hofmeister*) to an aristocratic family in 1793. According to Lukács, while residing in the capital city of Switzerland between 1793 to 1796 Hegel had the chance to start elaborating some useful ideas that would later be incorporated into his system of philosophy.

To begin with, one has to emphasize the fact that during his Swiss period Hegel slowly came to terms with the fact that the history of human existence should be seen through the prism of the developments within a triadic structure that encompasses: 1.) The fundamental freedom and self-activation of human society. 2.) The loss of this freedom under the hegemony of positivity. 3.) Moreover, the recovery of the lost freedom. Subsequently, in this respect, Lukács points out that while in Bern, Hegel engaged in more in-depth investigations of classical antiquity that according to his writings from this period were deeply romanticised, as he saw this period as an irreplaceable golden age of beauty. It is also underlined here that he was under a strong impression of the free and beautiful lives of the Greeks and Romans; the Greek model of the old republic, its democracy and freedom, and this thinker was also captivated by the vibrant public life of the ancients. For this reason Hegel sees antiquity as an eternal model for the development of humanity, and this fascination was so intense during this period that he even made a suggestion that posterity should treat antiquity as an idealized picture of the Republic of the future, and the place for creating the conditions for the democratic regeneration of man. In this respect, Lukács suggests that Hegel's early view of classical antiquity could have been affected by traditional festivals of Greece that were taking place precisely at the time when he was present in Switzerland. In his later writings, Hegel's sentimental attitudes towards classical antiquity would be replaced by his enthusiasm for the arid prose of the Enlightenment, the prose from which there is no escape.

Lukács makes sure to point out that while in Bern; Hegel dedicated a considerable amount of time to investigating Christianity and its central figure Jesus Christ from the perspective of some biblical teachings of Jesus' philosophical doctrines. In his writings of this period, Jesus is presented as a rationalistic philosopher who confronted various superstitions and the real religion of the Pharisees. Still, it has to be pointed out that Hegel had much more sympathy for the figure of Socrates than the figure of Jesus, that is why he visibly places the central figure of Christianity beneath the most famous figure of antiquity on his scale of importance. In order to justify this classification, Hegel accused Jesus of committing a sin of ignorance of the problems of the society he was part of, whilst Socrates focused a huge chunk of his philosophy on explaining them [Please see 'The Life of Jesus' (German: Das

Leben Jesu) and a manuscript titled 'The Positivity of the Christian Religion']. The reason behind this distinction in Hegel comes down to the fact that the interest of this philosopher in Jesus stops exactly with Jesus's crucifixion, and the paschal event is absent from his deliberations. In this respect, we can emphasise the fact that as much as he respected Jesus as the founder of the new religion, Hegel (possibly inadvertently) is guilty of downplaying the main message of Jesus' redemption, and the central message of Christianity, salvation that is associated with the atonement of the sins of humanity. Possibly this concept could be inconceivable for someone who had little respect for the notion of sin and evil seen through the prism of the separation of the individual from the universal.

As much as this thinker was visibly ignorant of the central truths of Christian faith, it has to be admitted that whilst in Bern, Hegel recognizes this religion as a critical factor in the development of continental thought, and correlated the decline of the states of antiquity in their primordial form with the rise of Christian religion. Subsequently, it is pointed out here that when one looks at this relation from the perspective of its genealogy and the evolutionary processes present in antiquity, one has a unique chance to recognize the fact that with time, Roman liberties were eventually overshadowed by the despotism of Roman rulers who attempted to banish the spirit of man from the planet earth. In this respect, a constant absolute demand for freedom came to the people's rescue as the deficit of freedom experienced by an ancient man had triggered their disappointment with the status quo and pushed them into the hands of the (Christian) God. In this sense, Hegel sees this incentive as an objective historical fact that could not be ignored. That being said, it is good to remember that Lukács draws our attention to the fact that whilst in Bern, Hegel still perceived Christianity as an imperfect system that on many levels enslaves humanity, the entrusting divine power with human liberty inadvertently results in the loss of human freedom, and framing individuals in the self-punishing process of a constant desire to redeem their earthly sins. In this sense, Hegel is of the opinion that this particular system of faith and worship develops into something much different from its founder's intention as it incorporates the presence of a superhuman or an almighty that controls the lives of the community of believers. Indeed, Hegel in this period learned to regard Christianity as a group of people with their own particular set of beliefs and practices that developed into a significant religious movement. Subsequently, Lukács maintains that when Hegel comes to examine positivity in the context of Christianity, he treats it as a product of the decline of humanity symbolized by the emergence of Christianity and civil society. On the other hand, it is also good to emphasize that Hegel saw Christianity as a necessary organic component of the process leading to the real present.

Finally, the other event that captured Hegel's attention while residing in Bern was the French Revolution of 1792, and the events that happened in the immediate aftermath of cutting the French king's head off in 1793. Hegel's philosophical development clearly coincided with very turbulent political events in neighbouring France (Bern lies just 500 or so km away from Paris, which even according to the eighteenth century's standards was considered to be a very close proximity), which had a massive impact on his future thinking. In this instance, it is important to point out that Hegel was indeed very optimistic about these events from their outset, as he saw the French Revolution as the recovery of lost freedom, the democratic regeneration of man, and the foundation of the approaching renewal of society. He even referred to this event as a real gift or even miracle for humanity. However, it is important to notice that Hegel's enthusiasm about these events perished very quickly–the moment the revolution ended up in the hands of the Jacobins after 1794. Still, the very fact that Hegel was so well acquainted with various dimensions related to the genesis and development of the events of the French Revolution gave him a significant edge compared with the situation of individuals in his native Germany that from his perspective at that time was very much backwards in comparison with France. Subsequently, according to Lukács, the young Hegel couldn't avoid individual errors and mistakes in his early philosophy and that is especially visible in his idealistic and very often contradictory vision of the evolution of the freedom and self-activation of people that comprises an element of specific development that originates in democratic Greece, the idyllic birth of the peaceful world of the Olympian gods, the indignity and debasement of life under late Roman despotism that in turn gives birth to the real religion of Christianity; at the same time, however, we see the opposite: the gods enter world history as real actors, freedom is not merely the origin of the Olympian gods, but also their gift to humanity, Christianity not only springs from the moral decadence of people governed by tyrants but equally, tyranny is pictured here as an effect brought about by the Christian religion. In this respect Lukács emphasises that for later Hegel, a triadic structure of freedom—loss of liberty—recovery of liberty will be replaced by a conception of the general growth of the idea of history: 1.) Freedom for one man (Oriental Despotism). 2.) Freedom for a few (Classical antiquity). 3.) Freedom for all (Christianity and modern times).

Frankfurt Period (1797–1801)

Consequently, the end of the Bern period marks the beginning of the Frankfurt period for Hegel which began in 1797 when he (after an absence of three years at the age of 27), returned to Germany to take up (similarly to the previous period) a house tutor position to one of the most influential local wine merchant's families in the city. In this respect, Lukács emphasizes that very characteristic to young Hegel is that as in the Frankfurt period, he would try various concepts, paradigms, and ideas, experimenting with them, modifying them and dropping them again, only to pick them up again at a later stage.

His thought in Frankfurt proceeded from his personal experience. While in previous periods he still had regarded the city-state of antiquity as a model for the present, in Frankfurt Hegel shows less enthusiasm for Greece. To be precise, he would depart from this assertion entirely in Frankfurt. From now on history would no longer begin with the Greeks, but with classical antiquity, even though it was irretrievably lost. Also, what is worth emphasizing in this respect is that he also shows a less extreme contrast between Greece and Christianity and starts treating Christianity more approvingly. According to Lukács, in this period we can witness Hegel's tendency to idealize Christian faith; he even begins to regard it as the prototype of religion. While in Bern Hegel made no secret of his resentment for Jesus, now he is slowly being transformed into a kind of guru for Hegel, and the most significant incarnation of love in history thus far. Having said that Lukács emphasises that Hegel's change of heart in this respect is not blind as he still finds many contradictions in Christianity (for example, Jesus, who is the son of God and is the son of man). As much as he was determined to build his philosophy as an atheistic system in Frankfurt Hegel came to terms with the fact that Christianity, in general, should be seen as the necessary product of social developments in the middle ages and in modern times, which also appears to him as the primary driving force of history (In this respect please also see: 'Fragments on Religion and Love' (1799) and 'The Spirit of Christianity and Its Fate', which was not published during Hegel's lifetime).

It is also important to point out that during this period Hegel also departs from his earlier enthusiasm for the events related to the French Revolution, which is no longer a primary preoccupation. What is noticeable is Hegel's attitudes towards this historical and social event is that despite the fact that he still associates much importance to the post–1792 political situation in France, he stopped regarding this event as the model or solution for present times. From now on, we can also witness Hegel's various reservations about Robespierre's political program, and his glorification of other French historical figures, Napoleon Bonaparte in particular. Importantly, what is even more characteristic of Hegel's Frankfurt's years that he has evidently shifted his attention towards matters related to contemporary German problems (as per Lukács' original suggestions), matters related to economy, Kantian ethics, the phenomenon of positivity, modern society and of course the idea of putting all of these insights into one coherent system.

Let us start with the deliberation on German problems as in this respect Lukács emphasises two significant developments: first, the fact that when Hegel left Bern for Frankfurt, he may have taken his firm Republican beliefs with him, but he definitely sympathized with Benjamin Constant, and Charles James Fox's faith in elections, and parliamentarian reforms, and that will have a massive impact on his further development in both Frankfurt and Jena. Secondly, Lukács draws our attention to the fact that Hegel did not hesitate anymore to speak out about political debate in his hometown (Württenberg), and Lukács in this respect emphasizes that Hegel also wrote a short political pamphlet that deliberated on local politics in the region he came from. It is being argued in this respect that although any recognizable publishing house never published this pamphlet, it had a very significant impact on both the local politics of the Württenbergian region and helped Hegel to connect specific dots in respect of the development of his philosophy and rational sense of history, and the history of the selected socio-political unity.

It is also being argued here that while in Frankfurt, Hegel also embarked on expanding his economic system. This desire was motivated by his belief that through the acquisition of more economic know-how he would attain a better understanding of modern society and Christianity in particular. Having said that it has to be pointed out that according to Lukács, we have no physical data suggesting how he studied economy and what texts he studied. In this respect, one can argue that Hegel's early economic studies must have been based on the purely empirical collections of sometimes unrelated economic data and various primordial approaches trying to capture the main ideas related to capital accumulation, trade, and various exchange relations. According to today's standard, writing about German economic backwardness seems like a bad science fiction novel but according to Lukács that was the reality at that time. For this reason, he allows himself to indulge a speculation suggesting that Hegel must have become acquainted with the essential microeconomy through his readings of Adam Smith because at that time the English-speaking economic methods of describing social reality were much more developed than the German ones.

Lukács also maintains that whilst in Frankfurt, Hegel was also profoundly interested in Kantian philosophy, especially his notion of morality, but that by the end of his time in Frankfurt Hegel would accuse Kant of a lack of social understanding of the concept of practical reason, and would object to the Kantian way of approaching this issue because it was framing a twisted reality of man being a slave against a tyrant and at the same time, tyrant against the slave. From Hegel's perspective, morality cannot be divided, and when it is fragmented, it cannot function harmoniously and free from conflict. Lukács emphasizes that despite these apparent differences, his awareness of the comprehensive Kantian system would, in turn, help Hegel to develop his dialectical method.

Subsequently, it is reiterated in these theses that when it comes to Hegel's view of positivity and the position of the individual in society, his attitudes had shifted in a different direction: while in Bern he still treated differentiations of society as a symptom of fragmentation and the decline of the state, but once he moved to Frankfurt Hegel elaborated an entirely different view on the arrangements in modern society that focuses more on various relations and multi-dimensional interactions between individual and society that Lukács sees as a much more comprehensive, realistic and mature attitude towards bourgeois society.

Finally, the deliberations on the way the Hegelian thought developed in his young period brought Lukács to a conclusion suggesting that while in Frankfurt Hegel made massive progress towards eventually establishing his first fragment of a system that would in the future be the first explicit formulation of the dialectical method, there are still many notions related to the process of this transition that are still not correctly interlined, and there is a very little evidence as to how Hegel arrived at the idea, but the research on the young Hegel continues so there is definitely a chance for further developments in this area in the years to come. These matters may be especially interesting when we look at them through the prism of in statu nascendi (*the process of creation*) of the Hegelian philosophy because even such sophisticated philosophical system had to undergo various stages of its internal development. Despite that it is commonly believed that Hegel put most of his grounding ideas together around 1805–1806, Lukács helps us to acknowledge that unlike what Aleksander Kojève wants us to believe Hegel started recollecting and forming some of his brightest ideas not whilst he was hearing the cannons from the Battle o Jena but much earlier than that, and there is a big likelihood that it was as early as at the end of his Frankfurt period.

Discussion on György Lukács' Method

During the course of these investigations, it was established that despite of the fact that many contemporary commentators try to cluster this thinker as a court Marxist, György Lukács could not be simply pigeonholed as some random commentator of someone else's thought. In fact, there is more into his contribution to the literature of the subject, than it is commonly understood, and in order to understand it we need to reach out to his "The young Hegel"; that exemplifies that the weight of Lukács' insights and his fascination with Hegel's philosophy.

In this publication, Lukács introduces us to an entirely new method of philosophical investigation by showing a great interest in the process of formation of Hegel's thought from the evolutionary perspective of his humble beginnings between 1793 and 1806. Subsequently, by applying such an enquiry into what has lead to shaping such a holistic and distinguishable system like the one of Hegel's, Lukács takes us on a tour aimed at investigating various stages of this philosopher's intellectual development in Tübingen, Bern, and Frankfurt up to the decision that led this philosopher to move to the University of Jena in 1801, at the age of thirty. Subsequently, by presenting us with distinguishingly early, mature and late period in Hegel life, Lukács has also managed to depict a process of formation (in statu nascendi) of a philosopher in general, and that can be used as transferable skill in investigation of other philosophers. By doing so, Lukács, on the one hand, shows reluctance to pay homage to one of the most world-renowned philosophers, but on the other hand he assigns an entirely new importance to a new type of exploration of what has been kept hidden or considered as irrelevant for far too long, namely the early stages in Hegel's philosophic development that are now approached in an entirely new way.

Naturally, in this respect, one could accuse Lukács of endorsing a particular shade of historical determinism, or of creating a very dangerous precedent aiming at trivializing this tradition. But this deconstruction of Hegel's thought was far from an attempt of undermining the integrity of this very sophisticated the system, in fact it actually allowed Lukács to present us with a unique opportunity to bring to the fore various hidden circumstances that led young Hegel to develop his central thesis, which could enable us to establish a method that should connect these findings with much broader philosophical debates; that could have a tremendous impact on the future development in the field and maybe even change the course of the contemporary philosophy.

For now, we can openly admit that the most crucial tangible finding related to Georg Lukács's publication "The young Hegel" is that, if we can deconstruct Hegel in such a way, we should be able to deconstruct any philosopher similarly and learn a great deal about the process of formation of his philosophy. By appropriately relating this data and by following Lukács's footsteps in investigating various developments encountered by the young Hegel on his road through different evolutionary stages of his development, as this philosopher presents us with a totally new method of investigation that turns the debate into question upside-down on many levels as it reveals the hidden complexity of Hegel's contribution to the literature of the subject.

The only requirement needed to mastering this method is to follow this method genuinely, by taking all elements in dissecting any period in the life of any given philosopher and assigning to it specific time frames. Doing so should allow us to separate one time-frame from another without any significant detriment to the integrity of the investigated tradition, or any given philosopher. So, as long as we have no personal agenda hidden behind our intentions and we aspire to study an objective truth about any given philosopher's development we should be able to bring more light into various hidden dimensions of the philosophy in general.

References

Arato, Andrew, and Paul Breines. (1979). The Young Lukács and the Origins of Western Marxism. New York: Seabury.

Bernstein, J. M. (1984) The Philosophy of the Novel: Lukács, Marxism, and the Dialectics of Form. Brighton: Harvester.

Corredor, Eva L., ed. Lukács After Communism: Interviews with Contemporary Intellectuals. Post–Contemporary Interventions. Durham: Duke University Press, 1997.

Feenberg, Andrew. Lukács, Marx, and the Sources of Critical Theory. Oxford: Martin Robertson, 1981.

Goldstein, J. D. (2006). Hegel's Idea of the Good Life: From Virtue to Freedom, Early Writings, and Mature Political Philosophy. Springer.

Gluck, Mary. (1985). Georg Lukács and His Generation, 1900–1918. Cambridge, Massachuset.: Harvard University Press.

Lukács, György (1975). The young Hegel: studies in the relations between dialectics and economics, London: Merlin Press, translated by Rodney Livingstone.

Osborne, Peter, (2000). Philosophy in Cultural Theory, London, and New York: Routledge.

Shafai, Fariborz. (1996) The Ontology of Georg Lukács: Studies in Materialist Dialectics. Avebury Series in Philosophy. Aldershot: Avebury.

Thompson, Michael J. (2011). Georg Lukács Reconsidered: Critical Essays in Politics, Philosophy and Aesthetics. London: Continuum.

Vazsonyi, Nicholas. (1997). Lukács Reads Goethe: From Aestheticism to Stalinism. Studies in German Literature, Linguistics, and Culture. Columbia: Camden House.

Williamson, Raymond K. (1984). Introduction to Hegel's Philosophy of Religion. State University of New York Press.

Piotr Pietrzak on 'Disenchantment and Re-enchantment': Chapter 3, The 'death of God' and the Crisis of Philosophy. Neascu, Michaela. (2010) 'Hans J. Morgenthau's Theory of International Relation: Disenchantment and Re-Enchantment

According to the traditional understanding of the meaning of "**Politics Among Nations**" (1948), its author Hans Morgenthau suggested that such ideas as the Kantian notion of Perpetual Peace should be considered as very naïve, delusional, and for these reasons, detrimental to global peace endeavors. Of course, he did not try to dismiss the possibility that at one point of our development we humans will enforce Immanuel Kant's vision of reality, but so far we are still not there, yet therefore it would be beneficial for us to stick to more realistic approaches, at least until we eventually get there. Indeed, we have a proven track record of starting wars every few decades for various somewhat irrational purposes, which are both resource- and human-life-consuming. Therefore the whole idea of a U.N.- based security system governing the maintenance of global peace and security remains very shaky at best. The sad truth is that we are doomed to keep repeating the mistakes of our predecessors and will be inclined to ignore the necessity of resolving our differences in a peaceful manner each time our interests collide (Neascu, 2010, p. 1–103).

According to Prof Morgenthau, what presupposes these types of behaviors can be explained by the way our human nature has been constructed as it turns human beings into greedy, selfish, sinful, power-hungry individuals who want to dominate other human beings and the end very often serves to justify the means of achieving this goal. Consequently, Morgenthau also elaborated in this publication the concept of national interest designed to provide the leader of any given state with a manual on what actions can be taken to secure a given country's survival, strength, and influence. This concept contains three elements: 1) The prime interests aimed at ensuring the country's survival that can be associated with the protection of the state's physical, political and cultural identity, the integrity of its territory and protection of its people, 2) The secondary interests of maintaining circumstantial power positions already acquired, defined as the crosscurrents of personalities, public opinions, local interest and partisan politics, and 3) the last but not least important element associated with the aggressive expansion of the country's influence and strength that could be directly related to finding a way to expand one's natural or strategic borders, access to the sea and natural resources, or the broader project of unification of national or territorial integrity. In this respect, Morgenthau maintains that primary interests of the state should never be negotiable, while the secondary interests are not to be pursued at the expense of the fundamental interest (Amstrup, 1978, p. 167; Behr and Rösch, 2012, p.16; Neascu, 2010, p. 67–100; Russet, 1969, p. 137).

Such interpretation of national interest has direct and indirect consequences for political leaders for whom Morgenthau sets very high standards of not only weighing the pros and cons of every vital decision carefully to fulfill national interests but also to do so if necessary at the expense of moral laws. Indeed, Morgenthau was of the opinion that there should be no question about it: political leaders should not be misguided into believing that they have some abstract right to decide whether they want to obey their moral principles or fulfil their responsibilities towards the state, as the interest of the polity should always come first over individual rights or beliefs. The implications of allowing prioritizing individual rights over the rights of the polity can be disastrous, as many nations have experienced for themselves the mistakes of such practices including the loss of statehood. For these reasons, individual morals, especially of those who govern the nation, should be considered as secondary, and ought to be surrendered to the interest of the whole community at large. These leaders subsequently are not to be judged for their moral choices but their ability and effectiveness in pursuing the national interest, and it is, therefore, their duty as the leaders of the community to pursue the national interest even if it would require using cruelty or breaking the law to accommodate these needs (Benson, 1951, p. 181; Kunz, 1948, p. 461).

As we can see in Politics Among Nations (PAN), Hans Morgenthau considers the realm of international relations as a very self-centered place where every single actor is deemed to first and foremost protect their own interest. For these reasons, counting on others in such an environment is naive only because it does not guarantee anyone's survival. In the opinion of this scholar, this relation is more visible on the international level as modern countries tend to be very unsympathetic to other international players' needs, especially when their national interests are at stake. Therefore, one should be skeptical about the ability of such organizations as the United Nations or the League of Nations to play the more significant role of a pillar of the global security system as their capacity to resolve conflicts in contemporary conflict zones is in fact limited. For sure, that is one way of looking at Morgenthau's theory of international relations, but according to Michaela Nescu, it is not the only way. Indeed, reading the third chapter of Hans Morgenthau's Theory of International Relations, Disenchantment, and Re-enchantment, written by Michaela Neascu, has changed many young scholar's understanding of this scholar's ideas and teachings (Neascu, 2010, p. 67–90).

In this respect, it essential to point out that Neascu suggests that treating Morgenthau like a hawkish academic concentrating his efforts only on proving how important it is for a country and its leaders to maintain their power in a very traditional sense is not rational for some reasons. Of course, it cannot be denied that this scholar was very interested in the notion of ensuring the survival of the state and projection of the power and influence of any given political regime, but that is just one part of the picture. In this instance, Neacsu explains that before we compare this scholar to Machiavelli and ascribe to his interpretations his account of a statesman's duties and obligations, in which ethics and morality have no place at all, we need to come to terms with the fact that Morgenthau committed his professional career to discovering the truth of international politics. For this reason, this scholar maintains that even if Morgenthau's political theories sound unsympathetic or cruel, they are infused with moral considerations deriving from the challenging postmodern time in which this scholar had published his opus magnum just few years after the end of the Second World War, when it was already clear that humanity could no longer guarantee the safety of an individual in society. It is due to the fact that we live in a fragmented universal realm of values that provokes global lust for power that has no mercy on the individual tragedies of those who suffer powerlessly, or are dependent on the uncertainties, unpredictability, unfavourable godlessness and morallessness of society at large (Neascu, 2010, p. 12–14, 25–28, 161).

The problem of misrepresentation of Morgenthau's contribution to the literature of the subject starts with the fact that we when we think about his concept of power, we treat it in particular static way through the prism of positive materialistic and tangible lenses that lead us to miss the forest for the trees. It has to do with the fact that this scholar's concept of power is much more flexible and less dogmatic than one may think. Furthermore, this idea comes down to the ability of a man to control the mind and actions of the other man, as an activity of imposing upon another man his will, but only by taking into the account the fact that the will of the object of power, in this case, must mirror our own. It is being argued in this parenthesis, that in order to correctly understand the notion of power in Morgenthau, one has to comprehend the intricacies of a particular triangular relation of morality, truth, and power, and the best starting point in order to achieve that is by not pigeonholing Morgenthau's work into the Realist tradition within the theory of international relations, especially, because this scholar has opened realist theory up to postmodernist reinterpretations, such as the plurality of truth, impositions of meaning, and various perceptions (Neascu, 2010, p. 118, 127, 134).

Admittedly, this problem is especially visible in the third chapter of Neascu's publication, where the author argues that Morgenthau sees the global reality at hand through the prism of a Western modern man's lenses, and the view he sees is not very appealing as he is faced with a fellow man who has lost sense of what is good and evil, what is right and wrong, in this postmodern anarchic and godless global environment (Strauss in Gilding, 1975, p. 81). This state of affairs has to do with the realization of the Nietzschean vision of the "death of the God": the vanishing of the supernatural being and coinciding disappearance of meaning, which initially grants him new opportunities and chances but at the end traps him in the "decaying house" without the common roof of Universal values that subsequently implies not only his loneliness but also desperation and nihilism. This unnatural transition from Deus Faber (God the Creator) to Homo Faber (Man the maker) has to be somehow undertaken, and the best way to do so would be to try to replace God with some higher structure in which an individual can strive. Indeed, an individual is not capable of living in a godless world, where there is no structure, no meaning, and no purpose, which is why, according to Neacsu, since there is no higher authority than the state itself, Morgenthau (influenced by Max Weber) turns his attention to the concept of the nation-state and statehood as a natural replacement, and a platform from which one can start searching for a truth (Amstrup, 1978, p. 167–174; Russet, 1969, p. 1–30; Neascu, 2010, p. 67–69, 76–78).

Consequently, it is important to mention that according to Neascu, Politics Among Nations cannot be solely constrained to the discourse on power and the global environment as there is much more to it than that. Considering that the author of this publication makes an attempt to explain the condition of the post–1945 man through the prism of Nietzschean philosophy: his belief that God is dead, and the need for Übermensch (Overman, superhuman) suggests that this track could also be read as a profound interpretation of the modern condition of man and humanity: current man in this setting who has either experienced or witnessed the cataclysms of both world wars and the Holocaust is likely to suffer from the syndrome of constant reevaluation of the moral standards and principles he was used to. Subsequently, such a man is also more inclined to be pessimistic about any accounts, visions or systems claiming to enjoy a divine authority, postulating a universal code of moral standards or any temporal powers that present themselves as capable of preventing humans from killing one another. That is precisely what makes a difference in Neascu's approach, that Morgenthau is shown here as an original scholar deeply engaged in a quest to find the meaning of truth, understood as a dynamic and complicated endeavour that involves researching various competing interpretations of truths in this uncertain world of ideas, adopting multiple non-classical new ways and standards of thinking, such as: the status of truth, the legitimacy of universal values, and engaging in the discussions of the collapse of a supranational ethics of Christian, cosmopolitan, and humanitarian elements and for these reasons, I strongly recommend this publication to anyone who is interested in rediscovering Hans Morgenthau's contribution to the literature of the subject (Neascu, 2010, p. 68–98).

References

Amstrup, Niels, The 'Early' Morgenthau. A Comment on the Intellectual Origins of Realism, Cooperation and Conflict, vol. 13, 2, First Published Jul 1, 1978.

Benson, Oliver, Dennett, Raymond, And Robert K. Tur Ner (Eds.). Documents on American Foreign Relations. Vol. XII: January 1–December 31, 1950. XXVI, 702. Princeton: Princeton University Press, 1952.First Published Jul 1, 1952.

Copper, John F.: Book Review: A New Foreign Policy for the United States, by Hans Morgenthau 1970 23:434 Political Research Quarterly 1970 23: 434.

Gilbert Alan, Must Global Politics Constrain Democracy? (Princeton University Press, 1999).

Herz, J., Political Realism and Political Idealism (Chicago, IL; University of Chicago Press, 1951), p. 200–5

Kunz, Josef L., Book Reviews and Notices : Politics Among Nations. The Struggle for Power and Peace. By HANS J. MoRGENTHAU. (New York: Alfred A. Knopf. 1948. xv, 489, xix. $5.50.), First Published December 1, 1948.

Pin-Fat, Veronique. (2008), How Do We Begin to Think About the World? Global Politics: A New Introduction.

Morgenthau, Hans J. (1978). 'Politics Among Nations: The Struggle for Power and Peace, Fifth Edition, New York: Alfred A. Knopf, 1978.

Morgenthau Hans J., To Intervene or Not To Intervene, Foreign Affairs, April 1967.

Morgenthau, Hans J., The Restoration of American Politics (Chicago. I L: University of Chicago Press, 1962), p. 237–9: see also,

Neascu, M. (2010) Hans J. Morgenthau's Theory of International Relation, Disenchantment, and Re-enchantment.

B.M. Russet and E.C. Hanson, Interest and Ideology (San Francisco, CA: W.H, Freeman, 1975), p. 126; see also, M. Kahler, op. cit, p. 62; F. Kratochwil, 'On the Notion of "Interest" in International Relations', International Organization (Vol. 36, No. 1, 1982).

The Concept of the Political (Palgrave Studies in International Relations) Paperback–6 Mar 2012.

Wong, Benjamin, Hans Morgenthau's Anti-Machiavellian Machiavellianism, Millennium–Journal of International Studies 2000 29: 389.

PART II:
POLITICS &
INTERNATIONAL RELATIONS

Krzysztof Żęgota

The Kaliningrad Oblast' of the Russian Federation: A Geopolitical Challenge for the Baltic Sea Region

Abstract: *The Kaliningrad Oblast of the Russian Federation is a unique area in East-Central Europe for the development of cooperation between the European Union and the Russian Federation as well as geopolitical conditions of security in the Baltic Sea region. For this reason the Kaliningrad Oblast is a crucial area for the security of the Baltic Sea region, as in this area of the Russian Federation intersect two critical processes for European security: on the one hand, the process of European integration, which is continued in the eastern part of Europe and the Kaliningrad Oblast—due to its geographical location—is involved in several nets of European cooperation. On the other hand, the Kaliningrad Oblast is part of the Russian Federation, which is carrying out a great project of reintegration of post–Soviet space and the Oblast is one of the key elements for the success of this project. The Kaliningrad Oblast might play the role of a particular tool for Russian authorities to threaten the states of the Baltic Sea region, as they do with other exclaves and separatist regions in post–Soviet space. The central thesis of the paper is an assertion that the significance of the Kaliningrad Oblast for the security of the Baltic Sea Region will rise with the ongoing process of integration in post–Soviet space. The indicator of this factor is the significance of the Kaliningrad Oblast in the system of national security of the Russian Federation as well as its geographical location, especially in the context of relations with the Baltic states. An essential factor in this process is also the goals of Russian foreign policy concerning the Baltic states as well as the Nordic countries.*

Keywords: Vladimir Putin, Geopolitics of the Russian Federation, Russian foreign policy, Kaliningrad Oblast, Baltic Sea Region, European Union, geopolitical wedge, Zbigniew Brzeziński

Introduction

The geopolitical situation observed in East-Central Europe after 1989 shows the importance of the Baltic Sea basin for the implementation of the objectives of Russian foreign and security policy. Observed political transitions in

East-Central Europe after 1989 have also resulted in a significant increase in the importance of the Kaliningrad Oblast of the Russian Federation for the stabilization and international security of the Baltic Sea basin[1]. For the Russian Federation, this region has become especially important given the integration processes occurring in East-Central Europe over the last 25 years. The European Union integration process has been ongoing, with significant milestones marked by two stages of the EU enlargement in 2004 and 2007, when a series of East-Central Eastern European states joined the European Union. An increase in the cohesion of this part of Europe was also affected by continuous Euro-Atlantic integration, a subsequent step of which was the eastward expansion of NATO in 1999 and 2004. Thus, the area of European and Euro-Atlantic integration significantly approached the borders of the Russian Federation and began to be a threat to Russian interests in Baltic Sea basin.

The aim of this article is to present the essential conditions for the security of the Baltic Sea region in relation to the Kaliningrad Oblast of the Russian Federation as well as to analyze the importance of the geopolitical dimension of two integration processes observed in Europe: the European Union (and Euro-Atlantic) integration and the integration of the post–Soviet areas carried out under the auspices of the Russian Federation. Given the above-presented circumstances, the thesis of the article should be to determine how the importance of the Kaliningrad Oblast of the Russian Federation, regarding the safety of the Baltic Sea region, will increase in the coming years. This may be substantiated as follows: the Kaliningrad Oblast is an area where the routes of two critical integration processes carried out in Europe are intersecting; the Russian Federation will strive towards maintaining its influence in the Baltic Sea basin and the Kaliningrad Oblast will play the role both of geopolitical wedge in Europe situated "behind the back" of the states participating in the processes of European and Euro-Atlantic integration as well as a factor in maintaining Russian influence on the Baltic Sea region.

---

[1] Potential threats from the Kaliningrad Oblast to the Baltic Sea region are natural consequences of Russian foreign policy toward all international regions of Eastern and East-Central Europe (including Ukraine, Georgia and other former Soviet republics). This approach was developed by the author in an article published in *Warsaw East European Review*. See: K. Żęgota, "The Kaliningrad Region – Key to Security in East-Central Europe" *Warsaw East European Review*, 2016, vol. VI.

Geopolitical Significance of the Kaliningrad Oblast

The geopolitical significance of the Kaliningrad Oblast in the Soviet Union, as well as in the Russian Federation, has evolved adequately to geopolitical changes occurring in East-Central Europe. To this article particularly relevant is the period after 2000, connected with Russia's internal consolidation and its return to the concept of reintegrating the post–Soviet area. It is worth noting that after 1991, it was mostly used as a collection point for Russian troops moved from East Germany and the Baltic republics to Russia. The Russian strategic concepts of that time did not foresee any particular role for the region regarding the Russian Federation's geopolitics nor defense. However, most of the Russian Baltic fleet was gathered in the area at the same time, which increased its military significance even more. The period after 2000 is connected with some intensified attempts of Russian authorities to reintegrate the post–Soviet area and reinforce Russian areas influenced by the Baltic Sea[2].

Here, it is worth analyzing the Kaliningrad Oblast more accurately as a crucial element of Russian policy in the post–Soviet area implemented and observed mostly after 2009. That time is characterised by intensified Russian actions aimed at increasing its influences in particular former Soviet republics, which would result in persuading them into participation in some integrational initiatives in the post–Soviet area, such as the Eurasian Economic Union, the Customs Union, or other actions of a political or defensive character. It is essential now to distinguish three critical groups of states, former Soviet republics that present different levels of acceptance towards the idea of post–Soviet area reintegration. The core of the integration processes should include Russia, Belarus, and Kazakhstan, which even today manifest their will to participate in the integration processes. The second group consists of the former Soviet republics that show a relatively ambivalent attitude towards the projects of post–Soviet area reintegration and whose attitudes towards those processes depends to a large extent on the current political conditions of those states. The third group, which includes Ukraine, Moldova and the countries of the South Caucasus, as well as the Baltic states to a lesser degree, forms a key challenge for the Russian objectives connected with the reintegration of the post–Soviet area. In the near future, the central attempts of the Russian authorities linked to the project of the post–Soviet area reintegration

---

[2] J. Affek, Potencjał militarny Rosji w obwodzie kaliningradzkim a możliwości wpływania tego państwa na sytuację geopolityczną w regionie, „Przegląd Geopolityczny" 2014, vol. 8, p. 192–194.

are directed towards building some mechanisms of destabilisation and forming regions/states which will be sources of threat for the critical areas of that reintegration. Those parts—being, in fact, sources of military and non-military threats–make some kinds of geopolitical wedges that threaten those areas of the former Soviet Union which are presently a part of the Euro-Atlantic integration process (Baltic states) or show such aspirations (Ukraine, Moldova, Georgia, Azerbaijan).

It is beneficial to look at this from the perspective of the paradigm of a geopolitical wedge in the scientific discourse on geopolitics and theory of international relations. The notion of a geopolitical wedge is used relatively seldomly by researchers of international relations and geopolitics. Nonetheless, it is a concept present in the scientific discourse on the geopolitical conditions of changes in the world's order. Based on these criteria, the idea of a geopolitical wedge may be applied to a politically and geographically separated region with a pivotal geopolitical and military significance from the point of view of one country/alliance located in the sphere of influence of a competitive country/alliance or in a neutral area. In a narrower meaning, one country's geopolitical wedge is located "behind the back" of another country/alliance[3]. In a broader context, a geopolitical wedge may also be interpreted as an area dividing spheres of influence owned by two (or more) world powers[4].

Subsequently, the studied notion is used in the literature on this subject in the context of some geographical regions of the world (presently as well as in the past), to which are attributed the characteristics of geopolitical wedges. Researchers define with that notion the United States' areas of influence in the post–Soviet regions: the republics of the Caucasus and of Central Asia[5], as well as Poland, which is, in fact, an American geopolitical wedge between Germany and Russia. From that point of view, a similar role may be played in future by Ukraine and the typical Polish-Ukrainian passage makes a potential focus for American influences in the area located between the Baltic Sea and the Black Sea, as well as in the Balkans[6]. Other researchers identify the geopolitical wedge with the significant areas between Euro-Atlantic and

---

[3] M. Malik, The Shanghai Cooperation Organization, in: S. Ganguly, A. Scobell, J. Chinyong Liow (ed.), The Routledge Handbook of Asian Security Studies, New York 2010, p. 80.
[4] L. Weijian, The September 11th Incident and Trends in Middle East Social Thought, in: Y. Xintian (ed.), Cultural Impact on International Relations, Washington 2002, p. 196.
[5] M. Malik, The Shanghai Cooperation Organization…, op. cit., p. 80.
[6] P. Gowan, The Global Gamble: Washington's Faustian Bid for World Dominance, London – New York 1999, p. 301.

Euro-Asiatic integrations[7] or with historical changes in East-Central Europe in the 19th and 20th centuries[8].

The paradigm of a geopolitical wedge should be seen as a useful category as it inscribes into the already formulated geopolitical concepts their creative development and supplementation. The value of that notion is especially visible in respect of one of the most critical geopolitical models of the world that focusses on competition between Halford Mackinder's Heartland and Nicholas Spykman's Rimland. Heartland understood as the central area of Eurasia, conditions the reign over the rest of the world. Rimland, on the other hand, forms a ring surrounding the central part of Eurasia and it is the competition between the states of the center and peripheries of Eurasia that shapes the world's order[9]. As for this article, the explanatory motif connected with the concept of Rimland by Nicholas Spykman is of particular importance. According to that idea, it is having an influence on the critical areas of Rimland—the Baltic Sea, the Black Sea, the Caucasus, and the Middle East—that conditions taking domination over the world by the Soviet Union, and then by Russia. That factor seems to justify the Russian authorities' determination in striving for making and maintaining their geopolitical wedges by the Baltic Sea (the Kaliningrad Oblast), the Black Sea (Transnistria, Crimea), and the South Caucasus (Armenia).

Furthermore, the concept in question should be situated between the theories explaining the geopolitical conditions of the world's order connected with the idea of choke-points and geopolitical pivots by Zbigniew Brzeziński[10]. A chokepoint is interpreted as a geographical object or an element of transportation infrastructure, possession of which gives a significant military and economic advantage and, further, a geopolitical one. From this point of view, it is a narrower notion that the paradigm of the geopolitical wedge as it refers to a particular geostrategic situation noted in a defined area. Interestingly, the concept mentioned above shares a number of similar features with geopolitical wedges: Firstly, while characterized by a relatively

---

[7] Ø. Tunsjø, Geopolitical shifts, great power relations and Norway's foreign policy, "Cooperation and Conflict" 2011, no. 46, p. 60–77.

[8] R. Pearson, European Nationalism 1789–1920, New York 2014, p. 187; F. J. Harbutt, Yalta 1945. Europe and America at the Crossroads, Cambridge 2010, p. 140.

[9] See: H. J. Mackinder, Democratic Ideas and Reality, New York 1981, p. 260; N. Spykman, The Geography of Peace, New York 1944, p. 43.

[10] The notion of a geopolitical pivot is used here according to the interpretation by Zbigniew Brzeziński, not by Halford J. Mackinder. See: L. Moczulski, Geopolityka. Potęga w czasie i przestrzeni, Warszawa 1999, p. 12–14.

small area, it is of a crucial geostrategic significance. Secondly, due to its significant geostrategic role, it is used to concentrate military potential (troops and army infrastructure), and finally, possessing a chokepoint makes it possible to influence the neighbouring areas/states[11].

A second significant notion connected with the issue of geopolitical wedges is the concept of geopolitical pivots developed by Brzeziński, according to whom geopolitical pivots are the states whose importance is derived not from their power and motivation but rather from their sensitive location and the consequences of their potentially vulnerable condition for the behavior of geostrategic players. Most often, geopolitical pivots are determined by their geography, which in some cases gives them a unique role either in denying access to critical areas or in denying resources to a significant player. In some cases, a geopolitical pivot may act as a defensive shield for a vital state or even a region. Sometimes, the very existence of a geopolitical pivot can be said to have very significant political and cultural consequences for a more active neighboring geostrategic player"[12]. A geopolitical pivot is, thus, an area including a state that does not play a stand-alone geopolitical role, yet, at the same time, influences the balance of forces in a particular region of the world. When formulated that way, a geopolitical pivot is a broader notion than the concept of a geopolitical wedge as it includes formally stand-alone political and spatial units. At the same time, the idea of geopolitical pivots is very often criticized by functionalist scholars as enclaves/exclaves or separatist areas may be of similar significance in the geopolitics of world powers/alliances.

The Kaliningrad Oblast of the Russian Federation accounts for a zone where various tendencies, as well as social and political phenomena, have emerged, on the one hand, reflecting the diversity of Russia itself and, on the other, specific features of this area of the Russian Federation. One of its primary features is its geographical location: the Oblast is an enclave "squeezed-in" between Poland and Lithuania (i.e., countries situated by the Baltic Sea) territorially disconnected from "big" Russia. This factor enhances geopolitical importance for the security of Baltic Sea basin. The peripheral nature of this region, especially in respect to other Russian territories, cannot be overlooked, especially if we take into account its geographical proximity to East-Central European states, which influences the opportunities for establishing

---

[11] J. J. Hobbs, World Regional Geography, Belmont 2014, p. 229–231.
[12] Z. Brzezinski, The Grand Chessboard. American Primacy and Its Geostrategic Imperatives, Basic Books 1997, p. 41.

economic and social contacts on various levels[13]. The Kaliningrad Oblast is an area with less than 70 years of historical tradition. No social or political structure of a similar territorial shape or national identity existed here before. The distinct character of the area under discussion is related to the fact that it was created as a result of decisions made by the allied superpowers at the end of World War II, conditioned mainly by geopolitical and geostrategic reasons and not for historical or demographic reasons[14]. As a result of the war, the demographic and material image of the region did not reflect any previous history or tradition of those lands. Subsequently, while the year 1946 marked the formal beginning of the existence of this area as part of the USSR and, currently, the Russian Federation, the legal sanctioning of the existence of the Kaliningrad Oblast and the establishment of its borders took place from 1945 to 1957.

The attitude of Russian authorities towards the Kaliningrad Oblast is based on the claim that it makes up an integral and significant part of the Russian Federation, particularly for national defense and security. All discussions—held over the last dozen years or so—concerning the special status of the region or the need to introduce economic privileges should take into account the inseparability of relations between the region and "big" Russia. The far-reaching dependence of the area on federal authorities has, first of all, political and systemic dimensions. Currently, the decision-making ability of the Oblast's government is highly limited. Most decisions concerning the social and economic development of the region are taken at the central level. Both the structure of the constitution of the Russian Federation and a series of other legal regulations at the federal and regional levels make the Oblast only a tool in Russian policy, depriving it of any vital importance as an autonomic political and spatial entity.

The dependence of Kaliningrad Oblast on federal authorities is also sanctioned by the formal and legal status of the region within the structural and political system of the Russian Federation. The Kaliningrad Oblast is one of 83 subjects[15] of the Russian Federation, and its political system is to a large extent determined by the structural system and the political scene of Russia.

---

[13] C. Wellman, Historische Miszelle. Die russische Exklave Kaliningrad als Konfliktsyndrom, „Die Friedens–Warte Journal of International Peace and Organization" 2000, no. 3–4, p. 404.

[14] G. V. Kretinin, V. N. Briushinkin, V. I. Galtsov et al., Ocherki isstorii Vostochnoy Prussii, Kaliningrad 2002, p. 452.

[15] Or one of 85 subjects – according to article 65 of the Constitution of the Russian Federation. See: The Constitution of the Russian Federation, Available at: <http://www.constitution.ru/en/10003000-04.htm>[Accessed on 19.02.2017, at 21:13].

Indeed, under the constitution of the Russian Federation of 1993, the Kaliningrad Oblast has gained the official status of the administrative-territorial unit. Subsequently, the strong relations between the Oblast and "big" Russia are also reflected in the provisions of the federal agreement of 31 March 1992 that provides a legal basis for the functioning of the region within the Russian Federation[16], and treated as a relatively important instrument for deepening the relations between the Kaliningrad Oblast and Moscow are mechanisms for integrating the political system of the arena with the federal authority system and a gradual reduction of the powers of regional authorities. In line with this legislation, the direct elections of Oblast governors were abolished in 2004, replacing them with appointments by the president of the Federation, with the consent of the regional legislature. This regulation was revoked in 2012, but the governor's political autonomy still depends on the political will of federal authorities.

A factor placing the Kaliningrad Oblast among the central regions of Russia—especially from the Baltic Sea region—is its military character. The Kaliningrad Oblast makes up a part of the North-West Federal District and the Western Military District of Russia. The region is also an essential component of the Baltic Naval Zone, the objective of which is to protect the Russian military presence in the Baltic Sea basin. The region is characterized by developed military infrastructure, based on a system of land, air, and naval military bases. A significant element of this infrastructure is the Russian Baltic Fleet, with naval bases in Baltiysk, Primorsk, and Kaliningrad[17]. Ground forces in the area of the Kaliningrad Oblast include infantry, missile, artillery and motor brigades stationed in Baltiysk, Kaliningrad, Gusev, and Chernyakhovsk. Major combat units of the air forces are located in air bases in Chkalovsk and Chernyakhovsk, and a helicopter regiment is located in Donskoye and Ljubino. To complete this picture, it can be added that the Kaliningrad Oblast is also an area where several reconnaissance and anti-aircraft units are located. The main centers are Pereslavskoye (radio-technical regiment), Gvardeysk and Znamensk (missile defense regiments)[18].

---

[16] See: Federalniy dogovor, (Moscow, 31 March 1992), Available at: <http://constitution.garant.ru/act/federative/170280/#220>[Accessed on 20.04.2013, at 21:00].

[17] A. Sakson, Obwód kaliningradzki a bezpieczeństwo Polski, „Przegląd Strategiczny" 2014, no. 7, p. 114.

[18] R. Ciechanowski, Rosyjskie siły zbrojne w Kaliningradzie, „Dziennik Zbrojny", 11.05.2014, Available at: <http://dziennikzbrojny.pl/artykuly/art,2,6,6819,armie-swiata,potencjal,rosyjskie-sily-zbrojne-w-kaliningradzie/> [Accessed on 18.06.2015, at 21:13]

Although after the collapse of the Soviet Union the number of troops in the Oblast was reduced, it remains one of the most significant clusters of military units in Russia, determining, to a considerable extent, the Russian military potential in the Baltic Sea basin. After 1991, the number of troops garrisoned in the region was estimated at 40,000–100,000 soldiers and sailors[19]. According to various data, these numbers were gradually reduced throughout the 1990s, and in the first decade of the 21st century the number of troops in the region was between 15,000 and 25,000[20]. However, the region still plays a significant role in Russian military strategy. After the fall of the Soviet Union, the Russian government supported the need to maintain the military nature of the region given its strategic importance. According to this concept, it was a vital interest of the Russian Federation to keep significant ground and naval forces in the area. Despite an apparent reduction in the military potential of this region, it should be expected that the Russian side will not refrain from taking advantage—at least in its political rhetoric—of this potential, as exemplified by repeatedly announcing the deployment of short- and medium-range missiles[21].

Arguments of a threefold nature are factors that indicate an increase in the significance of the Kaliningrad Oblast in Russian military doctrine as well as the geopolitical role of the region in the Baltic Sea basin. Firstly, Russian strategic documents on the sector of national security stress the significance of increasing the influence of the Russian Federation in the post–Soviet area identifying, at the same time, threats connected with the NATO's military infrastructure approaching the borders of Russia. Both in the National Security Strategy of the Russian Federation until 2020, accepted in 2009, as well as in its update of December 2015, it has been stressed that disturbances to the balance of military powers in the neighborhood of Russian borders or its

---

[19] V. Galtsov, Obwód Kaliningradzki w latach 1945 – 1991. Społeczeństwo, gospodarka, kultura, „Komunikaty Mazursko-Warmińskie" 1996, no. 2, p. 210; V. N. Abramov, Kaliningradskaya Oblast': socyalno–politicheskye i geopoliticheskye aspekty obshchestvennoi transformaciy 90–kch gg., Sankt Petersburg 1998, p. 27.

[20] I. Oldberg, The Kaliningrad region as a problem between Moscow and Europe, in: A. Żukowski, W. T. Modzelewski (ed.), Kaliningrad: its internal and external issues, Olsztyn 2016, p. 32.

[21] D. Szeligowski, Rosjanie rozmieszczą rakiety przy granicy z Polską, Available at: <http://www.uniaeuropejska.org/rosjanie-rozmieszcza-rakiety-przy-granicy-z-polska/> [Accessed on 19.04.2013, at 21:13]; I. Oldberg, Kaliningrad's difficult plight between Moscow and Europe, „Ulpaper", no. 2, p. 8–9.

allies make threats to state security[22]. Thus, the threats resulting from a possible infrastructure deployment in the NATO states neighboring Russia, especially the Baltic States and Poland, have been indicated. In that context, the Kaliningrad Oblast is one of the critical areas of Russian security strategy.

Also, the latest Security Strategy argues that ensuring strategic stability in Russia's direct neighborhood should be achieved by reinforcing integrational actions, political and military, in the post-Soviet area as well as by harmonizing the integrational processes in the European continent[23]. The content of the document is to be understood as a proposition to find a specific modus vivendi with the European Union and, at the same time, to obtain a more considerable freedom to implement the concept of the post–Soviet area reintegration. The Kaliningrad Oblast is a crucial element of that concept as a wedge that closes the post–Soviet area off from the west. Furthermore, a practical dimension of the role played by the Kaliningrad Oblast in the Russian security strategy, and war doctrine is also worth noting. The majority of military maneuvers conducted in recent years in the Russian Western Military District had their Kaliningrad episodes[24]. Apart from the military potential of the region, shown before, it should also be pointed out that it is located in one of the critical areas of Russia from a geostrategic point of view. In the case of a hypothetical military conflict with the West, the Kaliningrad Oblast is to form a Russian gate to the southern part of the Baltic Sea region, making it possible to cut Baltic States (Lithuania, Latvia, Estonia) off territorially from the rest of the NATO member states. An area of high risk is the so-called Suwałki Gap, the part of Polish territory that separates the Kaliningrad Oblast and Belarus[25].

---

[22] See: chapter II, pt. 12 of National Security Strategy of the Russian Federation to 2020, no. 537, 12.05.2009, http://www.scrf.gov.ru/documents/99.html 24.02.2016]; pt. 15 of National Security Strategy of the Russian Federation to 2020, no. 683, 31.12.2015. Available at: <http://kremlin.ru/acts/bank/40391/>[Accessed on 24.02.2016, at 15:44].

[23] Chapter IV of National Security Strategy of the Russian Federation to 2020, no. 683, 31.12.2015. Available at: <http://kremlin.ru/acts/bank/40391/>[Accessed on 24.02.2016, at 10:30].

[24] The following Russian military exercises had their Kaliningrad episodes: Zapad 2009, military exercise of Russian Western military District in 2012, Zapad 2013, exercises of rocket forces in 2014 as well as Union Shield 2015. See: J. Norberg, Training to Fight – Russia's Major Military Exercises 2011–2014, Report no. FOI-R--4128—SE, 2015. Swedish Ministry of Defence; L. Zdanavičius, M. Czekaj (ed.), Russia's Zapad 2013. Military Exercise. Lessons for Baltic Regional Security, Washington 2015; Rosyjsko-białoruskie ćwiczenia „Tarcza Związku". Available at: <http://przegladmilitarny.blogspot.com/2015/09/rosyjsko-biaoruskie-cwiczenia-tarcza.html>[Accessed on 24.02.2016, at 21:13].

[25] This area was defined by General Ben Hodges, commander of US Army Europe, as another NATO 'gap' to worry about. See: P. McLeary, Meet the New Fulda Gap. Foreign

Although the role of the Kaliningrad Oblast in the political stability and security of the Baltic Sea basin has already become important today, it seems that the geopolitical importance of the region will grow even more in the future. This will not only be the result of the specific geographical location of the region but, above all, the effect of the intersection mentioned above of two great integration processes in the area of the Kaliningrad Oblast: Euro-Atlantic integration and Euro-Asian integration carried out under the auspices of Russia. On the one hand, the Kaliningrad Oblast, as a part of the Russian Federation, will be an element of a broader political plan carried out by Russian authorities, aimed at political, military and economic domination of the post–Soviet space. On the other hand, the Kaliningrad Oblast is and will remain in the future, a participant in intensive cooperation with states of Baltic Sea region, which are also member states of the European Union and NATO. In this context, it is worth attempting to create alternatives for the region given the changing international conditions that can be observed in Europe. Those alternatives can be presented as four scenarios: 1) status quo with regard to the geopolitical role of the Kaliningrad Oblast in the Baltic Sea basin; 2) improvement of EU-Russia relations—in this scenario the Kaliningrad Oblast will play role of laboratory and a specific testing ground for these relations; 3) activity of regional authorities in the Kaliningrad Oblast aimed at wider sovereignty or self-reliance as part of Russia; 4) the Kaliningrad Oblast of the Russian Federation as a tool in the hands of the federal authorities, used in order to "hold in check" member states of the EU and NATO in the South Baltic region. Although we can now observe a mixture of the above-mentioned scenarios in the present geopolitical situation, particularly in the context of the conflict in Ukraine and the implemented project of integrating post–Soviet areas under the auspices of the Russian Federation, it should be expected that the fourth scenario is more likely, since it is related to the use of the geographical location of the Kaliningrad Oblast as an element of the geopolitical game carried out with regard to the Baltic Sea region. However, it should be expected that, at the social and economic level, the federal authorities will still allow the region to keep, to some extent, independent contacts with its European partners.

Policy, 29.08.2015, Available at: <http://foreignpolicy.com/2015/09/29/fulda-gap-nato-russia-putin-us-army/ [24.02.2016]; R. Sisk, Poland's Suwalki Gap Replaces Germany's Fulda Gap as Top NATO Concern, Available at: <http://www.military.com/daily-news/2015/12/10/polands-suwalki-gap-replaces-germanys-fulda-gap-top-nato-concern.html >[Accessed on 24.02.2016, at 15:13].

It is important to mention in this respect that the southern part of the Baltic Sea region is one of the critical geostrategic areas in Europe. According to many experts, the enlargement of NATO to the east from 1999–2004 has redefined the previous directions of geostrategic interests of the policymakers in Moscow, which, apart from the western course (Poland, Lithuania, the Czech Republic), now includes, among others, the southern (Crimea, Donbass, the Caucasus), south-western (Carpathians, Balkans) and north-western directions (Baltic states, Scandinavia)[26]. Furthermore, the internal political and military consolidation of Russia (especially since 2000), has resulted in the strengthening of integration tendencies in the post–Soviet area, primarily visible in respect of the conflict in Ukraine that has reinforced the importance of the above-mentioned geostrategic directions of interests of the Russian Federation. The geopolitical transformations in East-Central Europe presented above have resulted in the Russian authorities identifying areas of particular importance through which Moscow could protect its interests in this part of Europe and somehow "hold in check" the states participating in European and Euro-Atlantic integration—or aspiring to participate in those processes—by controlling the areas situated somehow "behind the back" of those states. In this context, the key areas of geopolitical interest to Russia can be treated as specific geopolitical wedges in relation to countries participating in the European network of relations. It should be emphasized that one of the crucial geopolitical areas for Russian authorities is Baltic Sea basin[27].

This is the way in which the incorporation of Crimea into the Russian Federation, as well as more or less official support for separatists in eastern Ukraine, should be interpreted, as a potential warning to Ukraine about demonstrating pro-European Union aspirations. A similar role is currently played by Transnistria, both in relation to Ukraine and Moldova, as well as by Armenia (with which the Kremlin maintains exceptionally warm ties) in relation to Georgia and Azerbaijan. It might be expected that a similar role—at least as intended by the Russian authorities—can be played by the Kaliningrad Oblast towards the Baltic Sea region, as a source of a permanent

---

[26] A. Sakson, Obwód kaliningradzki w otoczeniu NATO i Unii Europejskiej, „Rocznik Bezpieczeństwa Międzynarodowego" 2015, vol. 9, no. 1, p. 45; D. T.

[27] A. M. Dyner, Back to the Difficult Past: Central and Eastern Europe's Relationship with Russia, „PISM Policy Paper" 2015, No. 16 (118), p. 3–4; I. Wiśniewska, M. Domańska et al., Kaliningrad Oblast 2016. The society, economy and army, OSW Report 2016, Centre for Eastern Studies, p. 20–21.

(more or less real) threat, helping Russia to preserve its influence in a southern part of the Baltic Sea basin.

Conclusion

Thus, the factors that may define the role of the Kaliningrad Oblast as the Russian Federation's geopolitical wedge toward the Baltic Sea region according to the thesis presented in the introduction to this article should be singled out. Firstly, the geographical location of the region predestines it in a particular way to play the role of a specific guard of Russia's interest in the region of the southern Baltic Sea. Although the size of its area, population, and economic structure do not indicate its crucial role in the federal structures of Russia, the significance of the region attributed in Russian strategic documents, and including the Oblast in Russian plans connected with military maneuvers prove the significant geopolitical potential of that region. Secondly, its role in Russian military doctrine is an indicator of the significance of the Kaliningrad Oblast for security in Baltic Sea basin: even today, the region is a place of concentrated troops and military infrastructure and the military manoeuvres carried out in recent years on the territory of the Kaliningrad Oblast and those that used the military units stationed there have been of an expansive (and not defensive) character. Thirdly, the nature of actions by the Russian authorities in the international arena, including the expected aims of Russian foreign policy connected with post–Soviet area reintegration indicate that using the territories belonging to the Russian Federation or tightly attached to it economically, militarily, and politically is to be one of the tools for advancing Russian interests in that area.

Bibliography

Abramov V. N., Kaliningradskaya oblast': socyalno-politicheskye i geopoliticheskye aspekty obshchestvennoi transformaciy 90–kch gg., Sankt Petersburg 1998.

Affek J., Potencjał militarny Rosji w obwodzie kaliningradzkim a możliwości wpływania tego państwa na sytuację geopolityczną w regionie, „Przegląd Geopolityczny" 2014, vol. 8.

Brzezinski Z., The Grand Chessboard. American Primacy and Its Geostrategic Imperatives, Basic Books 1997.

Ciechanowski R., Rosyjskie siły zbrojne w Kaliningradzie, „Dziennik Zbrojny", 11.05.2014, Available at: <http://dziennikzbrojny.pl/arty kuly/art,2,6,6819,armie-swiata,potencjal,rosyjskie-sily-zbrojne-w-kalini ngradzie/> [Accessed on 18.06.2015, at 21:13].

Dyner A. M., Back to the Difficult Past: Central and Eastern Europe's Relationship with Russia, „PISM Policy Paper" 2015, No. 16 (118).

Federalniy Dogovor, (Moscow, 31 March 1992), Available at: <http://cons titution.garant.ru/act/federative/170280/#220/> [Accessed on 20.04.2013, at 21:13].

Galtsov V., Obwód Kaliningradzki w latach 1945–1991. Społeczeństwo, gospodarka, kultura, „Komunikaty Mazursko-Warmińskie" 1996, no. 2.

Gowan P., The Global Gamble: Washington's Faustian Bid for World Dominance, London – New York 1999.

Harbutt F. J., Yalta 1945. Europe and America at the Crossroads, Cambridge 2010.

Hobbs J. J., World Regional Geography, Belmont 2014.

Kretinin G. V., Briushinkin V. N., Galtsov V. I. et al., Ocherki Isstorii Vostochnoy Prussii, Kaliningrad 2002.

Kronenfeld D. T., Kaliningrad in the Twenty-First Century—Independence, Semi-Autonomy, or Continued Second-Class Citizenship?, "Washington University Global Studies Law Review" 2010, vol. 9, issue 1.

Mackinder H. J., Democratic Ideas, and Reality, New York 1981.

Malik M., The Shanghai Cooperation Organization, in S. Ganguly, A. Scobell, J. Chinyong Liow (ed.), The Routledge Handbook of Asian Security Studies, New York 2010.

McLeary P., Meet the New Fulda Gap. Foreign Policy, 29.08.2015, Available at: <http://foreignpolicy.com/2015/09/29/fulda-gap-nato-russia-pu tin-us-army/> [Accessed on 24.02.2016, at 22:30].

Moczulski L., Geopolityka. Potęga w czasie i przestrzeni, Warszawa 1999.

National Security Strategy of the Russian Federation to 2020, no. 537, 12.05.2009, Available at: <http://www.scrf.gov.ru/documents/99.ht ml/> [Accessed on 24.02.2016, at 14:20].

National Security Strategy of the Russian Federation to 2020, no. 683, 31.12.2015, Available at: <http://kremlin.ru/acts/bank/40391/> [Accessed on 24.02.2016, at 21:13].

Norberg J., Training to Fight—Russia's Major Military Exercises 2011–2014, Report no. FOI-R--4128—SE, 2015. Swedish Ministry of Defence.

Oldberg I., Kaliningrad's difficult plight between Moscow and Europe, „Ulpaper," no. 2.

Oldberg I., The Kaliningrad region as a problem between Moscow and Europe, in: A. Żukowski, W. T. Modzelewski (ed.), Kaliningrad: its internal and external issues, Olsztyn 2016.

Pearson R., European Nationalism 1789–1920, New York 2014.

Rosyjsko-białoruskie ćwiczenia „Tarcza Związku", Available at: <http://przegladmilitarny.blogspot.com/2015/09/rosyjsko-biaoruskie-cwiczenia-tarcza.html> [Accessed on 24.02.2016, at 20:15].

Sakson A., Obwód kaliningradzki a bezpieczeństwo Polski, „Przegląd Strategiczny" 2014, no. 7.

Sakson A., Obwód kaliningradzki w otoczeniu NATO i Unii Europejskiej, „Rocznik Bezpieczeństwa Międzynarodowego" 2015, vol. 9, no. 1.

Sisk R., Poland's Suwalki Gap Replaces Germany's Fulda Gap as Top NATO Concern, Available at: <http://www.military.com/daily-news/2015/12/10/polands-suwalki-gap-replaces-germanys-fulda-gap-top-nato-concern.html> [Accessed on 24.02.2016, at 20:15].

Spykman N., The Geography of Peace, New York 1944.

Szeligowski D., Rosjanie rozmieszczą rakiety przy granicy z Polską, Available at: <http://www.uniaeuropejska.org/rosjanie-rozmieszcza-rakiety-przy-granicy-z-polska/> [Accessed on 19.04.2013, at 14:15].

The Constitution of the Russian Federation, Available at: <http://www.constitution.ru/en/10003000-04.htm> [Accessed on 19.02.2017, at 20:15].

Tunsjø Ø., Geopolitical shifts, great power relations and Norway's foreign policy, „Cooperation and Conflict" 2011, no. 46.

Weijian L., The September 11th Incident and Trends in Middle East Social Thought, in: Y. Xintian (ed.), Cultural Impact on International Relations, Washington 2002.

Wellman C., Historische Miszelle. Die Russische Exklave Kaliningrad als Konfliktsyndrom, „Die Friedens-Warte Journal of International Peace and Organization" 2000, no. 3–4.

Wiśniewska I., Domańska M. et al., Kaliningrad Oblast 2016. The society, economy, and army, OSW Report 2016, Centre for Eastern Studies.

Zdanavičius L., Czekaj M. (ed.), Russia's Zapad 2013. Military Exercise. Lessons for Baltic Regional Security, Washington 2015.

Żęgota K., The Kaliningrad Region—Key to Security in East-Central Europe, „Warsaw East European Review" 2016, vol. VI.

Piotr Pietrzak

The Kremlin's Reaction to the St. Petersburg Metro Attacks seen through the Prism of Russian Intervention in Syria

> ***Abstract:*** *This report investigates the 2017 Saint Petersburg Metro bombing from the perspective of similar attacks: in the Sinai Peninsula (November 2015), the assassination of the Russian ambassador to Turkey (December 2016), and a very peculiar Russian plane crash near Sochi (December 2016) that was carrying the members of the Alexandrov Ensemble to perform to Syria. These terrible events are compared to determine who was more likely to stand behind them, whether the Islamic Caliphate or the Caucasus Emirate, in order to test the validity of the primary hypothesis of this project which suggests that these attacks wouldn't have happened if it were not for the Russian President Vladimir Putin's decision to intervene in Syria in September 2015. Subsequently, the final analytical part of this report tries to determine what would be the best policy of responding to the current resident of the Kremlin and to this unexpected outbreak of political violence in his country.*
>
> **Keywords:** Vladimir Putin, Russian Federation, terrorism, "St. Petersburg Metro Attacks", "Sinai Plane Crash", "Assassination of Russian ambassador to Turkey," "Russian military plane crash near Sochi", Islamic Caliphate, Caucasus Emirate.

Introduction

On Monday, 3 April 2017, the international media reported a terrorist suicide attack carried out in the St. Petersburg metro between the Sennaya Ploshchard and Technologichesky Institute stations at around 2:40 p.m. This attack resulted in ten casualties and approximately 50 people wounded. Reportedly, within just two days of the initial explosions, the condition of the four people severely injured in this attack severely deteriorated and resulted in their unfortunate deaths, contributing to the attacks' overall death toll of 14 people. Despite these regrettable figures, one has to emphasize that the Russian authorities stepped up to the challenge and responded to these attacks in the best possible manner. To illustrate this fact, let us point out that within just a few hours of the initial explosions, both President Vladimir Putin and Prime Minister Dimitri Medvedev were able to plausibly confirm that a terrorist attack, in fact, caused the blast in the metro. In the meantime, the fire brigades along with groups of volunteers started coordinating their efforts in helping the survivors of the explosion, and engaged in a tireless operation aimed at clearing out the rest of the potential explosives, whilst the relevant security services launched a thorough investigation to determine who stood behind this assault (Please see combined reports by ABC, Al–Jazeera, BBC, CNN, The Guardian, The Telegraph, France–24, 2017).

Subsequently, within just hours of these attacks, it was twice confirmed that the most probable culprit responsible for planting the explosives was a suicide bomber named Akbarzhon Jalilov, identified as a Russian national, born in Kyrgyzstan who was recently exposed to a very persuasive campaign of jihadist indoctrination, that resulted in his radicalisation and adopting hazardous methods of achieving his political objectives. Even more important is the fact that Jalilov's responsibility for undertaking these attacks was quickly confirmed by traces of his DNA found on the second device located in a different location in the underground which relevant security services, fortunately, deactivated. Still, the very fact that the perpetrator of this attack managed to plant two sizable explosives in one of the most scrutinized places in the country suggests that he must have coordinated his actions with third parties, as the level of complexity needed to put this plan into practice must have surpassed the capabilities of a proverbial lone wolf attacker (BBC, CNN, Guardian, 2017).

Nevertheless, despite the fact that the group responsible for this premeditated attack must have gone to exceptional lengths to launch such a sophisticated attack aimed at wreaking havoc among the residents of the second most significant city in the land, they failed to intimidate them; within just a few days, once their beloved metro was reopened, the citizens of this proud city used it to go to work as if nothing had ever happened. Even though one should not compare pears and apples, on certain levels, the citizens of this city showed an urban resistance to give in to their fears similar to their grandparents and great-grandparents who suffered a great deal of hardship during the almost 900-day-long siege of Leningrad during the Second World War. Having said that, it has to be admitted that as much as the contemporary citizens of St. Petersburg dealt with their fears with remarkable courage, the problem that the country's leadership now faces is the fact that this attack cannot be considered as an isolated incident, as it resembles a vital link in a critical series of recent terrorist attacks that have terrorised Russia for the last couple of years ever since President Vladimir Putin made the decision to intervene militarily in Syria to prop up his major Middle-Eastern ally President Bashar al-Assad in September 2015 (Brzezinski, 2015).

The Side-Effects of Russia's 2015 Intervention in Syria

It is being argued that the list of unexpected consequences of the Russian intervention in Syria are proliferating, and first in the file of these examples is one of the most tragic plane disasters in Russian aviation history, the detonation of the bomb on board the passenger flight Metrojet 7K9268 from Sharm el-Sheikh to St. Petersburg that killed 217 passengers and seven crew members in November 2015 and for which the Egyptian faction of the Islamic State took full responsibility. Although this group has not indicated directly that this assault should be seen as a direct response to the Kremlin's Middle East policy that is precisely how Russian policymakers, as well as the rest of the world, have chosen to perceive it.

Sadly, the Russian plane crash in the Sinai peninsula was followed by the assassination of the Russian ambassador to Turkey Andrey Karilov, who was shot dead in Ankara by a jihadist insurgent impersonating a Turkish police officer on 19 December 2016, at which time the gunman acknowledged his motives in a more explicit way by repeatedly shouting "Allah Akbar" and "Aleppo revenge" during the attack, which clearly indicated that he, as well as the people who helped him, not only disagreed with Russia's efforts to organize a military intervention aimed at prolonging the political life of Bashar al-Assad as Syrian president, but also showed that he was willing to take lethal action against the legal representatives of the country that had helped to create the diplomatic conditions for this state of affairs. Indeed, considering the fact that Mr. Karilov was personally responsible for improving Russia-Turkey bilateral relations after the period of hostility in the aftermath of Ankara's downing of a Russian jet that accidentally crossed Turkish territory in 2015, we can be confident that this political murder was by no means an accident.

Just a few days after the assassination of the Russian ambassador in the Turkish capital, on 25 December 2016, an even more significant tragedy happened as a Russian military jet carrying 92 people, including 64 singers, dancers and orchestra members of the Alexandrov Ensemble, commonly known as the Russian Army Choir, crashed into the Black Sea near Sochi. Furthermore, it has to be emphasized that despite there still not being irrefutable evidence suggesting this was an accident or an intentional act of terrorism, the very fact that this plane was carrying the members of one of the world's most acclaimed choirs, a potent symbol of Moscow's military and cultural might, to Syria to perform in front of Russian soldiers operating there, speaks volumes about the probable linkage between this assault and the ISIS-organized bomb explosion on flight 7K9268, and can be seen as yet another retributory action for the Russian military involvement in Syria.

Are we Certain That It Was Isis That Was Responsible for the St. Petersburg Metro Attacks?

Taken together, we need to admit that from the three above-listed examples one can see a direct linkage to the activity of ISIS, as all of these attacks were organized in the immediate area of this organization's operations. When we consider the 2017 St. Petersburg Metro attacks, it has to be admitted that Islamic State responsibility for this action looks far less convincing, as St. Petersburg is located in a northern part of the country that is not considered to be a traditional area of Islamic State operations and has previously proven be too challenging to be infiltrated by the members of this organization. Considering that for the last 5 years (between 2012 and 2017) we were able to witness the increasing capability of this organization to penetrate even the most demanding environments and organize the most unexpected and elaborate terrorist attacks in places such as France, Belgium, Germany, the US, Canada and even Australia, one can argue that it would be irresponsible to treat geographic proximity as a factor in these deliberations. Still, the way the St. Petersburg attack culprit organized his attack suggests that there is a stronger connection between his methods and tactics used by the members of the so-called Caucasus Emirate than the methods used by the members of the Islamic State of Abu Bakr al-Bagdad.

The problem with this argument is that the members of the Caucasus Emirate have not been very active in recent years, especially after the most charismatic leaders of this group, Dokka Umarov, Aliaskhab Kebekov, Magomed Suleimanov and Zalim Shebuzkhov, were liquidated by the Russian security services. The new leader of this organization has not yet revealed his true identity in public, as he most probably does not want to end up like his predecessors. However, we cannot disregard the possibility of the culprit being linked to the Caucasus Emirate (which emerged around 2007) only because the global media has decided to bombard us with the vast arsenal of examples of daily cruelties organized by the members of ISIS. Maybe the new leader of Caucasus Emirate decided to wait patiently to strike at a time when no one would have expected it, which is possible because this group has been known for its thorough planning capabilities.

As a background, this organization took actions in the late 2000s in Russia, by which time the Russian authorities had already been doing their very best to upgrade the security measures in the country to the highest possible level, as Russia had been subjected to such terrorist attacks as the Dobrovka Theatre hostage crisis in Moscow in 2002, which resulted in 170 casualties, and kidnappings of hundreds of students, their parents and school teachers in the Beslan School attacks of 2004 that caused 330 fatalities. Therefore the Russian authorities had been engaged in protecting every single strategically prominent location in the country: the airports, train stations, bus depots, administrative buildings, theatres, cinemas, and any other public space of particular importance. These measures, to a large extent, could even be compared to the methods applied by the U.S. authorities in the aftermath of the 9/11 events, yet the members of the Caucasus Emirate managed to overcome these difficulties and stage terrorist attacks at Moscow Domodedovo Airport in 2010 and various incidents on the Chechen-Dagestani border in February 2012 (Shterin 2012; Vatchagaev, 2015).

In The Search to Uncover the Rationale Behind the Actions of the Culprit

Although we cannot be sure what the incentive for Akbarzhon Jalilov's actions was, we can assume beyond a reasonable doubt that Russian policymakers' recent intervention in Syria has inadvertently exposed the country's security to various unforeseen hazards and dangers that might originate from multiple places in the global architecture of power. Even though to some political commentators the recent adoption of a much more assertive foreign policy proves that Russia is no longer on its knees and has assumed a commanding position, to others this is a clear sign of weakness since by embracing more militaristic attitudes in its neighbourhood, Russia's policymakers have proven that their soft power skills and powers of persuasion have failed them miserably, and for these reasons they had to resort to the country's arsenal of hard power. By doing so, they have inadvertently put the positive trajectory of the country's development at considerable risk, as the hawkish behavior of the Kremlin has been met with a Western sanctions regime that has negatively affected country's economy and has created a lot of resentment and hostility towards the Russian Federation in general. Unfortunately for the policymakers in Moscow, this atmosphere may work as a boomerang that will return to strike Russia at the least expected moment.

Yet, it is important to emphasise that the relative costs of those seemingly dissimilar interventions will inevitably be weighed differently, and as much as Russia's intrusions in Georgia (2008) and Ukraine (2014–) are not going to make Moscow many friends in those respective countries, they are unlikely to undermine Russia's internal security in any drastic way, as the political actors involved in those conflicts can be considered if not rational at least predictable. However, when it comes to the Kremlin's involvement in Syria, this operation will produce much more severe consequences to the Russian Federation than its combined intrusions in Georgia and Ukraine taken together due to the fact that in this instance we are dealing with much more unpredictable political actors who can and very often do employ extreme measures in their fight for their political goals. Indeed, this group involves radicalized Muslims, and after September 2015 the Russian leader further infuriated not only some Syrian and Iraqi tribal leaders but also a significant proportion of a 1.6-billion-strong community of brothers and sisters in faith around the world. In the Quran, this community of believers is called Ummah, a word that comes from the Arabic root word for "nation" (Quran 49:10)[1].

This problem can be seen from a different perspective if we take into account the fact that Russian Federation's Muslim community is growing very fast. Therefore, we can assume beyond a reasonable doubt that should Russia's policymakers choose to continue their current Middle Eastern policy it will inevitably produce even further tensions between the Kremlin and Muslim Russian citizens. The members of this minority have every reason to feel insulted by the actions of their authorities towards their brothers and sisters in faith in the not so distant Middle East. Subsequently, one may argue that in order to fully comprehend the causes, dynamics and implications behind the increasing radicalization of Russia's Muslim community and why this problem has evolved into a home-grown issue, it is worth bringing to the fore research by Giada Tardivo from the International Institute for Counter-Terrorism who made a plausible argument in 2015 that although the radicalization of local Muslims is still a relatively new phenomenon in Russia,

---

[1] "I possess not for myself any harm or benefit except what Allah should will. For every nation is a [specified] term. When their time has come, then they will not remain behind an hour, nor will they precede [it]". Quran 49:10, Available at: <https://quran.com/10 >[Accessed on 20/05/2017, at. 18:21]

this issue is likely to slowly but surely get out of control in the foreseeable future. According to Tardivo, this problem is noticeable especially in the northern Caucasus directly because this region has been traditionally exposed to various terrorist networks active in the EMEA area (Europe, the Middle East, and Africa). Unfortunately, the metro attacks in St. Petersburg seem to fulfil this scholar's predictions and suggest that the situation in this region is likely to deteriorate further because the Russian intervention in Syria is probably not helping to change the perception of Russia as a country interested only in achieving its geopolitical imperatives, in this case at the expense of Muslim people. If the current trend continues it is rather unlikely that those young, vulnerable and poorly-educated members of the Russian Muslim community from the most affected regions can be shielded from the various jihadi and Salafi recruiters who endeavour to turn southern parts of the Russian Federation into safe havens for their organizations (Malashenko, 2009, p. 30–34; Tardivo, 2015, p. 1–67).

Naturally, it has to be emphasized that Russian involvement in Syria in 2015 has had a very unsettling impact on the development of the situation in the north and south Caucasus, both in Russia and neighboring counties. In this respect, we can add that the very fact that Russia used its Caspian Sea flotilla as a launching pad for its Syrian operations in 2016 has also not helped to stabilize the region because it apparently throws more fuel onto the fire. Still, it has to be emphasized that however shocking the consequences of these events may be, blaming it on for the ongoing tragedy of the civilian population in the region and the Russian Federation would be inappropriate. After all, we were all turned into reluctant witnesses of the events that have had an unhealthy tendency to repeatedly erupt in this region ever since the break-up of the Soviet Union, namely the First Chechen War, the Nagorno-Karabakh War, The Second Chechen War, the Georgia War of 2008, and the Second Nagorno-Karabakh War. One also has to add to this ticking bomb scenario the hostilities between Turkey and Armenia, mutual hatred between Azerbaijan and Armenia, the unresolved tensions between Georgia and Russia, a rivalry between Turkey and Iran for regional domination, and the unstable Syrian—Iraqi as well as Turkish—Iraqi border areas. All of those unresolved tensions have affected the way in which the situations in the northern and southern Caucasus have been unfolding in recent years.

Despite the fact that both the Middle East and the Caucasus are considered to be of pivotal geopolitical importance in the calculations at the Kremlin, these regions are extraordinarily volatile and thus it was advisable to deal with both of them like with eggs. But Russian policymakers have decided to disregard this unwritten rule entirely and not only start behaving like an elephant in a china shop but also to intervene at the very heart of it. In order to illustrate this relation, let us recall possibly the most accurate example of dangerous playing with fire in foreign policy that contemporary history can offer us: President George W. Bush's strategic mistake of invading Iraqi in 2003, removing from power the local leader, followed by an attempt to force the local Muslim populations to embrace an unfamiliar Western style of democracy. That is how the cure for every single malady for the Iraqi society has turned into its poison and has turned into one of the most controversial foreign policy initiatives of any U.S. president in history. Within just a few months of this intervention, intervening forces started to be perceived not as liberators but as oppressors, whilst the 43rd President of the United States and his neo-conservative administration slowly began to acknowledge that the arbitrary intrusion in the internal affairs of an independent Muslim country may have opened a Pandora's box that will be very difficult to close (Pietrzak, 2014, p. 187–194).

Besides, one can argue that when it comes to Putin's intervention in Syria it has had an entirely different character that the U.S. intervention in Iraq, primarily due to the fact that the leaders of Syria explicitly asked the Kremlin for help, and as far as international law is concerned this changes the situation, yet the direct area of operations of the Russian forces has been a Muslim country. The leader of this country is considered by the majority of the people in Syria and the Muslim world to be an illegitimate, morally questionable despot who lost his credibility the moment he started gassing his fellow citizens (Brzezinski, 2015). In this case one can argue that if Prime Minister Yevgeny Primakov[2] was alive in September 2015, he would most

---

[2] **Yevgeny Primakov** (1929–2015) was a Russian politician, diplomat and academic known amongst the specialists of literature on the subject as "Russia's Henry Kissinger", as he acquired an incredible reputation and unquestionable authority on both Russia's internal and foreign policies. Primakov graduated in 1953 from one of the most prestigious universities in the land: the Arabic Department of the Moscow Institute of Oriental Studies in "Regional geography of the Arab countries". He served as prime minister of the Russian Federation between 1998 and 1999 and a minister of foreign affairs (from 1996 until 1998) and a member of the Presidium of the Russian Academy of Sciences. During his time as a foreign minister he became known for steering the country toward stability after its worst economic collapse in 1998, whilst showing the first signs of assertiveness in foreign policy. For instance, on 24 March 1999, whilst this politician was flying to the U.S. for an official visit, the moment he learned that NATO in the meantime had started its retaliation operations in former Yugoslavia for Serbian activity in Kosovo, he ordered the plane to turn around over the Atlantic Ocean and returned to Moscow in a manoeuvre popularly known as "**Primakov's Loop**". Along with Gennadii Ziuganov and Aleksandr Dugin, **Primakov** is consided to be a leading notable of one of the most influential geopolitical schools in

certainly have counselled President Putin against intervening in Syria in the first place, as this brilliant Arabist would have known that this intervention would inevitably appear to the Muslim people as nothing more than a disingenuous attempt to prop up a politician who is widely considered to be a walking dead, in the sense that al-Assad continues to be in charge of the country only thanks to his foreign patrons' help; if this patronage stopped, he would be ousted from power. This can be argued because Prime Minister Primakov considered his homeland to be a bridge between Europe and Asia, and as a result he would most probably take into the account the fact that whilst the leaders of countries come and go, the nation stays, so Russian policymakers need to apply a long-term strategy that excludes the idea of engaging in a military operation that could require staying in the country for decades to come only to prop up an ally who seems to be hated around the world. While Primakov's approach could be considered as strategic and respectful, he was also pragmatic. Meanwhile, Putin and his administration are tactical; their every move is well-played like a very sophisticated grandmaster, but not a champion, because of their impatience. For Primakov, the agenda of restoring Russia's pride and glory was meant to be achieved step by step, whilst the current resident of the Kremlin has decided to act like as if he knew that his time is limited and the majority of his work has to be achieved during his presidency and not the administration of his successor, even at the expense of an eruption of backlashes either in Syria, in the region or in the Russian Federation itself (Basin, 2006, p. 278–280, Riveong, 2005; Smith 2013).

---

the Russian Federation called Eurasianism, which acknowledges that after the end of the cold war this country has lost its superpower stature, and therefore its foreign policy imperatives should reflect this state of affairs. This approach acknowledges that Russia's most pressing security concerns lie in the countries that border Russia, many of them republics formerly in the Soviet Union. Consequently, according to this theory, policy should pursue rapprochement with the "further abroad countries," that are located further away from Russian territory, but are still deeply connected by shared geostrategic imagination and historical recollections. Euroasianist strategists normally bring to the fore such countries as Pakistan, India, Japan, Afghanistan, Iran, Iraq, Syria, Serbia, Bulgaria, Romania, and Slovakia. When it comes to Primakov it has to be emphasised that his approach greatly differed from Dugin's "Eurasian Dream" that suggests using more hawkish measures to attain Russia's goals and objectives. Primakov was of the opinon that the best way for Russia to restore its geopolitical status was through active participation in the agenda to build a more multi-polar world where Russia would be one of the leading powers, which would be achieved by the combination of closer ties with the West and China, and its more active engagement in other important regions in the world, such as the Middle East. This version of Eurasianism is known as **the Primakov Doctrine** (Basin, 2006, p. 278–280; Riveong, 2005; Smith 2013).

That may explain why President Putin behaves as if he were blissfully unaware that Bashar al-Assad expects now the Kremlin will provide Syria with long-term assistance to rebuild the country from the seven-year-long war and to take more vigorous actions in restoring law and order to the land that was left by almost half of its citizens, who have been either killed, internally displaced or had to seek a refuge in various countries around the world. Considering the current status quo in Syria the responsibility in question may entail providing economic, political, diplomatic and military assistance to Syria for the next five, ten or even 15 years, yet any attempts to stabilise Syria may be undermined by the fact that some parts of this country had been ungovernable even long before the outbreak of the Syrian uprising in 2011, or the U.S. intervention in neighbouring Iraq in 2003, or the growth of al-Qaeda as well as Islamic State in Iraq and Syria, and the Russian intervention is not going to miraculously resolve this situation (Levitt, 2009, p. 14–20; Fisk 2012; Grobe 2017; Unesco 2017).

The question remains what the best course of action is for Russia to respond to the St. Petersburg metro attacks, the terrorist attacks, and Syria that would discourage any future terrorist attacks in Russia. Possibly the best possible policy would be just to leave the country similarly to how policymakers in Spain reacted to al-Qaeda's ultimatum to leave Iraq after the state was subjected to the 2004 Madrid train attacks[3], or how the government of Saudi Arabia responded to ISIS blackmail after the downing of the plane of Jordanian Lieutenant Moaz al-Kasasba. Faced with similar dilemmas to Russia's, these governments would most probably consider showing humility and would withdraw from Syria altogether. For Russia it is not an option, mainly if the Kremlin is seriously thinking about regaining its superpower status, as its leaders cannot afford to be threatened by anyone, and neither can they afford to play the hit-or-miss game (Adams, 2007, p. 186; Khan 2015). That is why when we look into the Russian leader's handbook in the search for the best answer as to how to deal with the St. Petersburg metro attacks, we can be confident that Putin is not going to use rushed measures to deal with this

---

[3] In the direct aftermath of the **Madrid Bombings** there was a parliamentaty election in Spain. The Socialist Party led by José Luis Rodríguez Zapatero had promised that in the event of winning this contest, his Government would remove of Spanish troops from operations in Iraq. He won the election, formed the Government and consequently delivered on his main campaign promise. Yet by agreeing to this withdrawal, the newly elected Spanish leader inflicted on his country a massive blow to its international reputation as a regional leaders as he gave the impression that Spain can be compelled to change its foreign policy imperatives only because it cannot deal with internal threats of terrorist attacks.

issue, and he is likely to task Russia's security services with moving "earth and heaven" if necessary to establish who stood behind the terrorist attack in his home city. Once it is determined who is responsible for it, Russia will embark on the quest to hit the organizers of this strike hard, with either elaborated rapid reaction force anti-terrorist operations or (should the group responsible for these attacks prove to be more resilient) a combination of a ground offensive and air strikes. That is precisely how Vladimir Putin reacted to terrorist attacks in Moscow in 2002 and Beslan in 2004 and how his forces annihilated those who fought against his most loyal ally in the Middle East Bashar al-Assad in Aleppo in 2016. This proves one rule only that Vladimir Putin should be considered as a genuinely Machiavellian leader for whom the end always justifies the means, even if this policy creates a massive humanitarian disaster.

Conclusion

A careful analysis of Russian policymakers' options in response to the recent attacks in St. Petersburg illustrates that the current resident of Kremlin has been locked in a catch–22 situation, as the way Putin and Russian authorities react to this situation will inevitably trigger a reaction from abroad and from within the Russian Federation. Not reacting or advocating a weak response exposes Russia to vulnerability to further attacks, while pursuing a hawkish response and playing hardball against alleged (either or Caspian or Middle Eastern) enemies may inevitably push the young members of the local Muslim community in Russia into the hands of religious extremists. It is still difficult to determine whether Akbarzhon Jalilov acted as a lone wolf or associated with a much more extensive terrorist network, but considering the sophistication of his action, we may determine that the danger posed by similar actions in Russia is real. The literature on the subject offers ample evidence showing that applying violence as a response to such acts of terror almost always translates into new waves of hostility in the future. On the other hand, we need to remember that the costs of ignoring such a threat clearly outweigh benefits, so Russian policymakers have to take active steps in the forthcoming months aimed at stabilizing the situation at home and in its regional environment. That is why it will be essential to observe domestic developments in Russia in the forthcoming months and years.

Paradoxically, what adds to the complication of the domestic situation in Russia is the fact that the US and Iraqi forces have driven ISIS out of their regional commands in Mosul and Raqqa (both situated very close to Russia's southern border). For these reasons we may expect that any extreme developments in this area may inadvertently cause massive detriment to the stability of the Russian Federation and the Caucasus in particular (Associated Press, 2016; Persio, 2016). It has to do with the fact that (according to many verifiable sources) former ISIS leader Abu Bakr al-Baghdadi has been neutralized, Iraqi-US coalition forces have retaken Mosul, and for these reasons, it is expected that large groups of ISIS fighters will soon be on the move. Some of these rebels who still enjoy a certain degree of anonymity will try to go back to Western Europe, where they came from, but for the majority of the Islamic State's members who in one way or another have been exposed to Western intelligence, they will no longer enjoy such an option, and they would have to think about different escape routes. For these reasons, we may soon turn into reluctant witnesses of the increased activity of groups of stateless and compromised militants heading north to the southern and northern Caucasus in the hope of creating save heavens for their organization. Moreover, should they choose to follow in al-Qaeda's footsteps in this respect, it is reasonable to expect that they would try to establish their future safe havens somewhere in the northern Caucasus to be in a position to spread the dangerous jihadist and Salafi ideology in this vulnerable region. As we remember, the biggest paradox of the century was the fact that soon after the attacks of 9/11 and the US-led intervention in Afghanistan, Osama Bin Laden, and other al-Qaeda leaders were able to find safe havens in Pakistan in a compound in Abbottabad just 1.3 km southwest of the Pakistan Military Academy in Bilal. Therefore we may expect that those who are now trying to escape the epicenter of the Middle East's conflict and those who have assisted Akbarzhon Jalilov in his actions may try to establish their presence in the Caucasus these days and attract masses of brainwashed young people from this region to follow them (Riedel, 2013).

Bibliography

Abrahms Max, Why Terrorism Does Not Work, International Security, Fall 2006, Vol. 31, No. 2, Available at: <http://www.mitpressjournals.org/doi/abs/10.1162/isec.2006.31.2.42#.WRwKAGiGPIU/> [Accessed on 17.05.2017, at 11:05].

Associated Press: End of ISIS? Battle of Mosul begins (OCTOBER 17, 2016),Available at: <https://thehornnews.com/end-isis-battle-mosul-begins/> [Accessed on: 15.05.2017, at 22:05].

Bassin Mark, Eurasianism "Classical" and "Neo": The Lines of Continuity; & Bassin Mark, "Eurasianism and Geopolitics in Post–Soviet Russia," in Andrei Tsygankov, "Hard-Line Eurasianism and Russia's Contending Geopolitical Perspectives" 2006, Available at: <http://srch.slav.ho kudai.ac.jp/coe21/publish/no17_ses/14bassin.pdf/> [Accessed on 17.05.2017, at 13:07].

Braginskaia Ekaterina, "Domestication" or Representation? Russia and the Institutionalisation of Islam in Comparative Perspective. Europe-Asia Studies (2012).

Brzezinski Zbigniew, Russia must work with, not against, America in Syria, Financial Times (October 4, 2015, 7:55 pm). Available at: <https://www.ft.com/content/c1ec2488-6aa8-11e5-8171-ba1968cf791a/> [Accessed on 17.12.2016, at 16:10].

Carr C., 2002, The Lessons of Terror: A History of Warfare Against Civilians: Why it has Always Failed and why it will fail again, London: Random House.

CBC News, Pakistan denies bin Laden complicity: PM rejects claims intelligence agency 'in cahoots' with al-Qaeda, Available at: <http://www.cbc.ca/news/world/pakistan-denies-bin-laden-complici ty-1.110-310 /> [Accessed on 17.05.2017, at 11:10].

Dannreuther Roland, March Luke, Russia, and Islam: State approaches, radicalization, and the 'War on Terror.'

Dershowitz A., (2002), Why Terrorism Works: Understanding the Threat Responding to the Challenge, New York: Harvard.

Dugin Aleksandr, Osnovi geopolitiki. Mislit' prostranstvom (The essentials of geopolitics. Thinkingspatially) (Moskva: Arktogeia-tsentr, 2000, 925 expanded edition).

Fisk Robert: Syria's ancient treasures pulverised; Available at: <http://www.independent.co.uk/voices/commentators/fisk/robert-fisk-syrias-a ncient-treasurespulverised8007768.html/>[Accessed on 17.07.2014, at 11:10].

Ginsberg Marc, The Battles for Dabiq & Mosul: Not the Beginning of the End of ISIS, but the End of Its Beginning. Available at: <http://www.huffingtonpost.com/amb-marc-ginsberg/the-battles-for-dabiq-mo_b_12543086.html> [Accessed on 17.05.2017, at 16:30].

Grobe Stefan, Report chronicles deliberate destruction of Aleppo by Russia and Assad, (last updated: 13/02/2017). Available at: <http://www.euronews.com/2017/02/13/report-chronicles-deliberate-destruction-of-aleppo-by-russia-and-assad> [Accessed on 17.05.2017, at 16:30].

Group of strategic vision "Russia-Islamic world", Available at: <http://project65436.tilda.ws/page338152.html> [Accessed on 17.05.2017, at 12:30].

Holy Quran, Available at: <https://quran.com/10> [Accessed on 20/05/2017, at 18:21].

Khan Maria, Jordanian pilots, daub messages for Isis on missiles: 'For you, the enemies of Islam.' Available at: <http://www.ibtimes.co.uk/jordanian-pilots-scribble-messages-isis-missiles-you-enemies-islam-1486834> [Accessed on 17.05.2017, at 12:01].

Levitt Matthew, Foreign Fighters and Their Economic Impact: a Case Study of Syria and al-Qaeda in Iraq (AQI); Available at: <http://www.terrorismanalysts.com/pt/index.php/pot/article/view/74/> [Accessed on 10.04.2013, at 07:17].

Malashenko Alexei, Islam in Russia, Russia in Global Affairs, No. 3, 2014.

Malashenko Aleksei, Yarlykapov Akhmet, Radicalization of Russia`s Muslim Community, Microcon Policy Working Paper 9, May 2009.

McDermott Roger, Putin Approves Draft Strategy for Countering Extremism in Russia to 2025, Jamestown's Eurasia Daily Monitor, volume: 11, issue: 211 November 25, 2014, at 08:26 PM, Available at: <https://jamestown.org/program/putin-approves-draft-strategy-for-countering-extremism-in-russia-to-2025/> [Accessed on 17.05.2017, at 10:17].

Mufti Imam Kamil, Ummah: The Muslim Nation, Available at: <http://www.newmuslims.com/lessons/284/>[Accessed on 20.05.2017, at 18:17], (Published on 06 Apr 2015 - Last modified on 08 Jun 2015).

Persio Sofia Lotto, Battle for Mosul is a crucial turning point in the war against Isis, (October 17, 2016, at 18:05 BST), Available at: <http://www.ibtimes.co.uk/battle-mosul-crucial-turning-point-war-against-isis-1586830/> [Accessed on 17.05.2017, at 11:01].

Pietrzak Piotr, American "Soft Power" after George W. Bush's Presidency, in: The United States and the World. From Imitation to Challenge. Edited by Andrzej Mania, Łukasz Wordliczek, Kraków: Jagiellonian University Press 2014. Available at: <https://www.cambridge.org/core/books/united-states-and-the-world/american-soft-power-after-george-w-bushs-presidency/92C28B90B6768A74A8FF8123E5A81E-5F/> [Accessed on: 17.05.2017, at 14:17].

Reuters and Haaretz, ISIS Video Shows Captured Jordanian Pilot Being Burned Alive read, (03.02.2015) Available at: <http://www.haaretz.com/middle-east-news/1.640631/>[Accessed on 17.05.2017, at 11:01].

Riedel Bruce, Pakistan's Osama bin Laden Report: Was Pakistan Clueless or Complicit in Harboring Bin Laden? Friday, July 12, 2013, Available at: <https://www.brookings.edu/opinions/pakistans-osama-bin-laden-report-was-pakistan-clueless-or-complicit-in-harboring-bin-laden/> [Accessed on 17.05.2017, at 11:08].

Riveong Daniel, China, Russia tries quasi-NATO? Dugin's Eursia or Primakov Doctrine?, (October 26, 2005), Available at: <http://www.danielriveong.com/2005/10/china-russia-tries-quasi-nato-dugins-eursia-or-primakov-doctrine/> [Accessed on 10.05.2017, at 15:05].

Sagramoso, D., Violence and conflict in the Russian North Caucasus, International Affairs, 83.4, 2007. Available at: <http//www.onlinelibrary.wiley.com/doi/10.1111/j.14682346.2007.00647.x/abstract> [Accessed on 10.05.2017, at 15:05].

Goble Paul, Why are Russians Converting to Islam? [Pochemu russkie prinimayut islam] Available at: <http://www.islamicity.org/3551/why-are-russians-converting-to-islam/> [Accessed on 17.05.2017, at 10:05].

Sedgwick Mark, The Concept of Radicalization as a Source of Confusion, Terrorism and Political Violence 22, No. 4 (2010). Available at: <http://www.tandfonline.com/doi/abs/10.1080/09546553.2010.491009/> [Accessed on 01.04.2017, at 12:05].

Shterin Marat, Religion, Extremism, and Radicalisation in post-communist Russia: issues, public policy, and research: Available at: <http://www.radicalisationresearch.org/debate/shterin_2012_religion-2/> [Accessed on 10.05.2017, at 19:05].

Smith Gordon B., Russian Exceptionalism? Putin's Assertion of Sovereignty at Home and Abroad, (Paper Presented on April 20, 2013 at the Conference on Sovereignty and the New Executive Authority at the Center for Ethics and the Rule of Law at the University of Pennsylvania Law School). Available at: <https://www.law.upenn.edu/live/files/1882-gordon-smith-russian-exceptionalismpdf/> [Accessed on 17.05.2017, at 14:01].

UNESCO, International Conference "Heritage and Cultural Diversity at Risk in Iraq and Syria" (3 December 2014). Available at: <http://www.unesco.org/culture/pdf/iraq-syria/IraqSyriaReporten.pdf/> [Accessed on 17.05.2017, at 16:01].

Vatchagaev Mairbek, Russian Muslim Militants Are Joining the Ranks of Rebel Fighters in Syria, Eurasia Daily Monitor, vol. 10, issue 117. Available at: <https://jamestown.org/program/russian-muslim-militants-are-joining-the-ranks-of-rebel-fighters-in-syria-2/> [Accessed on 17.05. 2017, at 11:01].

Vatchagaev Mairbek, Counter-Terrorism Operations Take Place in Dagestan Virtually Non-Stop, Jamestown's Eurasia Daily Monitor, volume:12, issue: 92 (May 15, 2015): Available at: <http://www.jamestown.org/programs/edm/single/?tx_ttnews%5Btt_news%5D=43922&tx_ttnews%5BbackPid%5D=786&no_cache=1#.VW2rV1bGA6V> [Accessed on 16.05.2017, at 16:05].

Walt, Stephen, What Should We Do if the Islamic State Wins? (10/06/2015) Foreign Policy Magazine Available at: <https://foreignpolicy.com/2015/06/10/what-should-we-do-if-isis-islamic-state-wins-containment//> [Accessed on 13.08.2015, at 09:10].

Zyuganov Gennadiy (1999), Geografiya pobedi. Osnovi rossiyskoi geopolitiki (The geography of the victory. Introduction to Russia's geopolitics) Moskva: unknown publisher.

Global Media Reports Regarding St. Petersburg Metro Attacks:

ABC: St Petersburg metro explosion: At least 14 dead in underground blast in Russia: http://www.abc.net.au/news/2017-04-03/at-least-14-dead-in-st-petersburg-metro-explosion-russia/8412634.

AlJazeera: St Petersburg metro bomb blast kills 11, wounds dozens: http://www.aljazeera.com/news/2017/04/blast-hits-st-petersburg-metro-carriage-170403120753707.html.

BBC: St Petersburg metro attack: Russia police arrest eight: http://www.bbc.com/news/world-europe-39514694.

BBC: St Petersburg metro bombing a possible suicide attack: http://www.bbc.com/news/world-europe-39486640.

CNN: St. Petersburg bombing carried out by 'suicide' attacker: http://edition.cnn.com/2017/04/04/europe/st-petersburg-russia-explosion/index.html.

Counteriedreport: St Petersburg metro attack: 'Bomb' found in city raid: http://counteriedreport.com/news/st-petersburg-metro-attack-bomb-found-in-city-raid.

The Guardian: Shaun Walker, St Petersburg bomb suspect identified as 22-year-old born in Kyrgyzstan: https://www.theguardian.com/world/2017/apr/04/st-petersburg-metro-bombing-suspect-kyrgyzstan-akbarzhon-jalilov-says-security-service.

The Telegraph: St Petersburg Metro explosion: Russian investigators believe suicide bomber caused a blast that killed 14, a suspect named: http://www.telegraph.co.uk/news/2017/04/03/saintpetersburg-bombing-casualties-explosion-metro-train.

Piotr Pietrzak

Interview with Francesco Trupia on the Nagorno-Karabakh Conflict

Piotr Pietrzak (PP) – This interview was recorded on behalf of International Relations Daily. Our today's guest is **Francesco Trupia**, who is a PhD Candidate at the University of Sofia "St. Kliment Ohridski" and our South Caucasus expert at In Statu Nascendi. Francesco is a research fellow at the Alpha Institute of Islamic Strategic Affairs and a fellow at the Alpha Institute of Geopolitics and Intelligence; formerly, he was associated with CRC Armenia. Most recently, he has cooperated with some local NGOs based in Bulgaria, Serbia, Ukraine, Armenia, and Kosovo. This scholar is also interested in geopolitics, post–Soviet affairs, conflict resolution strategies, and issues related to the policy of multiculturalism and theories of minority rights in the former Communist Bloc.

This interview was conducted to discuss the reasons behind both territorial and ethnic conflicts between Armenia and Azerbaijan over the disputed region of Nagorno-Karabakh. It also aims at exploring various issues related to this dispute, such as the notion of "frozen conflict"; "otherness"; collective imaginary; and psychological trauma that have haunted the bilateral relations between the nations for the last 25 years; ever since the first significant outbreak of the hostilities in this region in the early 1990s. Our guest is known for seeing Nagorno-Karabakh as one of the most protracted conflicts in Europe and one of most vigorous confrontations in the former Soviet sphere, a proverbial ticking time bomb that can explode at any time, and last year's escalation, known in the literature as the Second Karabakh War, is a perfect example. Good morning, Francesco, can you tell a little bit more about this rivalry?

Francesco Trupia (FT) – Good Morning, Piotr. First of all, let me thank you for this interview. I couldn't agree more, Nagorno-Karabakh should be seen as the longest-running conflict in Europe. Although it is unusual to mention the European continent in reference to the south Caucasus, a region that, to a certain extent, is disconnected with a classical idea of Europe, Armenia and Azerbaijan, the countries involved in the conflict, deal with the EU through the Eastern European Agreement that they signed together with Georgia, Ukraine, Moldavia, and Poland. Both Caucasian countries began to take part in the political area of the European Union since they are involved in the EU's foreign policy strategies through the process of EU enlargement, despite, regarding the issue of Nagorno-Karabakh, a general lack of interest that Brussels shows in the regional rivalry. In my opinion, there is only one explanation: wealthy economic interests are trying to hide the issue of Nagorno-Karabakh in order to make the Karabakh Armenians' struggle for recognition unvoiced as they step towards more cooperation and relations with Azerbaijan's economy within the pivotal area of the Caspian Sea. Azerbaijani gas resources seem paradoxically, or perhaps controversially, to be more important than condemning one of the worst democracies worldwide whose authoritarian regime has ruled the post–Soviet country since the collapse of Communism and even before that, with impressive domestic violations of human rights currently taking place alongside Nagorno-Karabakh's Line of Contact (LoC). Addressing the Nagorno-Karabakh issue might risk legitimizing a de facto entity where local Armenians demand the recognition of their region which was de jure allocated to Azerbaijan and remains an Azeri region according to international law. In political terms, we can describe the situation as a "frozen conflict" even though such definition implies only an inability to "unfreeze" the conflict, as far as I understand the state of affairs. Many experts, scientists, and PhD researchers have paid attention mainly on "how to reach" a sustainable resolution for the two-decade-long conflict, which seems unsolvable because neither Armenia nor Azerbaijan is ready to compromise. For Armenians, for instance, Nagorno-Karabakh is one of their motherland's regions in deep connection with their communitarian idea of nationhood and history. The worsening experiences Armenians have been passing through, such as the 1915 Genocide, the loss of so-called "Western Armenia", that is, contemporary Eastern Turkey, as well as the Soviet takeover of their independent State of Armenia and Nakhichevan, which was allocated to SSR Azerbaijan, have made the struggle over Nagorno-Karabakh "something" unnegotiable. On the other side, Azerbaijan also reclaims the integrity of its de jure national territory, accusing Karabakh Armenians of being "illegal occupants" of the region and Armenia of being guilty of supporting separatists in the area.

_PP_ – *(Let us dig a little bit deeper into this issue): Can you tell us more about this particular point, from the perspective of history and in particular Joseph Stalin's policy in the region, as not everyone may be familiar with what happened during the Sovietization of the South Caucasus in the late 1940s and the beginning of the 1950s? This policy has* had a massive impact on the way local politics is still being shaped after all of these decades. Is this accurate?

FT – Very briefly, when the south Caucasus began geo-politically to represent a Soviet strategy between the two world wars, the region itself was on the south-western outskirts of the Soviet Union. With the rise of the Cold War and Turkey's joining NATO in 1954, the South Caucasus became a frightening area from which military escalations and interferences would take place. Besides history, there are nowadays many ethnic issues in the region, and Nagorno-Karabakh is only one of them. The "Black Garden" was historically occupied by Christian populations, such as Armenians and those nomadic peoples (e.g., an Albanian population living in the Caucasus without ethnic connections with those of the Balkan region) who had been living side-by-side until their total assimilation through common faith in the Christian religion. Since then, the region was included in the Persian Empire, which named the region "Karabakh" (i.e., Black Garden), and then Sovietized at the beginning of the 1920s, when the Soviet Union allocated it to Azerbaijan, which was formed in 1920, until the breakup of the union in 1988 and the first war between Armenia and Azerbaijan from 1992–94. For the Soviet administration, the allocation of the Autonomous Oblast of Nagorno-Karabakh was only a win-win strategy to take control over the region, and Stalin was the authority that decided to allocate Nagorno-Karabakh to SSR Azerbaijan.

PP – *For sure, when we take into account historical and geopolitical relations in such situations, we are more able to grasp the extremely convoluted political backdrop of both domestic and international consequences of various regional conflicts. On many levels, situations in Nagorno-Karabakh can be compared to the recent developments in Afghanistan, Iraq, Syria, Ukraine, Yemen, Egypt, or even Central Africa, for one straightforward reason – namely the fact that ethnicity plays a crucial role in the internal developments of these conflicts. It is also fascinating that very often various groups, sects, and minorities after decades of living in peace side by side with each other decide out of the blue to start being hostile to each other. I wonder whether we could explain it through the notion of frozen relations. That is precisely what interests me the most here with Nagorno-Karabakh, how the conflict that by many political commentators has been described as "frozen" for over twenty or even twenty-five years broke out to the extent that we started calling it in the Second Nagorno-Karabakh conflict. How can you explain it?*

FT – With all due respect, I really think that you are wrong when you label the conflict in Nagorno-Karabakh as a "frozen conflict". The former was defined "frozen" due to the lack of willingness to put Armenians and Azerbaijanis in a position to compromise and figure out the best resolution for unfreezing the military conflict. Many strategies have been employed; however, all of them have been failing in time. I would turn—and this is what I would like to point out—your idea of a "frozen conflict" into the idea of a "frozen relation" between Armenians and Azerbaijanis, going beyond the frozenness of the conflict and aiming to open up a point of view from which to look for a sustainable and stable solution for the future.

As a matter of fact, many renowned experts in the field have compared the Nagorno-Karabakh case with Kosovo rather than Middle Eastern case studies, since Kosovo was a majoritarily inhabited Albanian region within post-Yugoslavian Serbia as Nagorno-Karabakh was majoritarily Armenian within the Autonomous Oblast of Nagorno-Karabakh in the SSR Azerbaijan in the Soviet space. Interestingly, despite Russia and China officially refusing to recognize Kosovo as an independent state, it is recognized as the newest sovereign State in Europe by the majority of the international community, whereas the *de facto* entity of Nagorno-Karabakh does not exist internationally. Still, I need to admit that in my opinion, the Nagorno-Karabakh is a very unique case.

PP *– This seems to be a good comparison (...), but whereas most of our readers can relate to the post–1999 developments in Kosovo, as we consider those developments relatively recent, the genesis of the latest developments in the north Caucasus very often escapes our attention. Can you explain to us the current events through the prism of the previous military escalations in Nagorno-Karabakh in the early 1990s?*

FT – Indeed, the 1994 ceasefire agreement reached in Bishkek brought Armenia and Azerbaijan to decide to stop fighting after the two-year war. The result, in theory, should make the region and its locals relatively safe; however, the ceasefire did not work within the area, where hostilities along the Line of Contacts (LoC) have never ceased to take place. There is a war within the inhabited Armenian region of Nagorno-Karabakh, with a wide range of ceasefire violations triggered by both sides. This is why is inaccurate to name the region as a place of a "frozen conflict". I won't say that only Azerbaijan is conducting military operations and violations of the ceasefire against Armenians because Armenians are currently defending the positions they gained in the 1992–94 war by occupying the region militarily. According to what Armenians consider their motherland, their main aims have remained to protect their belongings and Armenian faith and nationhood from others.

Moreover, Lines of Contact show physically and even ideologically that military positions between which *de facto* Republic of Artsakh's and Azerbaijan's soldiers face each other are the places where the Nagorno-Karabakh conflict takes place randomly along its borders. Even though since 1994 Armenians have militarily shown no interest in taking more territory from Azerbaijan, the situation has severely deteriorated.

Consequently, in April 2016, there was a massive escalation; especially in the north-eastern part of Nagorno-Karabakh along the Armenian borders by the modest village of Talish, in which Azeri soldiers conducted human rights violations against civilians which triggered a military reaction from the Armenian side. This escalation, which began on 2 April and ended 5 April 2016, is nowadays well-known and called by Karabakh Armenians the "4 Days War", as well as the "Second War", due to the worst military clashes that took place after those between 1992 and 1994. Because of that, a new chapter of the conflict was written because it meant that Azerbaijan is able to attach the Armenian region and, in the meantime, it showed the Armenians' ability to defend the territory despite the loss of a couple of hundreds of square kilometers in the direction of Talish.

_PP_ – *Who in your opinion triggered this recent outbreak of conflict? Who pushed the button to escalate this situation in April 2016? How do you perceive the "time-bombs" that seem to be waiting to explode in a region that has a wealth of similarities from Abkhazia and South Ossetia to the Turkish-Azeri brotherhood and Armenia, that are in proximity with another unstable region, namely the Middle East, where Iraq and Syria are under the threat of jihadi movements?*

_FT_ – Firstly, there are a couple of explanations as to "who pushed the button". Besides those adhering to nationalistic and propagandistic explanations with any analytical explanations, in my opinion, the "4 Days War" in Nagorno-Karabakh was launched by Azerbaijan in order to move public attention from the Panama papers scandal, in which the Aliyev dynasty was involved, to the region of Karabakh, that is, a sensitive issue for Azerbaijani IDPs and the whole population. Secondly, the South Caucasus is one of the most interesting regions in the sphere of international relations since it is a region which geopolitically bridges Europe and Asia and the Middle East. There are three de facto entities within the region: two of them are in the *de jure* territory of Georgia where Russia is assuming a critical role along the Georgian external borders, and then the Nagorno-Karabakh entity. At the same time, the Azeri exclave of Nakhichevan, which Armenians campaigned a lot during the Soviet period to have reallocated to the SSR Armenia, brought to light the lack of relations between Azerbaijan and Armenia, and, in turn, between Armenia and Turkey. Both of them are dealing with a current process of diplomatic reconciliation, which is still lacking because of the Turkey's unwillingness to recognize the Armenian genocide in 1915 during the collapse of Ottoman Empire where Ottoman Armenians were murdered and forcedly moved from the "Western Armenia", historical Anatolia, contemporary Eastern Turkey, to the former Empire's outskirts. So far, Turkey has not recognized the 1915 genocide on the one side while Armenians have been strongly campaigning and calling for an international recognition of the 1915 genocide where 1.5 million Armenians lost their lives during the so-called operation of "resettlement" of the Armenian population conducted by Turkish Ottomans. This is why the Turkish-Armenian reconciliation process has often been interrupted without the possibility to move forward.

_PP_ – *In this respect, it is worth emphasizing that the European Union very strongly supports the Trans-Anatolian Pipeline (TAP) project, and as one may expect the current resident of the Kremlin does not very much appreciate it, would you agree with that?*

_FT_ – Surely it is. The TAP pipeline was initially a sub-regional project between Azerbaijan, Georgia, and Turkey, that aimed to bypass Armenia, which was the only country left out due to regional rivalries. However, after the decision to stop the South Stream pipeline, which was supposed to pass through the so-called Balkan corridor (Bulgaria, Greece, and Albania) in southeast Europe, all the way up to Italy and Austria. In this respect, it is worth emphasizing that the EU sanctions against Russia after its annexation of Crimea and "aggression" in southern Ukraine has situated the TAP project as one of the EU's most important energy projects. Once again, by having a quick look over the south Caucasus, even the TAP pipeline shows how "frozen relations" between Turkey and Armenia, and Armenia and Azerbaijan, are negatively affecting the whole region and its economic development. Interestingly, the friendship between Armenians and Georgians based on religious heritage seems also to be very fragile due to historical reasons that have paradoxically exposed both countries to further issues in the light of current phenomena. The historical alignment between Armenia and Russia leaves Georgia out of further cooperation with Moscow due to the disputed regions of Abkhazia and South Ossetia, and makes Armenia quite isolated in turn, surrounded by enemies, such as Azerbaijan and Turkey. Here, precisely *de facto* entities and "frozen" conflicts are seriously interplaying between the three South Caucasian Republics from within, and even regionally the presence of Turkey and Russia does not reduce the dangerous threats of escalation in future. I am very skeptical about any type of improvement that interregional relations and cooperation might effect between those countries that are involved in conflicts for disputed territories. I am saying so because it seems to be impossible to solve regional issues without trying to recognize problems over disputed territories. According to Nagorno-Karabakh, the question is as follows: should we acknowledge the region as an independent State? For Azerbaijan, however, this future perspective cannot be even taken into consideration for diplomatic discussion. Hence, why does Armenia not recognize the de facto entity also though the new constitution allows Yerevan to support the region in case of escalation? In this case, for example, Georgia is very carefully maintaining its impartial position over the conflict. Tbilisi, indeed, does not want to take the risk of losing Azerbaijan as regional partner on the one hand, and at the same time, it does not want to make the diplomatic relations with Yerevan vulnerable, on the other hand, since an important Armenian minority lives in the southern part of the country and both countries have mutual interests.

PP *– A quick slightly off-topic question – what in your opinion is happening in the region at the moment regarding the increasingly assertive Russian foreign policy? How, in your opinion, do Tbilisi, Yerevan, and Baku see the increasing Russian interest in so-called near abroad and how do they perceive Moscow's recent involvement in the Syrian conflict (especially considering that Russian policymakers have recently decided to use its Caspian Sea fleet to launch missiles towards Syria)?*

FT – Starting from the Syrian war, the most important phenomenon that currently concerns Armenia is the inflow of Syrian Armenians. Those who have been leaving Syria to be "back home", with some of them going to resettle in Nagorno-Karabakh, is a concern for sure. In Armenia, I have seen one of the first protests in front of the Russian Embassy in Yerevan because of the overwhelming usage of Russian weapons and militarily equipment sold by Russia to Azerbaijan, which in turn used them against Armenians in April 2016. The Georgian position is not very relevant here, even though Tbilisi does not regard positively any Russian intervention in foreign countries due to the wars in Abkhazia and the fragile scenario in South Ossetia. At the same time, jihadists use the Georgian Pankisi Gorge for training. From the

Azerbaijani point of view, it was proved that many IS supporters have joined the Syrian battleground in the last two years, and, once again according to Karabakh, some researchers show an involvement of jihadi fighters in Karabakh. Is the conflict between Armenia and Azerbaijan comparable to Ukraine and Russia? I do not think so because to me the rivalry of Nagorno-Karabakh is a unique case study due to many historical, political and sociological reasons. Of course, Ukraine's conflict is changing the Ukrainians' idea of national identity, which is going to play an essential role in social life, but it remains different from the scenario in the south Caucasus.

PP – *Let us just come back (for a second) to your recent research in Nagorno-Karabakh? Could you tell me more about your personal experience of living in a war zone?*

FT – I have been living away from the direct Line of Contact (LoC). In Stepanakert, *de facto* capital of Nagorno-Karabakh, the situation is quite safe, and this was my impression when I have been in the region, frankly speaking. Of course, the ongoing recollection of war is almost everywhere and is shaping the identity of Karabakh Armenians. From the past, when the mountainous region was not an issue for Armenians and Azerbaijanis to a certain extent, Armenians are now celebrating the "Day of Victory" on 9 May, which since 2016 will take place a month after the escalation triggered in the "4 Days War" of April. There was a photo exhibition in the main square of Stepanakert, for example, where pictures from the 1992–94 War have been collected and shown to everybody to underline the relevancy of the "Second War" of April 2016. Thereby, this idea of recollecting warfare situations where the attempt to fight in defense of the motherland is expressed has shaped the Armenian community's consciousness, creating an Armenia-ness that will be affecting (positively and negatively) every single characteristic of being part of the Armenian population. In this case, it is worth emphasising that Armenians living in Nagorno-Karabakh, as well as those communities of Azerbaijani and Armenian civilians residing along the Line of Contact (LoC) constantly feel the pressure of the war within a region where the second and third generation of locals have no idea how to conduct a peaceful life. From the first generation of Armenians and Azerbaijanis that have faced the first turmoil in the region, almost everyone has lost relatives, parents, sons, and friends. This worsening aspect has become crucial and existential for both communities. As far as I understood, Nagorno-Karabakh does not mean for Armenians and Azerbaijanis a war, it has come to take a place in every single part of Armenia's and Azerbaijan's everydayness: from mass media to the political landscape, from private to public life, and, most important to me, the loss of understanding the "Other" and otherness as well. This explains why, for instance, the last and current Armenian prime ministers and most important authorities in charge have familiar or personal experiences and linkages with the mountainous region of Karabakh. In Azerbaijan, too, the Aliyev family that is ruling the country belongs to Nakhichevan, the Azeri exclave that has been becoming very popular as it was another disputed land between Azeri and Armenian culture since the Sovietization of the region. Currently, because of the "frozen relations" with Armenia, Azerbaijanis living in the exclave are not allowed to reach the other side of Azerbaijan by crossing Armenia. Because of the Nagorno-Karabakh state of affairs, those Nakhichevan's locals who would like to reach Baku, for example, have to bypass Armenia by going through Iran to the other part of Azerbaijan.

PP – *Can you tell us more about your recent publication: "Unfreezing the "other": collective trauma and psychological warfare over the Nagorno-Karabakh rivalry", published by Journal of Liberty and International Affairs, where you elaborate on the role of the other in the conflict of Nagorno-Karabakh? Interestingly you have based some of your arguments on secondary research about Armenian and Azeri reluctance to marry one another. Can you elaborate a little bit more about your claim that the conflict cannot be solved currently due to an ongoing "frozen relation" between the communities?*

FT – Under certain circumstances in the Soviet time, Armenians and Azerbaijanis had interethnic marriages and families with the presence of Armenians and Azerbaijanis living in the SSR Armenia and SSR Azerbaijan. For me, it is fascinating to try to understand when exactly everything went wrong between two populations that have been living and sharing the same place and their everyday life. The Sumgait Pogrom in Azerbaijan against Armenians and the tragedy (or possibly "genocide") of Khojaly have misshaped the mentality of both populations, which nowadays show an unwillingness to think about a new possibility to living together again. Here, the ways that Armenian and Azerbaijani rulers and politicians, in general, are shaping collective memory and rewriting history by using collective drama and manipulating the warfare contest is and will be paramount. Historically, it was the breakup over the region of Nagorno-Karabakh that immediately changed everything and—in my opinion, – it became the main issue for dealing with when we start to think about a sustainable resolution of the two-decade-long war. The national identity of young Armenians and Azerbaijanis, especially those who have been born in the post-Soviet time, is connected with the regional rivalry and conflict in Nagorno-Karabakh, in which the "Other" is seen as an enemy, a killer of one's brothers and sisters, and so forth. If older generations remember (even with nostalgia sometimes) the Soviet time when Armenians and Azerbaijanis shared their everyday lives, the new generations in Armenia and Azerbaijan seem to be thoroughly brainwashed by the storytelling of the war, and the heroism behind the acts of fighting for Karabakh.

_PP_ – *I am not sure if a similar study has attempted to assess the relations between Ukrainian man and Russian women, and vice versa, or Turkish Cypriot and Greek Cypriot couples, or similarly relations between the two sexes within Sunni and Shia communities living in Iraq, Syria, and in the broader Middle East region, but this study seems to be quite relevant in showing the complexity of these relations…*

FT – Indeed, that is why I have used the Caucasus Barometer 2012 data concerning marriages to exemplify that in these post-conflict societies it will be challenging to start a business with the Other. I also claim that in order to go behind what the data I used shows, we have to work on a reconciliation process between Armenians and Azerbaijanis. Although it is impossible to imagine the conclusion of the conflict, neither community is ready to live side by side once again. This is what I meant when I phrased the ongoing situation as a "frozen relation", instead of re-addressing the definition of "frozen conflict" that has always been ongoing and never "frozen".

_PP_ – *Thank you very much for your time.*

FT – My pleasure.

Further Reading

Gramsci, Antonio. "Armenia, 1916". In Gramsci's Circle of Humanity and Armenia, Yerevan Prin.

Ayunts, Artak and Zalyan, Mikayel and Zakaryan, Tigran. "Nagorno-Karabakh Conflict: Prospects for Conflict Transformation", The Journal of Nationalism and Ethnicity, Routledge, Great Britain, <http://dx.doi.org/10.1080/00905992.2016.1157158>, 6 May 2016.

Kirvelyté, Laura. "The Conflict Over Nagorno-Karabakh: Is There A Way to "Unfreeze" The Resolution Process?" In The Margins of the Nagorno-Karabakh Conflict: In Search of Solution, Centre for Geopolitical Studies, Vilnius, 2015.

Glavanakova, Alexandra. Trans-Cultural Imaginings. Translating the Other, Translating the Self in Narratives About Migration and Terrorism. Critique and Humanism Publishing House, Sofia, 2016.

Krüger, Heiko. The Nagorno-Karabakh Conflict, a Legal Analysis. Heidelberg, Springer, 2010.

Lorusso, Marialisa. A Deepening and Widening Conflict: The Nagorno-Karabakh Dispute and the Regional Context. Istituto di Scienza Politica Internazionale (ISPI) Italy, June 2016.

Savinas, Igor. "The Conflict of Nagorno-Karabakh Between Armenia and Azerbaijan: Peculiarities of the Perception of the Conflict Outside the Region" In The Margins of the Nagorno-Karabakh Conflict: In Search of Solution, Centre for Geopolitical Studies, Vilnius, 2015.

Trupia, Francesco, Unfreezing the "other": collective trauma and psychological warfare over the Nagorno-Karabakh rivalry, In Journal of Liberty and International Affairs 2 (2017), 3, p. 30–44. URN: Available at: <http://nbn-resolving.de/urn:nbn:de:0168-ssoar-50092-2> [Accessed on 11.06.2017, at 21:13].

Christina Korkontzelou,
Evangelos Koumparoudis

Was it Greece's Lost Decade (2007–2017) or just a Culmination of the Process that has led Athens to the Brink of Economic Collapse?

Abstract: *The last decade (2007–2017) has been anything but rewarding for Greece, for both its socio-political development within the European Union and its geopolitical position in general. During this time, Greek people have been subjected to a prolonged period of economic austerity that had been imposed on them by the so-called troika–a group; formed by the European Commission (EC), the European Central Bank (ECB) and the International Monetary Fund (IMF). In theory, the application of these measures, combined with the introduction of very harsh fiscal reforms, were supposed to put the Greek economy on the right track of development and sustainable growth, in a relatively short period. However, this expectation was not be met with reality as the consequences of the Global Financial System have resulted in a massive negative impact on the condition of the Greek economy. Also, contrary to the expectations of the country's new creditors, the combination of both the austerity measures and the monetary reforms have impacted the abilities of the state actor to intervene in the local economy. For decades, the Greek state who has been seen as a reliable actor keen to stimulate the local economy started being now very absent from the economic horizon and that in turn has created a massive vacuum on the economic condition of the entire country that strongly depended on the state actor. In turn, the atrophy of various functions of the Greek state, combined with the lack of the economic investment on the macro level, have resulted in the massive unemployment, depression and deterioration of the living conditions in virtually every single sphere of social life in Greece: from the state pension system to health system. The same austerity measures that were supposed to resolve the economic problem of this Southern European country have started being perceived in Athens as too-harsh, counter-productive, and discriminatory. Not to mention the fact that, within days, the masses of the ordinary Greeks had to adjust to the conditions of new reality of enforced transformation from their beloved welfare state into the wild west-type of the variety of capitalism, and accept an extreme deterioration of* *the living conditions. That in turn, resulted in a great deal of anxiety, disillusionment and alienation about the way the situation in their country has started unfolding amongst the majority of the population that have been further troubled by the so-called refugee crisis in Europe that broke in 2015 as this country has also inadvertently turned into the first European nation hosting massive waves of refugees. This article aims at analyzing the essential structural contradictory elements and paradoxes of the Greek capitalistic development that lead to the debt crisis of 2010 and the immediately linked problem of an unstable environment for investments. It is endeavored to focus our attention on investigating the austerity policies, referring to the essential changes in the working and living standards, and focus on the issue of the alienation in the workplace in both private and public sector, and between the Greek citizens and newly arriving refugees and economic migrants from the Middle East, North Africa and Central Asia. Subsequently, it is also aimed at finding a suitable solution to the Greek Issue from the local perspective and the perspective of the European Union.*

Keywords: Greek variety of capitalism, Global financial crisis, The Greek government-debt crisis, the European Union intervention, Bailout & Economic Austerity Measures, Socio-Economic Crisis, Skyrocketing Unemployment, European refugee crisis

Introduction

In the first part of this essay, we will try to analyse the essential structurally contradictory elements and paradoxes of Greek capitalistic development that lead to the debt crisis of 2010 and the immediately linked problem of an unstable environment for investments, mainly after the debt crisis, based on data collected by the Hellenic Statistical Authority, OECD, and Eurostat. Consequently, in the following part of this essay we shift our attention to investigating the austerity policies, referring to the essential changes in working and living standards, and focus on the issue of alienation in the workplace in both private and public sectors, and between the Greek citizens and newly arriving refugees and economic migrants from the Middle East, North Africa and Central Asia.

This subject-oriented analysis endeavors to explain the Greek issue in a more lucid and more profound way, revealing the intercalary relations between capitalist development and the social field to also touch on the possibility of the emergence of a so-called alternative society in response to the economic and political challenges Greece has faced since 2007. We will look at the issue from the perspective of the national GDP that has shrunk almost 28% during that period. We will discuss the rationale behind wage and pension cuts and the new legislative framework for work in the private sector as a response to mass unemployment which according to the Hellenic Statistical Authority reached at least 23%. Furthermore, we will scrutinize the reasons behind the parallel malfunctioning of banking and credit systems and the deteriorating living and consuming standards of an increasingly impoverished Greek society at large. That will lead us to discuss the so-called social competition between the former highly paid and "state protected" employees by the welfare/insurance systems, and the new employees suffering from a much deteriorated social base and working standards.

Subsequently, we will focus on investigating matters related to the state's refugee and migrant policy and the response of ordinary Greek people who have grown increasingly frustrated with the way both Athens and Brussels are dealing with the issue, and that leads some segments of the Greek society into increasingly more Eurosceptic and radical views, reflected for instance by the recent entry of the neo-Nazi party Golden Dawn to the parliament.. Finally, in summary, we will discuss a possible solution to the Greek issue from the local perspective and the perspective of the European Union to prepare the ground for real changes at hand and social cohesion in the country.

The Background

Sunday, 6 December 2008 and the following events known as Greek December should be considered as it was one of the most defining dates in contemporary Greek history[1]. On the one hand, we could talk about a "political rupture", a break in the field of political events happening in Greece that started

---

[1] The revolt of Greek December (2008), was the response of a large variety of Greek people (not only to the Greek youth, but of persons coming from different class and educational strata as well as immigrants, to the mass corruption of the NEW DEMOCRACY (conservative party) and PASOK (socialistic party) governments of that period, as well as to the effects of the global economic crisis of 2008, like the mass unemployment and work under unfavorable and unstable terms (flexible forms of employment, "black" employment without public insurance etc.). The overall background and the issues affiliated to Greek December can be seen in Panagiotis Sotiri's work Reading Revolt as Deviance: Greek Intellectuals and the December 2008 Revolt of the Greek Youth, (a journal for and about social movements Article Volume 5 (2) 47–77, November 2013) and the collective work: Revolt and Crisis in Greece: Between a Present Yet to Pass and a Future Still to Come, Edited by Antonis Vradis and Dimitris Dalakoglou, (Co–Published by AK Press and Occupied London, 2011). Furthermore, as the events, covered by the press: Robert D. Kaplan, "Those Greek Riots", The Atlantic, accessed by December, 2008. Available

between 2006 and 2007 and concern social, mostly student movements and mass protests against the new legislative framework for the privatization of higher education[2]. If we consider the fact that after the Greek December, Konstantinos Karamanlis' conservative government fell and the Socialist Party (PASOK) came into power, which under the leadership of George Papandreou, imposed the first memorandum policy, many academics admitted that Greek December was a total bubble that deflated quickly and could not be seen as a revolt, but as an uprising of the Greek youth or a social movement without any deeply rooted social and political imaginaries that refused to acknowledge its potential as a very appealing form of collective action[3]. However, beyond the deflation of the revolt, a new political state of affairs has started to be established; that of counter-memorandum movements, political formations and forms of urban social organization. All these worked on the ground that brought the SYRIZA party[4] to the front and finally as governing party, incorporating most of the radical social-poetics and from the other imposing the third memorandum[5].

---

at: <https://www.theatlantic.com/magazine/archive/2008/12/those-greek-riots/3072 25> [Accessed on 20/05/2017, at. 18:21].

[2] "Greek Student Protest Turns Violent-Europe-International Herald Tribune", New York Times, accessed by June 27, 2007. Available at: <http://www.nytimes.com/2006/06/27/world/europe/27iht-greece.2066776.html.

[3] See Panagiotis Sotitiris': Reading Revolt as Deviance: Greek Intellectuals and the December 2008 Revolt of the Greek Youth, (a journal for and about social movements Article Volume 5 (2) 47–77, November 2013).

[4] SYRIZA (Coalition of Radical Left) entered a new stage in its life and action after its first (Founding) Congress (10–14 July 2013), as a single party. There were 3,568 Congress delegates, who had been elected by 491 organizations of members in Greece, by Greeks abroad and youth groups. The Congress elected **Alexis Tsipras** President of the party, as well as a 201–member Central Committee. Some of the component organizations of the initial coalition did not agree with the transformation of SYRIZA into a single party and retain their relationship as allied groups (Active Citizens, led by M Glezos, Democratic Social Movement: DIKKI, DEA, KEDA).This was the Founding Congress of the new party that declared itself a party of the democratic and radical Left, which has its roots in great independence, anti-fascist, democratic and labor movement struggles in Greece, comprises many different ideological currents and left cultures, while building its identity through a **synthesis** of the values of the labor movement with those of the ecological, feminist and other new social movements. This is why there are three flags on the SYRIZA logo: red, green and purple [...] For more information, please see the official site of the party. Available at: <http://www.syriza.gr/page/who-we-are.html#.WRN3IvnyjGg> [Accessed on 10.06.2017, at 23:13].

[5] For the turn of SYRIZA: from a working-radical left party to a party oriented to social democracy and serving the Greek civil society as well as imposing memorandum policies please see the work of John Milios: The Greek Left Tradition and SYRIZA: From "Subversion" to the new Austerity Memorandum, Available at: <http://users.ntua.gr/jmilios/Milios_Delphi_2016.pdf/> [Accessed on 10.06.2017, at 20:00.

These are close to the analysis of Alain Badiou in his book Being and Event. Badiou speaks of the event, a particular state (état) that breaks the field of historical or political continuity. Before the event, there is a prepolitical state (état), in Greece, the student mass protests and the resentment for the conservative party policies and corruption as well as the signs of the global economic crisis that started to be apparent. That pre-political state (état), has been torn by the event, the Greek December and the fall of the conservative government. The inner social contradictions and polyphonies lead to deflation of the social movement and its integration, with the election of the Socialist Party, according to its primary motto: "There is plenty of money"[6]! Then the first memorandum came[7]. In the Greek case, as we will exemplify it, we will show that there may be mass incorporation of the radical elements of the society with PASOK or with SYRIZA, but on the other hand,

---

[6] [...] Greece is by far the most striking example of how easily a "socialist" government can become an agent at the service of the global neoliberal project. In its 2009 electoral campaign, Greece's socialist party, PASOK, led by George Papandreou, offered the model of "participatory democracy" as the foundation of a new politics. Yet, the first action Papandreou took as new prime minister was to prepare the ground for turning Greece over to the IMF—and hiding this hideous fact from the Greek citizenry until the last minute.[...] article by C. J. Polychroniou, An Unblinking Glance at a National Catastrophe and the Potential Dissolution of the Eurozone: Greece's Debt Crisis in Context, (Working paper No.688, Levy Economics Institute, September 2011) An extended version of the analysis and critique on neoliberalism that just followed can be found in the online article by C. J. Polychroniou, "Europe in the Iron Grip of Neoliberal Fiscal Discipline and Anti-Labour Measures", published in Truthout (June 8, 2010).

[7] [...] But a multiple is in turning multiple of multiples. If it is normal in the situation in which it is presented and counted, the multiples from which it is composed could, in turn, be singular, normal or excrescent with respect to it. The stable remaining-there of a multiple could be internally contra-dictated by singularities, which are presented by the multiple in question but not re-presented. To thoroughly think through the stable consistency of natural multiples, no doubt one must prohibit these internal singularities, and posit that a normal multiple is composed, in turn, of normal multiples alone. In other words, such a multiple is both presented and represented within a situation, and furthermore, inside it, all the multiples which belong to it (that it presents) are also included (represented); moreover, all the multiples which make up these multiples are also normal, and so on. A natural presented-multiple (a natural situation) is the recurrent form- multiple of a special equilibrium between belonging and inclusion, structure and megastructure. Only this equilibrium secures and re-secures the consistency of the multiple. Naturalness is the intrinsic normality of a situation.(Being and Event, p.128)[...] We make use of the Badiou's theory to reveal that Greek December although it has not reached a final outcome (the socialist party came to power and turned Greece over to IMF), despite its short duration and its inner features and contradictions, worked as the mean (rupture of political continuity), by establishing new forms of mass social self-organization and counter austerity urban movements, as well as new forms of perceiving urban action and space, such as public squats etc. (unfolding of new representations). For further information on Greek December 2008, please see: comment No 1, above. Please also see: Alain Badiou, Behind and Event, translated by Oliver Feltham, (London: Continuum, 2009), p. 173–261.

the political state that has been formed after Greek December until today, is a mixture of two debating parts: a majority that suffers from the memorandum policies and tries in its poetics to be expressed and debate with the normative political thinking of the austerity policies revealed by the government.

Consequently, to proceed to a subject-oriented analysis of the Greek issue, we ought to refer to the aspects that concern the distinguishing character of the Greek capitalistic formation, which following the global and European tensions, adopted an urban-oriented development. This mass turn to urbanism in strong interconnection with social, political and economic factors has led both to the imbalances and contradictions of Greek capitalism and to the occurring urban social movements against national capitalist integration, or after the first memorandum, against the austerity measures. We should mention that in the past, before the austerity measures and the Greek December, the political debate was mainly about the ways through which the social welfare policy could be imposed. The last seven years, due to the political and social developments, the anti-EU and anti-capitalistic front has gained ground. However, beyond that, the populist far-right, the neo-Nazis tend to be attractive to a majority of citizens, which is revealed by the fact that the neo-Nazi party Golden Dawn entered the Greek Parliament in 2012. This situation has worsened since the refugee and immigrant crisis.

Between Two Worlds

The Greek example is much more profound than the issues related solely to the public deficits and debt management; it is also something far more complicated than the problems revealed to statistical indicators concerning capitalistic development in Greece. These issues are also inadvertently related to inner contradictory elements associated with the question of capitalistic reproduction in Greece. The other aspect of this situation comprises such issues as social and political problems related to the question of social coherence and the social-political representation of the Greek people. We will, therefore, refer to parallel historical events in a subject-oriented way to precisely explain what the valid reasons for the current problem are.

1961	13,2	1971	7,8	1981	-1,6	1991	3,1	2001	4,2
1962	0,4	1972	10,2	1982	-1,1	1992	0,7	2002	3,4
1963	11,8	1973	8,1	1983	-1,1	1993	-1,6	2003	5,6
1964	9,4	1974	-6,4	1984	2	1994	2	2004	4,9
1965	10,8	1975	6,4	1985	2,5	1995	2,1	2005	2,9
1966	6,5	1976	6,9	1986	0,5	1996	2,4	2006	4,5
1967	5,7	1977	2,9	1987	-2,3	1997	3,6	2007	4
1968	7,2	1978	7,2	1988	4,3	1998	3,4	2008	2,9
1969	11,6	1979	3,3	1989	3,8	1999	3,4	2009	-2,0
1970	8,9	1980	0,7	1990	0	2000	4,5	2010	[-4,0]

Figure 1. Greek GDP, 1961–2010 [Source: Hellenic Statistical Authority[8]].

As we can see in this diagram, the national GDP between 1961 and 1962 dramatically fell. It is a period that Greek economy was submerged in recession. In the past decades (starting from the 1950s), the general political and economic doctrine was based on the fact that Greece was recovering from the Greek civil war between the Democratic Army (left and leftist partisans) and the Greek Army with the strong evolvement of the British[9]. The subject is divided into different worlds, the one that is represented by the elected deeply conservative governments of 'Ethnikos Synagermos' ("National Alarm") and then ERE, another turn to more radical schemes like EDA (United Democratic Left), while there is a large part that is strongly connected with the "Enosi Kentrou" ("Centrists' Union") with no apparent political orientation but mainly around anti-conservative policies. So, we could talk about two dominant worlds at that time, those of the conservative and progressive powers in the Greek field. The lack of democracy and the strong stance against the former partisans and then members of the left and leftist groups by the conservatives worked as factors of social coercion. The public response to the conservatives was a mixture of supporting the industrialization under state protection (Milios, 2010), mainly in strategic fields like electricity, the production of sugar and fertilizers, etc. That is how the new working class has emerged in Greece, the first formation of lower and middle classes and consequently, this led to distributions in urban living by the mass buying of small private holdings by the social layers mentioned above. In this

---

[8] Γιάννης Μηλιός, Η Ελληνικη Οικονομια Κατα Τον 20ο Αιωνα, Available at:<http://users.ntua.gr/jmilios/Oikonomia_Eikostos1ab.pdf/>[Accessed on 10.06.2017, at 21:13], p. 16.

[9] Ed Vuillamy and Helena Smith, "Athens 1994, Britain's Dirty Secret", The Guardian, Available at: <https://www.theguardian.com/world/2014/nov/30/athens-1944–britains-dirty-secret > [Accessed on 30.11.2014, at 21:13].

part, we should say that mass urbanization was promoted as well as the rebuilding of the urban centers (see figure 2 and 3).

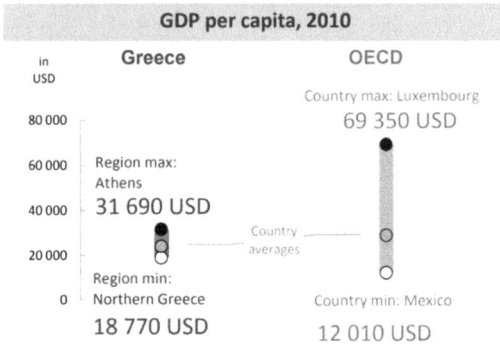

Figure 2. GDP per capita comparison between Greece and other OECD countries, 2010 [Source: OECD][10].

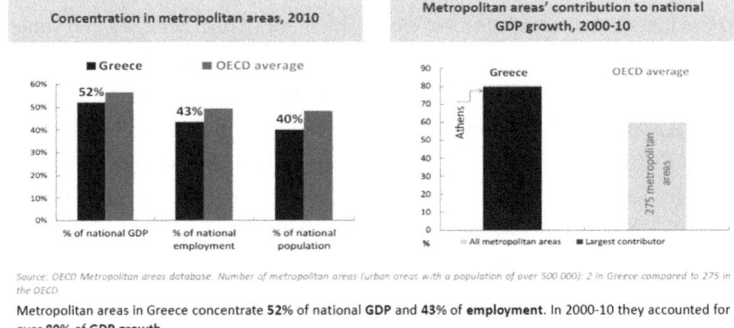

Figure 3. Metropolitan contribution to national GDP [Source: OECD][11].

One of the primary measures was that of "antiparoxi" ("exchange"). The small private houses of the working and lower classes were taken by the constructors of a large block of flats, and the payment to the smallholders was some units with surplus value compared to their previous holdings. This is very crucial for two main reasons: firstly, the idea of small private holdings worked as a factor of the lower- and middle-class consensus, and in that way, the danger of a capitalistic overthrow driven by the left and the leftists started

---

[10] Report on functional urban areas in OECD countries: Greece, Available at: <https://www.oecd.org/governance/regional-policy/Country-statistics-profile-Greece.pdf> [Accessed on 10.06.2017, at 21:13].

[11] Ibidem.

to be blunt; secondly, adverse wealth effects began to make their appearance, with a large number of private house holdings, a factor that is connected to the Greek debt crisis. However, commercial balances started to fall, and inflation began to rise in the late 50s. So Greece faced the recession of 1961–1962. A new politics of a second mass industrialization occurred, based on private capital, not state protected but funded in most cases by the banking system this time. The national turn to the European Common Market was also done in this period. Political instability, the evolution of the palace to democratic debate, and the mass enrolment in secret services of the far right group, on the one hand, caused social resentment. As a result of this social phenomenon, there were mass counter-actions, such as protests against the war, a new constitution with more democratic elements, and the rise of EDA. On the other hand, the far-right groups were earning a place in the army and a small part of the society[12]. These right-wing groups worked as the primary mediator for the military dictatorship to be imposed.

Subsequently, the military dictatorship was imposed between 1967 and 1974, under the effect of the United States, which had geopolitical interests in the Middle East during that period[13]. A new era of national division started. Many people who were against the dictatorship were jailed, exiled and tortured[14]. The military dictatorship, in every way, was promoting a two-sided economic and social dogma. The first one, concerned capitalistic development, mainly in the fields of industry, tourism, shipping, but also in strategic areas of the economy, like transportation, public construction, and services; it worth adding that the measure of antiparoxi, takes one of its most prominent dimensions in the years of Junta[15]. The second doctrine as to its core essence concerned an agenda of militarism, nationalism, anti-communism and adherence to tradition and the Orthodox Church. Beyond the apparent division of the society, the Greek economy seems to make stable steps. As it

---

[12] Cristina Politi, "American intervention in Greece 1946-64", Available at: <https://1pdf.net/american-intervention-in-greece-1946–64-during-the-_58fbe2ecf60 65d3b 0c985e8b/> [Accessed on 10.06.2017, at 21:13].

[13] Miller, James Edward. The United States and the Making of Modern Greece: History and Power, 1950–1974. (The University of North Carolina Press, 2009. Print), p. 134.

[14] Solon N. Grigoriadis, "Istroria tis Sigxronis Elladas 1941-1974", (Athens: Polaris, 2010) see also Tsoukalas, Kostas. The Greek Tragedy: From liberation to the generals. (Athens: Antonis Livanis Press, 1981). As to the exile and tortures see the report of Amnesty International Available at: <https://www.amnesty.gr/wp-content/uploads/2014/11/EUR-25-001-1968-2.pdf/> [Accessed on 10.06.2017, at 21:13].

[15] George Pagoulatos, Greece's New Political Economy State, Finance and Growth from Post war to EMU, (New York: Palgrave Macmillan, 2003), p. 37–38.

can be seen in figure 1, Greek GDP was increasing at a notable rate. Subsequently, in the years 1973–1974, the global economic crisis deeply affected the Greek economy. This factor leaves its stigma, in combination with the geopolitical redistributions in the Greek national territories. During this period Turkey also invaded northern Cyprus, an issue that is still ongoing today, affecting the geopolitical relations in the southeast Mediterranean, and, of course, between Greece, Cyprus, and Turkey[16].

It is interesting to notice that the crucial breaking point for the fall of the junta was the uprising of Polytechneion (the uprising of the students of Athens Engineering University and their brutal repression by the military tanks of the dictatorship government). The years after the uprising of Polytechneion on 17 November 1973were the years of political and social rehabilitation, known as the years of metapoliteusi ("post–political era or political change")[17]. The wounds of the past were starting to heal, and entry to the European Economic Community was achieved in 1981. During this period after the fall of the dictatorship, the left and leftist movement, (more reformist when it came to class war policy and which started to incorporate liberal elements), was extremely strong. The political façade and expression of this reformist left movement, was the formation of the Socialist Party "PASOK", which had already started to affect a majority of people. In its political program, PASOK promised an exit from the EEC, an anti-American and anti-NATO foreign policy, and social justice and prosperity. During these years, if we speak of the economic growth, the GDP was stably rising, as well as the GDP per capita. The strategic fields of the economy were under state control, like new technologies and the telecommunications, electricity, water, transportation, the airports and the ports. All of those factors contributed to political stability, the rehabilitation of democracy and the entry (or the procedures of admission) to the EEC, forming a stable environment for economic growth, national and foreign investments. Greece was on the way to European integration, and Greek capitalism made crucial steps that placed Greece on the map of the global economy.

When PASOK came to power, they were faced with some critical social problems such as excessive bureaucracy, official corruption in every sphere

---

[16] See: Prof. Giorgos Kentas work: A Period of Reflection for Turkey, (Cyprus Centre for European and International Affairs, Volume 6, Issue 4, Article 3).

[17] Phillip Chrysopoulos, "Greece Celebrates Anniversary of November 17, 1973 Student Uprising against Junta", Greek Reporter, Available at: <http://greece.greekreporter.com/2015/11/16/greece-celebrates-anniversary-of-november-17-1973-student-uprising-against-junta> [Accessed on 16.11.2015, at 14:13].

of life, as well as lack of real democratic representation of the people. Furthermore what was even more drastic was the fact that as a result of decades of negligence; the Greek economy had slowed down drastically as the public debt was agglomerating very rapidly. Having said that it has to be emphasised that thanks to its populism and adoption of radical mottos like: "Pasok-The People On The Power", "There Is No Authority But The People", " Eec And Nato Are The Same Syndicate", "Greece Belongs To The Greeks" PASOK managed to bring people from different walks of life to work together to overcome these difficulties and that is how one of the most significant social experiments in contemporary Greek history ended with being out of the woods for the Greek people. One of the essential social measures introduced during this period was the fact that PASOK offered social pension to the former members of Greek liberation army, partisans, and by doing so, the situation in the country was stabilized. Also, it is worth emphasizing that this social movement established a unique legislative framework for the children of their families and for them to be employed in the public sphere and state organizations.

Still, despite these social policies, the majority of the Greeks, like their Western colleagues, were allowed to embrace a new wave of consumerism, and consumption became the new dogma. During this time the Greeks have been transformed into the real consumer subject of the western world, oriented to spend on clothing, cars, nightlife, and holidays. (One of the central policies was the: "Bania Tou Laou"/"people's holiday baths" − the almost state-protected right to summer holidays in August. Sometimes the whole state was paralysed with mass vacation-taking by the public and private employees.) Driven by problems connected with the financial deficits we already mentioned, which the state tried to conceal under the ideological doctrine and false image of social prosperity and wealth, Greek capitalism was inevitably submerged in recession and inflation in the years 1980–1996. The large deficits led the government to take out big loans from private national and international banks. The deficit rate was rising while the GDP rate was decreasing, a situation which created even larger deficits (Milios, 2010). The civil society was undergoing a certain redistribution of relations. The former industrial elite and shipping elite started to lose their power and influence while the new entrepreneurs emerged. The latter had been in strong connection with the PASOK and New Democracy governments. (New Democracy is a party that appeared on the political scene during this era; they accounted for a loose conservative, a neo-liberal continuation of the former Ethnikos Synagermos. That is why the battle in the political field went on between the two main parties PASOK and New Democracy, which gave way to a semi-bipolar political system known as diaploki (loosely translated as politico-economic interweaving). Diaploki was very specific to Greece patron-client relationships and a commonly accepted state of affairs in which higher political party members, with the support of a certain part of Greek civil society and bankers, created mechanisms of loaning to big businesses on favorable terms, and in some cases on unexpected terms. That means that many of the people in the political and economic scene at that time had great relations with private television and press. Furthermore, some of the large construction corporations that had taken most of the public big construction projects, like state buildings, national roads, industrial parks, etc., also held private TV channels, newspapers, etc. In that way, on the one hand, they were controlling the public opinion and obtained the role of an ideological mechanism of State, and on the other, they became an immediate pressure lever for the politicians and their attitudes – they had a major role in the formation of political conscience and action in Greek society[18]. The state of Diaploki continued into the next decade. As for democratic representation beyond the electoral system, mainly two syndicates were reigning in that period, GESEE ("General Federation of Greek Workers") for the private sector, and ADEDY (Administration of State Employees' 'Unions") for the public sector. These two syndicates mostly expressed the voice of the two main parties, PASOK and New Democracy. For the years 1980–1996, we can mainly point out switching between stability and crisis of over-accumulation of capital.

Subsequently, in the years 1996–2008, Greek capitalism again turned to a new phase of development and reproduction. The new technologies and the informatization of industry brought a rise in the rates of competitiveness of the Greek economy. The third sector of services was also overdeveloped in that period. The GDP rate was on the steady rise, while GDP per capita was higher than the EU average. All these achievements in combination with entry to the Eurozone were significant factors for national and foreign investments. The truth is that during these years, the economic growth of the Eurozone periphery was higher than the center. The increase in the south in some way helped the central economies of Germany and France when it came to the export of capital flows for investments under the standard money and the economic and legislative framework of the EU. Subsequently, another interesting phenomenon that we were able to witness during this time

---

[18] Dimitri A. Sotiropoulos, "Civil Society in Greece in the Wake of the Wake of the Economic Crisis", Konrad Adenaeur Stiftung, December 2013.

had to do with the fact that once the integration within the Eurozone started, the Greek economy turned into an import-based economy, whilst country's export potential rapidly declined. It is worth emphasizing that by this time the strength of the country's industrial system had already been decimated by the economic reforms of 1990–1996. Despite all of those negative factors, the consuming habits of the Greek people and their confidence in the strength of their economy were dangerously reassured by the local politicians and fantasists. That can be considered one of the paradoxes of the Greek variety of capitalism[19].

Distinguishing Characteristics of Greek Capitalism (As Seen After the Debt Crisis of 2008 and Through the Current Austerity Years)

1. Greek capitalism is considered to be a core part of Western capitalism but combines features of both central and peripheral capital accumulation. The features that can be attributed to a central position in capitalistic integration are high levels of competitiveness and productivity[20]. The outer may be linked to the fact that the European south and Ireland, countries of the euro periphery, faced the highest deficits and increase in spreads after the debt crisis. The origins of the process can be found in the fact that first of all, the GDP rate may have been increasing stably, but the deficit rate was growing at a much quicker pace than the stable GDP, and secondly, for the reason that we explained above, because of the issue of imports and exports, and of an externally dependent economy. Lastly, when the spreads of Greek loans passed 1000 units, the economies of the center had negative interest rates, so under a standard monetary policy (and considering the externally dependent character of the economy), the occurring imbalance was a self-fulfilling prophecy.

2. There is the contradiction of mass urbanization and centrism in capital accumulation. As can be seen from the figures (3, 4, 5), there may not have been significant deviations between Athens (capital) and regional minimum (northern Macedonia) in GDP per capita, but the metropolitan areas concentrated 52% of national GDP and the 43% of employment. However,

---

[19] John Milios and Dimitris Sotiropoulos, Crisis of Greece or crisis of the Euro? A review from the European Periphery, Journal of Balkan and near Eastern Studies, Volume 12, Number 3, September 2010.

[20] Panagiotis Petrakis, "Ta paradoxa tis Ellinikis Oikonomias", Euro2day, Available at: <http://www.euro2day.gr/specials/opinions/article/594735/p-petrakhs-ta-paradoxa-ths-oikonomias.html> [Accessed on 16.07.2010, at 12:22].

the total investments, as is seen, were made by the central government and not by the sub-national governments, forming, in that way, a policy of centrism. Beyond that fact, there is a severe problem with decentralization in Greece as to the modus operandi of the flexibility and the governance of the public sector. The fact is that the 92% of the businesses are small (under 250 employees) and 1200 big enterprises contributed to the 55% of the national GDP[21].

3. Geopolitical competition with Turkey is a constant issue in the relations between the countries, in combination with the fact that Greece has never declared an exclusive economic zone. This competition was rising over the last period for three fundamental reasons: 1) Due to President Erdogan's propaganda on the Turkish referendum based on a boost to the national psyche 2) Still unresolved the Cypriot issue that goes back to 1974. 3) Also, the other problem relates to the fact that Turkey is deeply engaged in the Syrian and Iraqi civil wars and that may inadvertently expose Greece to various undesirable consequences, which would be beyond its control.

4. We can also notice in this respect a number of the fundamental contradictions of Greek capitalism, such as the so-called adverse wealth effect of public real estate holdings as well as of the private estate holdings. The state-owned and the public-owned real estate have created the networks with strategic administrative (ports, airports, national roads, telecommunication and electricity networks, etc.) or touristic value (The Ellinikon airport, the resort of Astir Vouliagmeni) that had been functioning relatively well until the beginning of the years of austerity. But still, these holdings were either severely underdeveloped or undeveloped and therefore not ready to face challenges ahead. Subsequently, after the closing of the first evaluation of the third memorandum, a mass plan for privatization was implemented. The adverse wealth effect was reinforced at that time because the construction sector was in recession, and many holdings obtained by loans after the crisis were not being repaid, so private debt has increased by default because unreliable public partners dragged it down the drain. Furthermore, in the years 1996–2008, the objective value of the real estate holdings touched its highest levels. Individual holdings with increased value worked as means of technical capital accumulation, so one part of the surplus values has been invested in other products like cars, etc., or as a guarantee for loans. After

---

[21] Thanos Tsiros, "1200 Megales Etairies Sygentronoun to 55% tou Epixeirein", Kathimerini. Available at: <http://www.kathimerini.gr/832520/article/oikonomia/epixeirhseis/1200-megales-etaireies-sygkentrwnoyn-to-55-twn-kerdwn-poy-paragei-to-epixeirein/> [Accessed on 27.09.2017, at 20:12].

2008, however, the over-investment and over-borrowing have resulted in the banking sector being unable to supply even individual consumers with lines of credit.

5. To summarise: The massive public deficits occurred, firstly because the state never proceeded to a socially fair and stable taxing system and taxation of the more substantial incomes. Secondly, private businesses first took large loans with favorable terms that in most cases were not repaid, so the banking system was seized by severe capital runs (The case of Diaploki). Thirdly, the consumerist subject, the lower and middle classes, in a way indulged in the general fake "Greek Dream", so the consuming or housing loans that they got, after the break of the crisis and the implementation of austerity measures, could not be repaid, and the banking system was suppressed again. A recapitalization was necessary, but the deficits were progressively getting higher and higher. Greece turned to the solution of PSI and haircut of the Greek Repos and Swaps[22], but the answer was not viable (2012). After many disasters, in order that a bailout of the banking system be avoided, a capital control measure has been imposed since 2015, and as for the public debt, a solution is still being debated today.

The Economic Consequences of Austerity in Greece

As we can see in figure 4, Greece has lost almost 28% of national GDP between 2008–2015. That coincided with the salaries and the pensions being reduced up to 48%, and also all the austerity governments have imposed a system of high taxation[23][24]. The production is based on the third sector of services which is dominant in the Greek economy, and the industrial production is mainly based on oils and minerals that are used in electric power and high-end technologies, as well as on the furniture sector.

---

[22] Yanis Varoufakis, "Five Lessons From the Greek PSI", Varoufaki's Thoughts for the post–2008 world. Available at: <https://www.yanisvaroufakis.eu/2014/03/12/lessons-from-the-greek-psi/> [Accessed on 12.03.2014, at 18:13].

[23] David Adams, "A Greek Tragedy", European Pensions, November/December 2011, Available at: <http://www.europeanpensions.net/ep/A-Greek-tragedy.php/> [Acessed on 06.06.2018, at 23:13].

[24] Heather Steward, "Greece's tax revenue collapse as dept. crisis continues", The Guardian, Available at: <https://www.theguardian.com/world/2015/aug/06/greece-tax-revenues-collapse-debt-crisis-continues-euro/> [Accessed on 06.08.2015, at 21:13].

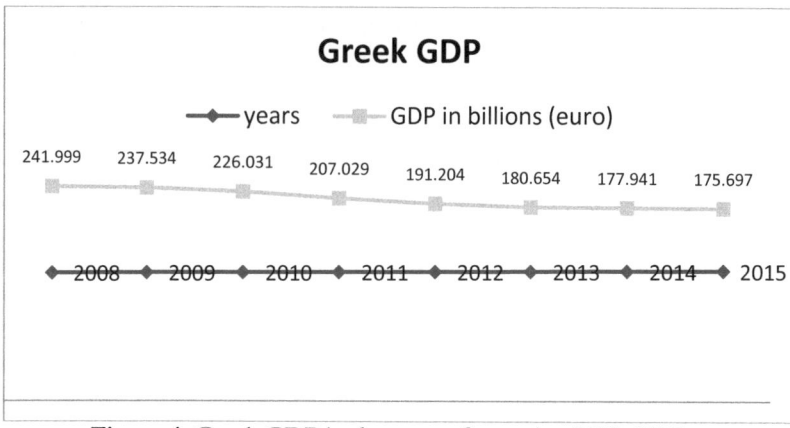

Figure 4. Greek GDP in the years of austerity, 2008–2015
[Source: Hellenic Statistical Authority].

The field of agriculture is also making a quite significant contribution to the national GDP[25]. The Greek subject in the years of austerity is gradually transforming into that of the post–consumerist society. The lowering of living standards and the overall instability reflected a new kind of consumption: that of non-addictive consumption, but of lasting − returning to the past (to the high values and quality of history), in response to the ephemeral. The other tension may be linked with an alternative consumption, mostly connected with urban and social movements as a response to austerity.

Greek Society in Austerity: Politics and Labor

In this part, concerning the social transformation of modern Greece, we will aim to adopt an analytical approach that will focus on dialectics of economic base and social-cultural-political superstructure and hegemony; figuring out some characteristics of the latter will be our primary goal, especially in connection with the direct and indirect relation of power and generated resistance, in the Foucauldian manner[26].

---

[25] Dimitris Paitaridis, "I Ekseliksi tis paragogik;otitas kai oi epiptoseis stin antagonistinotita tis ellinikis oikonomias", (Athens: INE/Paratiritirio Oikonomikon kai koinonikon Ekselikseon, 2015).

[26] Michel Foucault, "On power and class war - conversation with 4 members of the LCR", 1970. & Joseph Kay, Intellectuals and power: A conversation between Michel Foucault and Gilles Deleuze - discussion recorded on 4th March 1972; and published in a special issue of L'Arc (No. 49, p. 3–10), dedicated to Gilles Deleuze. It is reprinted here by per-

Talking about the political formation of modern Greece after 2008 we should first make a differentiation between politics[27], and the political. In other words, we will discuss the issues concerning political parties, governmental policies, economy, etc., dictated by national-border-international relations, and the vast variety of diverse political opinions and actions that can be clustered under the speculum of social counter-activity, radicalisation, and interpersonal relationships driven by the appearance of the Other. In this sense, the Other will be understood as either political, cultural, or national Other, which enters the traditional social formation. Subsequently, we will consider the period after the 2008 riots, which had been sparked off by the tragic accident that led to the death of a 15-year-old student, in which one policeman from Athens was directly involved. These riots stirred up a robust social discontent that has triggered an anarchic momentum directed against on the one hand the Greek state seen as mechanisms of oppression, entangled by the contemporary doctrines of the post–consumerist society, and on the other hand the global financiers, world capitalism and its regional representation the European Union[28].

That brings us to the finding that between 2008 and 2015 Greece suffered from an unstable political system as neither of the main political parties/coalitions PASOK or NEW DEMOCRACY was able to form a stable government that would last at least a year. Both the main political parties/coalitions acted as applicators of the memorandum policies and provoked an even broader mass rage. That rage was politically externalized through confronting trends noticeable within, such as the creation of a strong Marxist–Leninist anticapitalistic coalition with anti-European characteristics, expressed by ANTARSYA ("Anticapitalistic Left Cooperation for the Uprising"), and the reinforcement of SYRIZA (Coalition of Radical Left) expressing that time (2008–2015) mainly anti-memorandum views and an internal policy of solidarity, dignity and justice with a humanitarian orientation, as well as an external policy for democratic changes that should be implemented in the EU, for a program of relieving the lower and oppressed layers of both the Greek and the European people, to be achieved. With this agenda and under the leadership of Alexis Tsipras, SYRIZA managed to come to power

---

mission of L'Arc. Available at: </https://libcom.org/library/intellectuals-power-a-conversation-between-michel-foucault-and-gilles-deleuze/> [Accessed on 12.06.2017, at 00:05].

[27] Saul Newman, Power and politics in Poststructuralist thought: New theories of the political, (New York: Routledge, 2005), p.153–54.

[28] Aris Hatzistefanou, December 2008: history, here we come!, (Athens: Livanis, 2009).

in January 2015 and form a stable government with ANEL (Independent Greeks, a right-wing party), until today. We also have the appearance of minor right-wing neo-liberal parties that proposed a "painless" governmental alternative, such as Potami (River), and eventually, the rebirth of a strong anarchist and autonomist culture of civil resistance, with many squats opening to the public in big cities.

We need to mention in this respect a parallel reinforcement of the neo-Nazi, nationalist and Eurosceptic front as well, expressed by the party of Popular Association-Golden Dawn (a member of which is held guilty for the murder of an anti-fascist singer, Pavlos Fyssas, in 2013). In this respect it is worth emphasizing that the views of Golden Dawn tend to be appealing to some working-class voters who live in traditional patriarchal families that finds among this turmoil a social self-reflection, as expressed in itself, by the Golden Dawn party, which acts as a self-proclaimed savior, a patriarchal figure in the era of the father's betrayal, as Jacques Lacan asserts[29], for the period of the crisis. As the effects of disaster and austerity in Greece started to become even more apparent, social resentment and rage were rising in the first months of the SYRIZA–ANEL co-government. After the unproductive negotiations between the Greeks and the EU-IMF, the SYRIZA–ANEL coalition, to reinforce its negotiating position, promoted the idea of a mass referendum that was held in July 2015. The Greek citizens came to decide with their vote if the package of austerity measures of the third memorandum should be accepted or not by the Greek government. The final result of 62% against was not purely fully class-conscious. On the one hand we should consider the deepening of the crisis and its effect on the living standards and labor, as well as the radicalization of the society through mass protests and urban movements, but on the other hand the fact that the Euroscepticism cultivated in that period was not only based on radicalization but was a mixture of resentment, of pressures to the banking system after capital controls had been imposed in order that a bailout be avoided and its social reflection, the mass media propaganda, that were favorable to the yes vote, and finally of the Euroscepticism that had been promoted under the scope of populist far-right groups and the neo-Nazi Golden Dawn.

Today's Greek political scene has been dominated by, and at the same time, split by, the refugee issue: the massive waves of Syrian and the Middle East immigrants entering Greece, victims of the civil war in Syria, bring into

---

[29] Phlippe de Georges, "A psychoanalytic approach to modern authority", lecture in the Centre for Psychoanalytic Research in Athens, 2015.

the surface issues and public discussions of Greek territoriality in relation to the otherness of the border and the national identities it produces, of cultural integrity, of human rights, etc. A significant aspect of the situation is the EU-Turkey Agreement, which, on the one hand, serves the Turkish plan for entrance to the European Union, and on the other, has worked as the framework for the management of the refugee crisis for both Greece and Turkey: first, it secures the geopolitical presence of one country and the another. Secondly, it controls the policies of refugee relaunching from those countries to the European Union. As a result of this, the fence on the Evros River on the northern border of Greece has been reinforced, and refugees ended up jam-packed in the hot-spots of the Aegean Islands and the borderline territories, as a transitional stage before their relaunching to Central European countries, under the auspices of various NGOs; the living conditions in the hot-spots are deplorable, there is a lack of sanitary/health care and of essential food amenities, the presence of police and army is continuous, and the death of immigrants is not an uncommon phenomenon (in the Moria hotspot, in January 2017, three refugees died, not to mention those who do not even manage to reach a hot-spot and are drowned on the coasts of Turkey and the whole Mediterranean—230 people, according to UN, since the first months of 2017[30]).

In this case, it has to be admitted that Greek's people reactions to this issue have been diverse. On one hand, the humanitarian crisis that followed the over-accumulation of refugees in the hotspots has awakened a movement of solidarity, supported by left-wing organizations, squats, and united people from various backgrounds (even those who were politically uninvolved before) to not only help the refugees but also to form an anti-war movement that started protests against the civil war in the Middle East. It is important to mention that for the vast majority of Greek people, the vast groups of refugees coming to their homeland has meant the disintegration of the traditional, protected, orthodox, territorially-enclosed state, a direct enemy of the national identity, and a cause of all maladies[31]. These feelings have also contributed to the rise of xenophobia, racism, and bigotry amongst the urban

---

[30] "Friki sti Mesogeio To Periodiko", Available at: <http://www.toperiodiko.gr> [Accessed on 21.02.2017, at 21:13].
[31] See. Plateia Amerikis (Amerika Square). A 2016 Greek film that describes in an elaborate way the relation of the newly-arrived refugees with the Greek society in Athens, especially through the eyes of a middle-class 30-year-old man, unemployed, living with his parents, who confronts the immigrants as the reason of his own unemployment and poisons some

population. The local neo-Nazi party known as Golden Dawn has launched various political campaigns against the refugees and the involvement of some of its members in cases such as Oraiokastro and Perama: in the primary schools of both towns, parents of Greek pupils (Golden Dawn affiliated), official party members, and other more obscure fascist and nationalist forces, such as Patriot's Movement and Holy Army, broke into and prevented the entrance of refugee and immigrant children in the school courses, exercising violence on the people who resisted and blackmailing children with shouts and mottos[32]. In general, one could say that Golden Dawn's rhetoric on the issue is not so far from Donald Trump's in the USA concerning migration policy, or Marie Le Pen's in France concerning the Islamic threat; the three aim at the abolition of political correctness and human rights that was propagated throughout the years of the neo-liberalism and the urban democratic state, and look forward to ways of national economic/productive reform under the burden of the crisis, but the difference is that they represent different capitalistic interests, which will not be analyzed here due to the fact that the aim is to point out a structural increase in far-right concepts and practices in the western world, that covers both the politics and political field, as a symptom of the economic breakdown.

In addition, it is important to point out that the memorandum policies of the SYRIZA-ANEL government, part of this above-mentioned plan of capitalist reform in Greece and in the EU, have affected in a catalytic way the world of labor and the relations of production: with unemployment reaching almost 25% of the population and with the decadence of the state employment mechanism, it seems that the only viable working perspective for middle class, low class, and young people, is the private sector. The legislative framework imposed by the European Union institutions, about the changes in the relationship of employer-employee, being applied in parts since 2014–2015 until today (as of March 2017), manages to establish legally what is already called a "new working shift". The new working shift constitutes the ultimate liberalization of employment conditions which made its appearance during the first years of austerity and became prevalent as the crisis continued. It encompasses elements such as: working in private companies (mostly

---

of them ("they were stealing my job"!). The world of labor in Greece today will be thoroughly explained later, and some points about the connection of unemployment with social conscience and therefore, racism, will be illuminated.

[32] "Ethnikistes prokalesan episodeia sto Oraiokastro". Iefimerida, Available at: <http://www.iefimerida.gr/news/319919/ethnikistes-prokalesan-epeisodia-sto-oraiokastro-fonazan-lathraia-ta-prosfygopoyla/> [Accessed on 17th February, 2017, at 15:00].

in service sector) with limited hour or even zero hour individual contracts, white collar-blue collar type (the collective working contracts become absent), working without insurance provided by the employer ("high risk or black" employment), working without the opportunity to be organized in a syndicate or a trade union, or even to strike, since the employer now has the right to impose a lock-out, or also to mass dismissals without compensation.

That subsequently brings us to the issues related to the fact that a significant proportion of young people in Greece these days suffer the consequences of unemployment and working jobs that are beneath their qualifications, and this problem is affecting even university alumni, who are being absorbed by these types of work that are close to a new form of slavery and pay extremely low wages. In this sense, we can see that a new kind of social subject emerges here, defined by the alienation from the product it produces, in Marxian terms, and by the isolation from its own life and inner desire. The more the subject generates[33], the less it lives as a result, and the more it perceives itself through the dominant images of imaginative-accumulated capital, it can be seen as an inherent element of late postmodern capitalism[34]. The whole spectrum of existing becomes a countable commodity; the money transforms the worker/human into an object of productive force from which it obtains surplus value not only by means of labor but also by means of desiring (and thus consuming) and of self-perception: the power that is imposed onto the subject is multidimensional in its nature and could quickly turn it into either a social cannibal (in terms of work antagonism), or into a libidinally oppressed individual (according to Freudian psychoanalysis, when libido is suppressed it turns to neurosis)[35]. In this respect, it is also worth mentioning that the number of suicides, especially those of young people, has dramatically risen during the austerity years[36]. It is important to add here that the refugee waves are destined to be integrated (and many of them are already integrated) into the Greek social formation as a cheap workforce during their transitional stage, as an alternative to the hot-spot reality, under the same conditions described above, or even worse, to help the capitalist reforms[37].

---

[33] Guy Debord, Society of Spectacle, (New York: Zone Books, 1991), p.10.
[34] Ibid., p.3.
[35] Wilhelm Reich, Mass Psychology of Fascism, trans. Mary Boyd Higgins, (New York: Farrar, Straus and Giroux, 1970).
[36] Katie Allen, "Austerity in Greece caused more than 500 male suicides, say researchers", The Guardian. Available at: <https://www.theguardian.com/world/2014/apr/21/ austerity-greece-male-suicides-spending-cuts> [Accessed on 10.06.2017, at 21:13].
[37] "Is migration good for economy?" OECD, Migration policy debates, 2014.

Another side of the labor issue is that the establishment of the new working shift goes hand in hand with the privatization of a large part of the public wealth (water, ports, electricity, transportation), as well as of the private (from factories to houses), by banks or big companies, through the process of auctioning. During the last three years, a significant number of private-owned properties in debt have been seized and sold at auctions, leaving low-class families and individuals outside a social welfare system, which is intended to provide housing, insurance, healthcare, etc. In big cities, Athens and Thessaloniki, a protest movement against the auctions has arisen, mainly driven by left-wing or anarchist workers, students, and other activists, successfully preventing many of the state organized sales[38].

Conclusion: Greece, the European Union, and Resistance as a Public Demand for Changes in the Status Quo.

Thus far, we have tried to take a critical glimpse at the genesis of the contemporary Greek crisis, both from an analytical approach and our empirical studies on the situation of an individual in Greece from the perspective of the society one leaves and the view of the global village. In this sense, we have attempted to investigate the European Union from the perspective of a coherent economic, social, cultural and international ensemble with open, democratic ideas, seen as a representative mark of the emancipated western world. Yet, it has to be emphasised that framing reality in such a manner poses some serious issues as it opens up the scholarship to a number of dilemmas related to its role in the world capitalist plexus, its involvement in various morally questionable military interventions in the Middle East as well as Africa, and its humanistic facet. For these reasons, it is essential to see this problem through the prism of national perspective underlining such dilemmas like domestic economic relations on the semi-macro level, cultural independence, traits of secularism and fundamentalism and the variety of different politics, without forgetting about a composition of the human subject-citizen, which lives and acts in it. That is why to correctly conclude this debate we need to ask whether in fact the European Union can be seen as a well-thought mechanism of economic authority that strengthens the existing social stagnation and bans militarily from its political

---

[38] Helena Smith, "Greek activists target sales of homes seized over bad debts", The Guardian, accessed by March 11, 2017, Available at: <https://www.theguardian.com/world/2017/mar/11/greek-activists-target-sales-of-homes-seized-over-bad-debts/> [Accessed on 11.06.2017, at 23:30].

boundaries. Does it help us to overcome the potential dangers of nationalism, xenophobia, racism, anti-Semitism, sexism, bigotry, or is it deemed to end up as yet another failed organization that feeds its members with all of those essential phrases but in fact accounts for a utopian idea of those who want to turn Europe into a federation, the organization that looks after the global and regional interest of various interest groups but fails to look after the individual and the society that is in need? Finally, exposing these issues opens our debate on Greece and its place in such a union.

From our point of view, there is no easy answer to this dilemma as the drastically mounting debt plagues Greek society with a combination of social maladies that affect the ordinary people primarily. It seems to attest to the opinion of a leading economist who suggests that the Greek crisis is likely not to be overcome for the next 50 years. For these reasons, we believe that the answer to the various political and existential dilemmas that have been discussed in parenthesis does not lie in patient waiting for the historical continuum from a safe distance, but in the mobilization and functional self-organization of collective life. In order to bring some significant structural changes to any social formation, one should set off from the grassroots level, even if it means starting a level of Molecular Revolution[39] – of individual being, that could open itself to the public sphere of political engagement in the political realm, and that would be supplemented with the coordination with various desires, and the reassurance of the right of a decent existence for every individual living in Greece at the moment, not only bankers and the owners of the capital. That, in turn, could mean opposing a status quo that is fueled by an ideological fraud, bipolar action or manipulation, from any person subject to the authority and generally, to an oppressive social contract. We take our example from many squats/social centers and the anarchist subcultures or the various urban movements that made their appearance through the austerity years and shed some rays of sun on the haunted city[40]. In this sense it is essential to point out that a large number of these groups contributed to the well-being of the society at large by hosting homeless people, looking after the rights of sexual minorities (LGTBQI), supporting the work of various grass-roots activists, and looking after the fundamental rights of those most vulnerable members of our society: immigrants, refugees and those affected by poverty and abusive relations who suffered a lot over the

---

[39] Felix Guattari, Molecular Revolution, (Arizona: Peregrine Books,1984).
[40] Written by Renato Curcio and Alberto Franceschini, members of the Italian political organization Brigate Rosse.

course of the last decade and who were very often left on their own by the apparatus of the country that has almost ceased to exist in the way that it was designed. In this respect, it is important to offer these people a haven and a solid chance to chase their dreams and to reenter the society at large.

So, this kind of insubordination against the official organization of state and power mechanisms, both negative and positive[41], could serve as a creative force for the gradual construction of a network of self-sufficient zones outside of the dominant system; those zones that visualize an alternate mode of producing, consuming and living (horizontal organization under the model of collectivization of production), while embracing, in parallel, every type of anthropological otherness. As soon as it is achieved, the zones will have the capacity to work as laboratories of social resistance, which will be able to gain a stronger position that will allow them to address more practical issues of bio-power and habitus[42]. This development should enable the Greek society at large to open up to the upper political strata: to doubt economic and political sovereignty, to confront the war machine and eventually, to build the foundation of what could be called a multitudinous real democracy that transcends into a new beginning that does not fear radicalizing in order to attain a new social liberation.

Bibliography

Books (English)
Guy Debord, Society of Spectacle, (New York: Zone Books,1991).
Felix Guattari, Molecular Revolution, (Arizona: Peregrine Books,1984).
Saul Newman, Power and politics in Poststructuralist thought: New theories of the political, (New York: Routledge, 2005).
Wilhelm Reich, Mass Psychology of Fascism, trans. Mary Boyd Higgins, (New York: Farrar, Straus and Giroux, 1970).

---

[41] For more details please see: Michel Foucault, Discipline and Punish: The Birth of the Prison (1977) in which its author pictures power as a necessary precondition for the social formation, which penetrates and diffuses the social body in multiple ways. So, it could not only have a negative aspect (represented by the mechanisms of direct repression, such as police and law, who exercise violence, discipline, forbid), but also a positive-productive one (power which produces knowledge and truth, science, perception of objects, subjective reality). In our analysis, positive power held by the state, could be also loosely described as *ideological state propaganda*.

[42] Pierre Bourdieu, (1987): The sociologist Pierre Bourdieu sees *habitus* as the totality of unconscious or conscious embodied dispositions coming from social roles, acquired through the process of early -and later- mimesis, which mold in a definitive way the individual's perception of itself and of society, and therefore, shape its social action.

Books (Greek)

Aris Hatzistefanou, December 2008: history, here we come!, (Athens: Livanis, 2009).

Dimitris Paitaridis, "Ekseliksi tis paragogik;otitas kai oi epiptoseis stin antagonistinotita tis ellinikis oikonomias", (Athens: INE/Paratiritirio Oikonomikon kai koinonikon Ekselikseon, 2015).

Solon N. Grigoriadis, "Istroria tis Sigxronis Elladas 1941–1974", (Athens: Polaris, 2010).

Academic Articles (English)

Dimitri A. Sotiropoulos, "Civil Society in Greece in the Wake of the Economic Crisis", Konrad Adenauer Stiftung, December 2013.

Articles from the Press (English)

David Adams, "A Greek Tragedy", European Pensions, November/December 2011, Available at: <http://www.europeanpensions.net/ep/A-Greek-tragedy.php/>[Accessed on 10.06.2017, at 21:13].

Katie Allen, "Austerity in Greece caused more than 500 male suicides, say researchers", The Guardian, Available at: <https://www.theguardian.com/world/2014/apr/21/austerity-greece-male-suicides-spending-cuts/> [Accessed on 21.04.2014, at 21:13].

Phillip Chrysopoulos, "Greece Celebrates Anniversary of November 17, 1973, Student Uprising Against Junta", Greek Reporter, Available at: <http://greece.greekreporter.com/2015/11/16/greece-celebrates-anniversary-of-november-17-1973-student-uprising-agnst-junta/> [Accessed on 21.04.2018, at 19:13].

Robert D. Kaplan, "Those Greek Riots", The Atlantic, Available at: <https://www.theatlantic.com/magazine/archive/2008/12/those-greek-riots/307225/> [Accessed on 21.04.2018, at 19:13].

Helena Smith, "Greek activists target sales of homes seized over bad debts", Available at: <https://www.theguardian.com/world/2017/mar/11/greek-activists-target-sales-of-homes-seized-over-bad-debts/> [Accessed on 11.03.2017, at 22:13].

Heather Steward, "Greece's tax revenue collapse as dept. The crisis continues", Available at: <https://www.theguardian.com/world/2015/aug/06/greece-tax-revenues-collapse-debt-crisis-continues-euro/> [Accessed on 06.08.2015, at 22:13].

Yanis Varoufakis, "Five Lessons From the Greek PSI", Varoufaki's Thoughts for the post–2008 world, accessed by March 12, 2014, Available at: <https://www.yanisvaroufakis.eu/2014/03/12/lessons-from-the-greek-psi/> [Accessed on 06.08.2015, at 22:13].

Ed Vuillamy and Helena Smith, "Athens 1994, Britain's Dirty Secret", The Guardian, Available at: <https://www.theguardian.com/world/2014/nov/30/athens-1944-britains-dirty-secret/>[Accessed on 30.11.2017, at 22:13].

"Greek Student Protest Turns Violent-Europe-International Herald Tribune", New York Times, Available at: <http://www.nytimes.com/2006/06/27/world/europe/27iht-greece.2066776.html/> [Accessed on 27.06.2017, at 22:13].

Articles from the Press (Greek)

Panagiotis Petrakis, "Ta paradoxa is Ellinikis Oikonomias", Euro2day, Available at: <http://www.euro2day.gr/specials/opinions/article/594735/p-petrakhs-ta-paradoxa-this-oikonomias.html/> [Accessed on 16.07.2010, at 22:13].

Thanos Tsiros, "1200 Megales Etairies Sygentronoun to 55% tou Epixeirein", Kathimerini, accessed on September 27, 2015, Available at: <http://www.kathimerini.gr/832520/article/oikonomia/epixeirhseis/1200-megales-etaireies-sygkentrwnoyn-to-55-twn-kerdwn-poy-paragei-to-epixeirein/> [Accessed on 16.07.2017, at 19:13].

"Ethnicities prokalesan episodes to Oraiokastro". Iefimerida accessed on February 17, 2017, Available at: <http://www.iefimerida.gr/news/319919/ethnikistes-prokalesan-epeisodia-sto-oraiokastro-fonazan-lathraia-ta-prosfygopoyla/> [Accessed on 10.06.2018, at 11:45].

"Friki sti Mesogeio ." To Periodiko", accessed by February 21, 2017, Available at: <http://www.toperiodiko.gr/>[Accessed on 10.06. 2018, at 11:45].

Lectures/Interviews/ Other (English)

Michel Foucault, On power and class war—conversation with four members of the LCR, 1970.

Philippe de Georges, "A psychoanalytic approach to modern authority", lecture in the Centre for Psychoanalytic Research in Athens, 2015.

"Is migration good for the economy?" OECD, Migration policy debates, 2014.

Stavros Panagiotou

(Neo-)Liberalism and the Unresolved Political Problem in Cyprus: A Philosophical Perspective

Abstract: In this brief (commentary) proposal I argue that economic recession in Cyprus along with the political impasse of the inability of a resolution to reunite the two communities—philosophically speaking—emerged (and still exist) due to a continuation of adopting Western modernism in the political and social life of the island. Neo-liberalism and mass democracy severely affect all mechanisms that are responsible for the isolation of the island to find political ways for the unification of Cyprus. In this paper, I explain that the one-dimensional static role of rationality, through the liberal economy and mass production, leads not only to the wreckage of all political conversations (between Greek Cypriots and Turkish Cypriots) but also creates political amnesia for the people of Cyprus in general. After raising some objections to modernity, I suggest that social and political stability in Cyprus can be only achieved by adopting a multi-dimensional way of being through relationalism, morality and a return to metaphysics.

Keywords: Cyprus; morality; neo-liberalism; individualism; relationalism; metaphysics; modernism; post-modernism

Cyprus: Historical Background.

Cyprus, like several British and French colonies during 20th-century colonization, directly adopted several characteristics of modernism which gradually trapped the island in the chain of neo-liberalism. Cyprus' bank systems, as well as the Cypriot financial sector, were obliged to close the country's second-largest bank, the Cyprus Popular Bank, in 2013, 'haircutting' all deposits over one hundred thousand euros. In parallel, political, diplomatic affairs between Greek Cyprus (GC) and Turkish Cyprus (TC) have been wrecked for at least 40 years due to 'ethnic' issues. Turkey and Greece together with the UK signed a treaty in Zurich and London in 1959 to secure peace on the island after the inauguration of a new state, the Republic of Cyprus, which was formally established in 1960 (Hoffmeister, 2006, p. 4–10). However, 14 years later (15 July 1974) GC extremists from the Right Party prepared a coup to push Makarios III, the Archbishop, and president of the Republic of Cyprus to resign and flee Cyprus. Five days later (20 July 1974) the Turkish government announced a massive military 'intervention' in the island in order to secure the future of TC; from 1974 until now Turkish military powers have been established in the northern part of the island to secure the rights of TC (ibid., p. 34–47). All political conversations between the leaders of the two communities from 1974 until now as regards the reunification of the island have failed. In 2004 the former Secretary-General of the UN Kofi Annan suggested a plan of a referendum for the unification of Cyprus, but it was rejected by 76% of GC while it was approved by 65% of TC (Michael, 2009, p. 145–191).

From the year of Cyprus' independence, 1960, and onwards, several treaties, plans and diplomatic assembles have been tried in order to achieve a resolution for the case of Cyprus but unfortunately collapsed without functional and fair implications. The Cypriot Constitution in 1960 faced several objections from both sides. In 1963, intercommunal violence broke out, increasing tensions which were altered in 1974. The Treaty of Guarantee between Greece, the UK and Turkey (King, 1963) concerning security and internal trust collapsed when TC extremists assisted by the Turkish state manipulated a spirit of domination in the northern part of the island after the Turkish 'intervention' or 'invasion' in 1974. After this 'tragic year', suspicion, bias, and animosity emerged throughout the inhabitants of the island.

In the first decade of the 21st century, the UN together with the EU developed encouraging endeavors to resolve the case of Cyprus by nominating prominent and experienced technocrats on the island to cooperate with the two communities. After the failure of the Annan Plan (Pericleous, 2009, p. 281–321) several pacts have been suggested after the conversation of the two political sides with the involvement of the US and EU. However, the unresolved Cyprus problem has remained as a 'dark page' not only in the history of Cyprus but also against the prestige of EU itself.

A Philosophical Background of Cyprus Issue

Why does the 'Cyprus issue' remain unresolved? Is there any new political method or approach to suggest for the unification of the island? What is the main obstacle? Political and social problems are challenging to explain, especially when extremely different cultures are concerned. However, this is not the point. In this paper, I argue that tensions and conflict are increased in the political and social sphere due to the expansion of modernity. Neo-liberalism defends individualism which promotes the subject as a self-enclosed unit decentering the subject for the sake of the object. The problem of modernity is that individualism presupposes relationalism and not the opposite. Mass democracy, mass production, advertisement, marketing and liberal markets tend to vanish the *way of being* as a subject focusing mainly on the object. Societies develop a 'one-dimensional Man' (Marcuse 1964) ready to sacrifice his subjectivity for the sake of individuality. Politics thus decentering the subject ignores the importance of aesthetics and arts. Patriotism lost its meaning and creates different models of heroes (Matravers and Pike [ed.], 2003, p. 286–300). Heroes of our time need to merit specific individual, civilized criteria such as money, glory, property, and power. There are no 'heroes' anymore who are thirsty to share or to create *concepts*. Heroes nowadays are identical to individualism and not to relationalism (Chappell, 2013, p. 3–28).

Communities serve the human being not as a person but merely as an individual, as merely a biological logic animal. Arts lost their trace being integrated with politics and individuality. There is neither a vision nor a colored canvas to create concepts. Structuralism seeks to create dogmas and canonical methods, not concepts. Only through creative concepts will relations of human beings be sustained in a solid ground (Kearney and Rainwater [ed.], 2005, p. 402–410). Politics without aesthetics and eros cannot find relational solutions (ibid., p. 224–234). The Nietzschean despair (West 1997: 126–136) and the Hegelian desire of negation (Kojeve, 1969, p. 3–30) say nothing through the summits of the Great Powers' institutions. The target is justice but justice nowadays, unfortunately, must be construed through injustice. Justice and freedom for contemporary politics are extremely different from Platonic justice, Aristotelian προαίρεσις (proairesis) and Augustinian responsibility of freedom (Chappell, 1995, p. 56–61, 121–139). If the GC does not have a desire to create concepts together with the TC minority and vice versa tensions will remain. Summits and congresses around EU political circles and agendas are unable to create concepts on the basis of relationalism because they ignore and refuse to adopt the subject qua subject. Relationalism presupposes individualism and not the opposite. Reunification of such a peculiar region as Cyprus which includes extremely different cultures and religions such as GC's and TC's must develop relational and not merely individual criteria.

On the one hand desire for justice, even if this justice presupposes merely individualism, is a necessary condition for TC and GC to coexist peacefully. However, it is not a sufficient condition. What matters is to return to a metaphysical account of a justice imbued by ethics. There is a need to return to the real notion of democracy which focusses on the model of the ancient Greek πόλις or city-state (Yiannaras, 2007). Human beings need to participate (μετέχειν) in communities as persons and not as self-enclosed units (Matravers and Pike [ed.] 2003, p. 182–194). As Aristotle contends "τό ὀρθῶς διανοεῖσθαι διά τό ὀρθῶς κοινωνεῖν" (Yiannaras, 2011) which means rationality emerges through relationality. Several post-Hegelian thinkers intend to defend this thesis in the post-modern era where the aim to decenter the subject is of immense significance. It is through the face of the other, according to Emmanuel Levinas, that justice can find its moral notion (Levinas, 1969, 2009). Through morality and otherness societies can construe political justice and constitutions in a stable stance where subjectivity starts from the face of the other and not from the 'I' (Dimitrova, 2016). It is the face of the other that gives priority to 'me'. Without otherness, there is no meaning for the subject to exist. Liberalism without morality develops injustice through objectivism. There is an urgent need to return to a metaphysical progress of thinking. Logic through mere rationality of modernism is not enough. (Neo-) liberalism seems to have several severely awry points that need reconsideration.

Are there any challenges that fatally undermine (neo-) liberalism as a political theory?

At first, it is important to mention that, as has been clearly stated throughout the literature of political philosophy, there is not a 'fertile ground' to develop a sufficient definition of liberalism. Its terminology is quite harsh transmuting its meaning depending on the conditions and historical framework of each political period. I mean that several thinkers and scholars, specialized in political and social philosophy[1], insist on the distinction between the 'old classical liberalism' and the 'new revisionist liberalism'[2].

In order to understand the notion of liberalism and the debate as to whether there are challenges that fatally undermine liberalism as a political theory, several terms need to be explained and defined. Although, as I have

---

[1] I mainly refer to political philosophy and not to political theory as the former is normative, while the latter is not.
[2] A comprehensive interpretation concerning the distinction between the 'old classical' and the 'new revisionist' liberalism can be found in "Liberalism", *Stanford Encyclopedia of Philosophy*, ed. E. N. Zalta, *2.1–2.2,* First published Thu Nov 28, 1996; substantive revision Thu Sep 16, 2010.

mentioned above, it is quite difficult to provide a sound explanation concerning the definition of liberalism, I would say that the two major principles of liberalism are individualism and (moral) liberty. That is, society should allow individuals to reach their full potential without any interference[3]. In parallel, I might borrow a phrase from John Stuart Mill who says that liberalism is the only political theory that allows people—progressive beings—"to pursue our own conception of the good in our own way, so long as we do not attempt to deprive others of theirs or impede their own efforts to maintain it" (Mill, 1974, p. 72). Mill continues by underlining that the importance of the power of society over any individual who is a member of a civilized community must be limited. He thus argued that "the only purpose for which power can be rightfully exercised (by government or society) over any member of a civilized community, against his will, is to prevent harm to others" (ibid., p. 68). We can infer that—according to Mill—liberalists (both liberals and libertarians[4]) are against society's power over individuals and believe that no one should infringe their rights. Individual's rights are both inviolable and inalienable (Matravers, 2012, p. 39). As Friedrich Hayek argues, "There can be no freedom of the press if the instruments of printing are under government control, no freedom of assembly if the needed rooms are so controlled, no freedom of movement if the means of transport are a government monopoly" (Hayek, 1978, p. 149).

Liberal concerns such as toleration, the rule of law, freedom of thought, freedom of expression and autonomy, the ability of free market and the right to sell or buy property freely[5] in combination with the economic motto called laissez-faire[6] ('let it be') are the main characteristics of individuals' rights. As political liberalism states, individuals that adopt the above features are not

---

[3] A further historical analysis and consideration of liberalism can be found in R. Geuss, History and Illusion in Politics, Cambridge: Cambridge University Press, 2001.
[4] An excellent historical analysis of libertarianism can be found in J. Wolff, Entry on 'Libertarianism', in the Routledge Encyclopedia of Philosophy, ed. E. Craig, London, 1998, 2012, Available at: <http://www.rep.routledge.com/article/S036/> [Accessed on 10.06.2017, at 22:30].
[5] That is, private property is consistent with individual liberty (especially based on classical political liberalism).
[6] By the term *laissez-faire* in a liberal economic system we mean a system of trade that is free from government interference. The most significant, comprehensive treatise about economic liberalism was Scottish philosopher Adam Smith's *The Wealth of Nations*, first published in 1776. Smith adopted the policy of *laissez-faire* contrasting it with protectionism, which restricted trade between states. By protectionism we mean the policy of imposing high taxation on imports in order to protect small- and middle-scale domestic industries from foreign monopolies' competition. See A. Smith, *An Inquiry into the Nature and Causes of the Wealth of Nations*, Oxford: Oxford University Press, 2008 (first published in 1993).

necessarily harmonized with each other (Matravers 2012: 39). For example, an agent who pursues her own conception of the good in her own way can act freely pursuing her welfare no matter how it might increase inequalities in society. Therefore, according to liberals, selfishness is not a bad, immoral conception: by increasing self-ownership, one automatically increases rights over oneself[7]. Jon Pike provides an excellent historical analysis and definition of self-ownership and its confrontation in contemporary social and political philosophy[8]. Pike defines the self-ownership he wants to defend by saying that self-ownership is "the idea that I (rather than everyone else) own myself, and so I ought to determine the way in which my life proceeds, in the same way, that I determine what happens to my other processions" (Matravers, 2003, p. 117). If persons own themselves, then they own their various capacities and talents, and therefore they own the rewards derived from their endowments and natural assets. Hence, people will have different earning capabilities and in different parallel levels of wealth. So, we can infer that self-ownership is (probably) incompatible with equality. The latter argument is of immense importance to challenge whether liberalism is a complete political theory as, according to Gerald Allan Cohen, "substantial self-ownership and equality are incompatible because there is an inbuilt tendency in self-ownership towards inequality" (Matravers, 2003, p. 141).

Examining the literature which is related to contemporary social and political philosophy we can quickly identify several objections that come up from different political theories: multiculturalism, democracy, nationalism, the need for judicial punishment and communitarianism are some political theories which (fatally) challenge and undermine (political) liberalism as a political theory. In this essay, I will present how nationalism and the need for judicial punishment provide their arguments to point out that liberalism needs supplementation as a political theory.

Before starting to discuss objections under the broad heading of nationalism and punishment undermining liberalism as a political theory, it is worth

---

[7] See a significant graph indicating the thick and the thin concepts of self-ownership in D. Matravers, *The Postgraduate Foundation Module in Philosophy: Study Guide*, London: Open University Press, 2003, p. 119.

[8] The two main "rivals" concerning the debate of self-ownership are Robert Nozick and Gerald Cohen. The latter, contrasting his views with those of R. Nozick and J. Rawls, offers an extensive moral argument in favor of nationalism (socialism) rejecting Nozick's and Rawls's liberal-egalitarian position. See: ibid, p. 117–148.

to provide some information about communitarian critiques of (political) liberalism. Communitarianism[9] (a Marxist-inspired ideology which criticizes liberal individualism) is characterized by the view that liberalism for several reasons overestimates the individual as the bearer of value at the expense of goods inherent to the community (Matravers and Pike, 2003, p. 137) and that liberalism has more to say about the notion of individualism; communitarianism in relation with nationalism waits for liberals to explain who is this particular 'ego' who is being favored by liberal-individual privileges. Metaphysically speaking, liberalism must go further to give a more complete statement about the morality of individualism. Communitarian theory in parallel admits that on the one hand liberalism gives the free opportunity to individuals to live their lives as they prefer without harming others. On the other hand, according to communitarians and nationalists, this is not enough. A communitarian line of thought claims that liberalism lacks not only morality—"beings without purpose or incapable of moral ties"—but also that we cannot stand back and regard our conceptions of the good as a matter of choice (ibid: 135).

By saying that liberalism must further explain its morality, I mean that it is not necessarily sufficient to accept the universal theory of liberalism claiming that "all deserve equal consideration". The above argument comes under the broad headings of nationalism: the latter political thought is primarily a (historical) phenomenon that emerged during the early nineteenth century where several groups of people realized the urgent need to create independent nations in order to 'escape' from the bondage of monarchy (ancient regime). A nationalist is mainly someone who is a member of a group of people sharing four characteristic features with other persons: a shared language, shared associations, shared history and a common culture (ibid., 280, p. 1).

Philosophically speaking, nationalism finds the liberal 'unconditioned rational chooser' implausible providing a 'non-political idea of membership'. The latter term insists that individuals would have to regard themselves as a part of group adopting two major features: membership and patriotism. Nationalists and communitarians, moreover, claim that liberalism 'cannot command the kind of loyalty to the state that will inspire people to come to its defense or safeguard its public institutions' (Matravers and Pike, 2003, p.

---

[9] Communitarianism is not so much a clearly defined position as a tendency of thought. However, a very clear evaluation regarding the definition of communitarianism and its debate with liberalism can be found at A. Gutmann, "Communitarian Critics of Liberalism", in *Debates in Contemporary Political Philosophy: An Anthology,* eds. D. Matravers and J. Pike, London: Open University Press, 2003, p. 182–194.

267). The above statement—according to nationalism—shows that liberalism has some weaknesses in order fulfill its moral obligations to society. As far as nationalists are concerned, (moral) obligations in society are necessary for individuals. Membership, therefore, and patriotism are sources of obligation. It is a matter of pluralism: no one can survive in society's environment alone without getting involved with social institutions. In contrast, individualism implies atomistic traits which inevitably develop an 'egocentric' character focused on πλεονεξία (greed) rather than the common good. As a counter-argument, liberals reply that they do not 'care' about a wholly neutral position that means to take care the worst-off rather than to agree to a conception of an (individual) good.

The above debate needs further consideration. On the one hand, liberals claim that it is sound (and logical) to react as a free rational agent where, first, their goal is to reach a high standard of (their) personal potential being loyal to a legitimate 'treatment': that is, (a) not to harm others whilst pursuing (as a progressive being) the benefit of their conception of the good and (b) being loathe to agree to a national identity that negatively means they must have an obligation to society. Liberals, in short, underline that patriotism (and membership) is a lenient vice. On the other hand, nationalism raises its objection by insisting that the liberal self is not metaphysically plausible. As nationalists believe, "we have the obligation because we belong to the nation and we belong to the nation because we have this obligation" and the 'individuals who comprise a nation must believe themselves to share 'certain traits that mark them off from other peoples' (ibid., p. 269). Roger Scruton argues that liberalism is metaphysically implausible not only as to what gives it unity but also what gives it legitimacy (ibid., p. 271). Many thinkers distort the liberal individualist conception of the person because it insists on an 'unconditioned rational chooser' rather than a 'non-political', 'non-contractual' order. Scruton correctly (as far as I am concerned) underlines that the conception of the good and morality (based on an ethical community) are 'cultural rather than biological matters' (ibid., p. 267) and that every political order depends upon a non-political idea of membership.

It is worth defining membership and its notion concerning the debate whether liberalism is undermined as a political theory as it raises a major argument against liberalism (as a moral-political theory). By membership, I mean the three-dimensional feature of nationalism involving personal identity, the notion of an ethical community and the notion of the political community (regarding a pre-political contract). This three-dimensional unity relies on a kind of loyalty to a 'give and take' obligation. It is necessary and sufficient as a biological and moral member of a unity (nation) to share such a bond with others: to identify themselves regarding a common descent which is in parallel a feature of their pre-political unity. For instance, Jews, Arabs, and other prosperous ancient nations tied their nationality to a common descent community and to religion supported by a biological and cultural continuity across generations making a (moral) promise that must be open to all members of the community who have the capacity for obedience. That is, they share a combined moral-secular code: "The belief in racial inheritance construed as an endlessly transferrable set of benefits and burdens…rights and duties…the belief in the obligation of inheritance: we must receive from our forefathers what we also pass to our children…" (ibid., p. 274). Membership also is referred to a unity between the unborn and the dead; that is, a unity which is mainly based on a moral contract which has a continuity to all generations that are involved in a pre-political community preserving the proviso below: a shared history, shared language, shared geographical area and a common culture.

After discussing the notion of membership which is a major proviso of nationalism, it is urgent to construe another trait of nationalism: patriotism. There is a line of thought, liberalism that insists that patriotism is a vice without any moral or political structure. It is mainly a 'social doctrine' which derives from an extreme part of nationalism, that is, our duty to die for our country, to sacrifice our properties, families and ourselves for our nation. Liberals continue to characterize patriotism as immoral since they cannot express further arguments about its morality and its hypothetical value. They also believe that only 'liberal universalist' morality is the appropriate version of virtue. On the other hand, there is another line of thought, nationalism, that certainly is loathed to agree to that viewpoint: that is, patriotism is rather defined 'in terms of a kind of loyalty to a particular nation' (ibid., p. 268) with particular moral traits, and hence, it is a virtue. Patriotism opposes liberalism as a lack of interconnection and interrelation between individuals. I mean that patriotism objects to liberal individualism as the latter ignores not only the common social good but especially because it does not obey certain obligations to one's country. Liberals contrarily sacrifice national and ethical duties for the sake of atomistic welfare and personal success that aims only at prosperity and wealth. Patriotism, therefore, is "not only a mindless loyalty to one's particular nation" but, according to Alasdair MacIntyre, "it involves a peculiar regard for the particular characteristics and merits and achievements of one's nation". He continues by asserting that "these latter are indeed valued as merits and achievements, and their character as merits and achievements provides reasons supportive of the patriot's attitudes" (ibid., p. 287). However, a liberal account of morality raises a crucial (rhetorical) question in order to provoke confusion about patriotism: where and from whom do I learn and adopt the core principles of nationalist patriotism? MacIntyre answers that the principles of patriotism "are learnt from, in and through the way of life of some particular community" (ibid., p. 291), who probably wants to underline the major importance of national inheritance through the ages and also that the non-political social contract sometimes is being 'signed' by its members with "specific institutional arrangements", that is a "highly specific morality of some highly specific social order" (ibid., p. 291).

The question, however, remains unanswered: how can membership and patriotism show that liberalism ('liberal universalist') lacks morality and thus is not a complete political theory? The answer might be found by looking at the normative/epistemological sense of the debate: which factor is the most important in order to make autonomy, equality, consciousness, and responsibility coexist with a fair, moral, non-political redistribution of resources which can satisfy all social classes without infringing or violating individual and/or human rights? A potential (future) answer might be based on a reflective equilibrium between those features. Nationalism seems able to give substantial directions concerning this answer providing characteristics related to patriotism such as a deprivation of our welfare in favor of our community as a moral task, and as MacIntyre suggests: "It is within a community that individuals become capable of morality, are sustained in their morality and are constituted as moral agents by the way in which other people regard them and what is owed to and by them as well as by the way in which they regard themselves" (ibid., p. 292). As has been mentioned above, there is no need to supplant liberalism but an urgent need to supplement it with special traits from other political thought, such as nationalism and the need for judicial punishment. A wise suggestion of Amy Gutmann argues that liberalism "must give up some of its impartiality and favored some conceptions of the good over others" (ibid., p. 138). By this, it is meant that liberalism according to Gutmann needs to integrate communitarian attributes within its framework to treat others ethically and not only epistemologically.

Discussing materials above concerning how nationalism (and its similar attitudes such as membership and patriotism) undermines liberalism as a political theory, I paid special attention to terms such as impartiality, autonomy, morality, justice, and equality. Those terms are going to be used also to define and explain a second crucial phenomenon that might undermine liberalism as a political theory coming also from the broad heading of social and political philosophy which concerns the nature of the limits of legitimate judicial punishment and the (positive or negative) role of liberalism regarding penance, deterrence and the liberal state's justification of punishment.

Before defining punishment and its relation to liberalism in order to describe the argument as to whether punishment (the need for judicial punishment) challenges and undermines liberalism as a political theory, it is worth evaluating the relation between punishment and personhood. Unlike sticks, stones, and animals, individuals are rational persons[10]. Considered as persons, the individuals must be treated as persons, which means like equal, progressing beings and not like animals that need an animal tamer. I mean that offenders are persons and should be treated as such (Matravers, 2003, p. 9).

There is a general characteristic sense that nowadays that punishments should communicate with citizens, considering them as rational, autonomous agents. This is because it would be immoral to treat offenders as animals without an appropriate moral reason. It is of immense importance to figure out the notion of communicative theory and how it is related to autonomy and the justification of punishment. Moreover, I will argue that the need for judicial punishment does undermine liberalism as a political theory due to the fact that liberalism seems to find it problematic to confirm the 'general justifying aim' without judicial communicative punishment.

To understand the above argument (that judicial punishment undermines liberalism as a political theory) several terms concerning the institution of punishment related to liberalism need to be explained or defined. First, in order to explain punishment, I will borrow a phrase by Ted Honderich, who states that punishment is an authority's infliction of a penalty on an offender (Honderich, 1989, p. 19). By saying 'general justifying aim' (GIA), we mean the endeavor of the overall reduction of crime in society by deterring people, who are persons and not atoms (Hart, 1959, p. 1–27). By saying 'communicative theory' we mean a new version of 'retributivism'[11] which justifies pun-

---

[10] An individual in order to be named as person must fulfil some necessary conditions such as moral obligation and respect, values, responsibility, and autonomy: the agents must be able to act for reasons reflecting on facts and interests across time. See T.E. Jnr. Hill, "Kantianism", in The Blackwell Guide in Ethical Theory, ed. H. LaFollette, Oxford: Blackwell, p. 241.

[11] Retributivism is a theory of punishment which unlike deterrence and rehabilitation (other theories of punishment) is 'backward looking': it justifies punishment by looking at the

ishment on the grounds that it communicates a moral message to the offender (Matravers 2003: 247). The notion of the communicative theory is of immense importance to understand how judicial punishment challenges the liberal line of thought concerning the punishment of persons (even as progressive moral beings).

The communicative theory aims to respect the constraints of punishment. That is, it is to send a moral message to offenders. For instance, as Herbert Morris states, "The guilty wrongdoer is not viewed as damned by his wrongful conduct to a life forever divorced from others. He is viewed as a responsible being, responsible for having done wrong and possessing the capacity for recognizing the wrongfulness of his conduct…to have a society of laws that it should provide our good of moral persons" (Morris, 1981, p. 105). This is, from my point of view, the liberal line of thought concerning the notion of punishment and its justification. It is, therefore, an urgent need to treat an offender as a person without forgetting her rights of autonomy, evaluating the crime she committed by addressing her reasons and not ours. Treatment of an offender must not infringe her values, autonomy, and reflective reasoning but must regard her as an autonomous individual freely attached to her new meaningful life without being divorced from others due to her past crime (ibid., p. 99).

Liberals also argue that there are some problems with the notion of desert, as they claim justice in unjust where there is a lack of moral understanding. That is, they continue, we cannot make a right (desert) repaying evil with evil: two wrongs do not make a right. Providing this argument is plausible, liberalism tries to say that it is better to seek the actual inflicting of punishment (a moral necessity) than the feeling that offenders deserve (an inevitable and punitive) punishment (Walker, 1992, p. 160). Before assessing the opposing line of thought which is loath to agree with the liberal-moral argument, it is noteworthy to mention something important that derives from the Strawsonian theory of moral responsibility and reactive attitudes. Peter Strawson[12], an individualist and a thinker favoring autonomy and freedom in

---

nature of the offence that has been committed. It is mainly a punitive theory of punishment as it claims that anyone who contravenes the laws deserves a penalty. (Matravers 2003: 246). In short, it is mostly familiar with the Old Testament's quote: "an eye for an eye and a tooth for a tooth".

[12] Peter Strawson also analyses the notion of personhood as a matter of metaphysics. He claims that autonomy is the core principle of a rational agent and it is a necessary and sufficient trait for someone to be regarded as a person. Contrarily, he adds that there are individuals that are not persons such as atoms, wantons and people who are in a persistent vegetative state.

his works, argues that every individual who is regarded as a person has some necessary and sufficient attitudes which cannot be infringed upon or violated. Even though those reactive attitudes might be negative and harm others, they are still attitudes of personhood, such as demand, indignation, disapprobation, and condemnation. Strawson explains that a person does not lose her personhood by having those attitudes and feelings and she must continue to be regarded as a person. Thus, we can infer that Strawsonian theory is against the harsh treatment of persons and that punishing individuals is not justified.

In contrast, another line of thought, harsher to offenders, argues that persons no matter what attitudes or values they carry are responsible for their acts and their way of life. This specific line of thought disagreeing with the liberal thought on punishment invokes the need for judicial punishment. A more social, communitarian theory of punishment alleges that penal states must be strict and harsh, especially for severe offenses. Punitive deterrent punishment increases the average of annulling the crime. According to the German idealist philosopher George Wilhelm Friedrich Hegel, punishment is needed to eradicate the (severe) offense. To punish is to "annul the crime which otherwise would have been held valid, and to restore the right; the objective treatment of righting the wrong…is the primary and fundamental attitude in considering crime" (Matravers, 2003, p. 246).

Andrew von Hirsch, another legal philosopher, and penal theorist, asserts that crimes should be punished proportionally, but he insists on not the Strawsonian interpersonal attitudes but on the appropriateness of institutionalizing censure, arguing that the justification for punishment is that it censures the offender (ibid., p. 252). He underlines that punishments might be connected with the community and not with the individual herself, meaning that the state has the responsibility and the power to reduce, deter or annul crime using (always) impartial judicial punishment of the offenders. He concludes that punishment can be justified only in a social background adopting a communicative account of new retributivism based on the community and not on the individual liberal theory of punishment. The above account can respect without violating the means/ends and the reason constraint (ibid., p. 234, 240). Von Hirsch, as a communitarian thinker, raises a question whether any communicative account is compatible with liberalism. This is the core argument which will answer whether judicial punishment undermines liberalism as a political theory. The problem here is to define what it is to be illiberal in order to manage von Hirsch's claim that liberalism is not compatible with the communicative account of punishment. Von Hirsch believes that liberalism is committed to atomistic communities of individuals who have no broader social commitments. That is, being communitarian alleges correctly (from my point of view) that the broader social commitments to which liberals are entitled are not enough for a communicative theory. So, if this argument draws on some notion of the community such a community cannot be a liberal community but a community.

To conclude, it is prudent to make clear that Von Hirsch does not speak about a non-liberal penal state where personhood and moral reason should be infringed. His intention is to supply some further social constitutions to Anthony Duff's and Daniel Farrell's liberal theory of punishment. As I have mentioned above, liberalism, as a political theory, needs further supplementation, not a fatal rejection. One of its supplementations—according to Von Hirsch—is to accept some constitutive grounds to address certain coercive state institutions for punishment, where these coercive institutions might also be given specific supplemental functions, perhaps concerned with the offender's moral well-being (Matravers and Pike, 2003, p. 416–17). Summing up, von Hirsch provides his own criteria for proportionality of sentence, arguing that the offender should be punished proportionately to the seriousness of the crime committed under coercive state institutions.

Evaluating materials and views deriving from nationalism and the need for judicial punishment I have argued that the two latter political theories can provide arguments to challenge and undermine liberalism as a political theory. Liberalism seems to appear weak as regards its notion that the moral should aspire to the universal. The latter argument as I have tried to present it is metaphysically implausible. Liberalism has to loosen its liberal values by trying to adopt some constituents of nationalist and communitarianist political theories. Autonomy, moral reason and freedom remain the most essential features of individuals, and liberal theory must safeguard them. In parallel, it would be wise to add some other traits that will give a robust viability in order to give up some of its impartiality. As regards punishment, liberal theory also provides the sound argument that we have to engage with offender's reasons rather than ours before deciding on judgment. This is quite an important and solid argument since it defends the offender's autonomy and moral reason. In contrast, the liberal theory of punishment cannot react arbitrarily focused only on an individual's moral reason but ought to obey the state's institutions in order to reduce, deter, or annul crime in the future.

Comparing the future between liberalism, nationalism and the need for judicial punishment we can infer that the perfect outcome will be a reflective equilibrium among them, or at least an endeavor to 'collaborate' in order to respect first persons as individual progressive beings and not discriminate against them either as isolated liberals or as a group of people who obey a nation that may require a kind of loyalty and social obligations. Of course, to be optimistic, and realistic, it is a complicated effort to be just in an unjust society. Nowadays impartiality seems impossible isolate as long as people pursue the good and not the right. Capitalism as an economical ecumenical system based on monopolies provides, on the one hand, freedom of market and free commerce to all, but a crucial danger remains: an extreme form of liberalism which does not care about nations or citizenship may cause disastrous consequences to mankind in the future, even harming its own core principle: autonomy.

To sum up, summarizing the above arguments, I have argued that nationalism and the need for judicial punishment can provide logical arguments in order to challenge and undermine liberalism as a political theory. It has to be clarified that liberalism remains a solid political, social theory, but it would be better to find the courage to restore, amend or supply alternative views from other political ideologies. Taking into consideration the above thoughts we can infer that modernity through the *ratio* of the Enlightenment cannot implement any qualitative implications as regard the notion of justice. Justice needs to be interpreted through metaphysical and ethical perspectives in order to provide relational and not merely individual conditions of liberalism. The political status in Cyprus might change through a metaphysical framework in which GC and TC might coexist by sharing and creating concepts like the ancient city-state or *πόλις* in classical Athens together with the adaptation of morality.

References

Chappell, T., "Knowledge of Persons", European Journal of Philosophy of Religion, 5. 4 (2013), p. 3–28.

— Aristotle and Augustine on Freedom, London: MacMillan Press, 1995.

Dimitrova, M., Sociality and Justice, Stuttgart: Ibidem Press, 2016.

Duff, R.A. and Garland, D., eds, A Reader on Punishment, Oxford: Oxford University Press, 1994a.

Farrell, D.M., 'The Justification of General Deterrence', Philosophical Review, 94 (1985), p. 367–94.

Gaus, R., "Liberalism", Stanford Encyclopedia of Philosophy, ed. E. N. Zalta, Available at: <http://plato.stanford.edu.libezproxy.open.ac.uk/entries/liberalism/> [accessed on 3 September 2014, at. 14:10].

Geuss, R., History and Illusion in Politics, Cambridge: Cambridge University Press, 2001.

Gutmann, A., "Communitarian Critics of Liberalism", in Debates in Contemporary Political Philosophy: An Anthology, eds. D. Matravers and J. Pike, London: Open University Press, 2003, p. 182–194.

Hart, H.L.A., 'Prolegomenon to the Principles of Punishment', in Hart H.L.A., 1968. Punishment and Responsibility, Oxford: Oxford University Press, p. 1–27.

Hayek, F.A., 'Liberalism' in his *New Studies in Philosophy, Politics, Economics and the History of Ideas*, London: Routledge and Kegan Paul, 1978.

Hill, T.E. Jnr., "Kantianism", in The Blackwell Guide in Ethical Theory, ed. H. LaFollette, Oxford: Blackwell, 2013, p. 227–46.

Hoffmeister F., Legal Aspects on the Cyprus Problem, Leiden-Boston: Martinus Nijhoff Publishers, 2006.

Honderich, T., Punishment: The Supposed Justifications, Cambridge: Polity Press, 1989.

Kojeve, A., Introduction to the Reading of Hegel, Ithaca and London: Cornell University Press, 1969.

King, G. (ed.), Documents on International Affairs 1959, Oxford: Oxford University Press, 1963.

Levinas E., Totality and Infinity, tr. A.L. Pittsburg, PA Duquesne University Press, 1969.

—Otherwise Than Being, or, Beyond Essence, Pittsburg: Duquesne University Press, 2009.

Marcuse, H., One-Dimensional Man, London: Routledge Classics, 1964.

Matravers, D., Study Guide: A 850 The Foundation Module in Philosophy and A 851 Postgraduate Module in Philosophy, The Open University of London, 2003 and 2012.

Matravers, D. and Pike, J., eds, Debates in Contemporary Political Philosophy, Open University Press, London, 2003.

Michael, M.S., Resolving the Cyprus Conflict, New York: Palgrave MacMillan, 2009.

Mill, J.S., On Liberty, Harmondsworth: Penguin, 1974 edn.

Morris, H., 'A Paternalistic Theory of Punishment', in Duff and Garland 1994a, p. 95–111.

Pericleous, Ch., The Cyprus Referendum, London-Ney York: I.B. Tauris, 2009.

Rawls, J., Theory of Justice, Harvard: Harvard University Press, 1999.

Smith, A., An Inquiry into the Nature and Causes of the Wealth of Nations, Oxford: Oxford University Press, 2008 (first published in 1993.

Walker, N., 'Reductivism and deterrence', in Duff and Garland 1994a, p. 212–17.

West D., An Introduction to Continental Philosophy, Cambridge: Polity Press, 1997.

Wolff, J., 'Libertarianism', in the Routledge Encyclopedia of Philosophy, ed. E. Craig, London, 1998, 2012, <http://www.rep.routledge.com/article/S036> [accessed 3 September 2014].

Yiannaras Ch., Έξι Φιλοσοφικές Ζωγραφιές, Θεσσαλονίκη: Ίκαρος, 2011.

Piotr Pietrzak

Donald Trump's visit to Saudi Arabia, Saudi-Iranian Relations, and the Future of the Iranian Nuclear Deal

Abstract: *Over the course of the last decade, the Islamic Republic of Iran has gone a very long way to re-join the international community, and that happened at the expense of severely slowing down the development of its nuclear weapons program; but at the end (Unlike North Korea's Kim Jong Un[1]), the political leadership of this country has decided that it is in its country's best interest to abandon the development of its first nuclear weapon, and embark on the path of compliance with the international community's expectations. Naturally, this realization did not come quickly at first, it is more of the effect of the Barack Obama administration exercising its power of persuasion as the conditions offered to the Iranians were actually very favourable for the Iranian people: On one hand the former US president attracted the authorities in Teheran with various compelling economic incentives that have reasured them of the importance and tengibility of their new strategic choices, and on the other hand, this leader has also managed to persuade the other members of the international community that it was the high time for Iran to be given a realistic opportunity of re-entering into the international community. Yet, the results of the presidential election of 2016 has drastically changed the political backdrop in the United States, the Democratic president who persuaded Iranian authorities to enjoy the benefits of this new beginning in their relations with the outside world is no longer in office, and President Obama's influence over his successor is minimal at the best, as the new occupant of the White House Donald J. Trump has shown very little desire to understand the Middle Eastern policy and lacks patience for Iranian Foreign Minister Javad Zarif and his declarations that his country is still fully committed to fulfilling its nuclear disarmament obligations. For these reasons, many political commentators suggest that the future of the Iranian Nuclear Deal may be soon put into question. Thus far, President Trump has been*

---

[1] Please see the work of Balazs Szalontai and Sergey Radchenko, North Korea's Efforts to Acquire Nuclear Technology and Nuclear Weapons: Evidence from Russian and Hungarian Archives, Cold War International History Project, Working Paper 53, Cold War International History Project Woodrow Wilson International Center for Scholars & Kim, Jiyul. "Strategic Culture of the Republic of Korea." Contemporary Security Policy 35, No. 2 (2014):270–89.doi:10.1080/1352326 0.2014.927675.

only moderately vocal about the necessity of "ripping up" this deal and renegotiating it from scratch, but upon his recent visit to Saudi Arabia and Israel, the tone of his declarations has changed dramatically. Many political commentators have already suggested that the Trump Administration is in the process of checking its options before the inevitable implementation of its full-scale revision of the White House's Middle East policy. It is possible that US relations with Iran and its nuclear deal may soon account for the first casualty of this geostrategic reshuffle. The danger of such a scenario materializing is that it could potentially lead the international community to an eruption of a crisis that has never been seen before in the Middle East. Furthermore, it is also more apparent that the anti-Iranian attitudes in the USA in the post–2016 political circumstances are becoming increasingly stronger and stronger to the extent that it no longer matters whether the Iranian political leadership complies with international norms and regulations, or not, because no matter what they seem to lead Teheran to similarly negative results. The question remains how President Rouhani would react to this new unfavorable political environment? Would he show patience and composure or would he follow the footsteps of Ayatollah Khomeini in his relations with the West that had led the region to decades of chaos?

Keywords: Donald Trump, Barack Obama, Saudi Arabia, Iran, Israel, Middle East, Iranian Nuclear Deal

Introduction

There are many foreign policy initiatives in the Middle East of the former President Barack Obama that future historians will see as examples of blatant failures and disappointments of his strategic thinking and this list should start with his administration's involvement in the 2011 military intervention in Libya, due to the fact that the actual removal of Colonel Gadhafi from power in Tripoli has left this country in a state of political vacuum and yet another civil war. The next item on the list might be Obama's premature withdrawal of US forces from Iraq in the same year, as a lack of reliable stabilising power in this country has inadvertently created conditions for al-Qaeda in Iraq to evolve into ISIS that has lead this organization to take control of vast swathes of the borderland between Syria and Iraq. Subsequently, one can emphasise that Obama also showed a considerable reluctance to put any extra pressure on the Syrian government to stop abusing its citizens at the beginning of the Syrian uprising between 2011–2013, which consequently opened the window of opportunity to the Russian Federation to transform the conflict into almost a domestic issue when the intervening forces just joined the theatre of operations in this country in September 2015.

When it comes the US policy towards Iran and the so-called Iranian nuclear deal it can be considered as a cornerstone of the Obama foreign policy and one of the best international policy initiatives in generations that offered a healthy middle ground between Iranian nuclear ambitions and global uneasiness about the Tehran government obtaining a nuclear capacity. Therefore, the scale of this achievement can be indeed compared to the Camp David Accords for which Menachem Begin, Jimmy Carter and Anwar El Sadat were awarded the 1978 Nobel Peace Prize. It is possible that, by pushing for this deal so vigorously, President Obama has inadvertently undermined U.S. relations with Israel and Saudi Arabia, but according to many political commentators that was a risk that was really worth taking, as this initiative in the global sense presented White House officials with a unique opportunity to stabilise the Middle East and the global architecture of power itself for generations to come.

Indeed, under the Joint Comprehensive Plan of Action (JCPOA) agreed on 14 July 2015 between the Islamic Republic of Iran and the United States, the United Kingdom, Russia, France, China, Germany and the European Union, Tehran has agreed to reduce its enrichment capacity by 98% to 300 kg, keep the levels of its enrichment at not more than 3.67% for at least 15 years and has promised to retain no more than 6,104 out of almost 20,000 centrifuges it possesses. Secondly, it has committed himself to closing enrichment facilities other than Natanz and will conduct research and development on centrifuges only with an agreed scope and schedule, and consequently made a declaration that any other underground enrichment facilities would either cease to exist or would be converted into nuclear physics and technology centers. When it comes to reprocessing the existing heavy water stockpiles that had been ongoing in its facility at Arak, the rulers of Iran agreed that this plant would be redesigned and modernized into heavy water research reactor with no weapons-grade plutonium by-products, whilst all of the spent fuel would not be reprocessed but would be exported to countries that agree to dispose of it. Furthermore, the Iran has decided to submit to an International Atomic Energy Agency (IAEA) monitoring procedure which secured an enhanced access with modern technologies to clarify past and present issues with the modified Code 3.1 and provisional application of the Additional Protocol. In exchange for fulfilment of all of these commitments, Iran persuaded the IAEA officials along with the UN Security Council, the European Union, and the United States policymakers to terminate all nuclear-related economic and financial sanctions that had been imposed on this country until further notice (Morello & DeYoung Karen, 2015; Laub 2015).

The Political Situation in Iran after the Presidential Election of 2016

According to many political commentators, the Iranian nuclear deal (that had been reached at the end of Obama's second term in office) accounts for one of the most essential peaceful initiatives in generations in the Middle East. As we remember, the Democratic president at that time was instrumental in persuading the other members of the international community that this Middle Eastern country should be given a realistic and tangible chance of re-joining the community of nations should it choose to adhere to the norms and regulations of international law and non-proliferation policy. The enthusiasm of Democratic members of the U.S. political establishment after signing the deal was probably not shared by their Republican counterparts in both Congress and Senate. With the U.S. political backdrop changing very rapidly after the 2016 election, and the transition of power from the hands of the Democratic administration to that of the incoming Republican, the leading advocate of this deal has been replaced by President Trump, who is far less impressed by Iranian Foreign Minister Javad Zarif's declarations that his country is fully committed to fulfilling its nuclear disarmament, which will have a direct, tangible effect on the shape of the U.S. foreign policy in the Middle East and Iran.

Indeed, Donald Trump, both prior to and after assuming the office, has put into question the very rationale of signing this deal and emphasized the necessity of "ripping this deal up" and renegotiating it from scratch. In this respect, we can plausibly assert that as his recent visit to Saudi Arabia and Israel shows, President Trump's attitudes in this regard have not changed much. Both countries are considered to be Iran's most influential regional competitors, yet upon his visits to these countries, Donald Trump not only accused Iran of fuelling the fires of sectarian conflict in the region and supporting terrorists, but also chose to sign a number of mutually beneficial deals with Saudi King Salman bin Abdul Aziz Al Saud, and exchanged a number of friendly gestures with Iran's eternal enemy Israeli Prime Minister Benjamin Netanyahu. Undoubtedly, these actions account for a clear message to Tehran that the U.S. policy in the region has undergone a significant transformation into much a more hostile and unreliable one. Naturally, these declarations could not be unnoticed by the Iranian government as Mohammad Javad Zarif responded within just minutes of Trump's comment on Twitter with a suggestion that the US Government is milking Saudi Arabia for billions of dollars in newly-signed arms deals (Goldman-Eps, 2016; Ibrahim 2017; Laub, 2015; Melvin 2015).

Saudi-Iranian Hostilities Seen Through the Prism of the Greater Middle East Region

In order to give us some perspective on Zarif's outrage at recent actions of President Trump we need to try to wear his shoes for a moment, which starts with an acknowledgement that Iran's principal antagonist in the quest for regional supremacy is precisely Saudi Arabia and mutual Saudi-Iranian hostility is natural in this case. From this perspective Trump's Saudi Arabia visit that coincided with the Iranian Presidential Elections of 2017 gave a very peculiar timing to this visit. In this respect, it is worth mentioning that it is already a pattern in the international relations within the region that an improvement in Washington's relations with Riyadh and Tel Aviv happens at the expense of Iran and other Shiite countries. For these reasons, one can build on that rule of the thumb a plausible argument suggesting that the Trump administration has sent Iranian policymakers a powerful message implying that his administration will not be willing to continue with the much more balanced and predictable Middle Eastern policy of his predecessor, and therefore the future of the nuclear deal itself may be at stake. There is ample historical evidence suggesting that when one of these countries manages to improve its bilateral relations with Washington, it is always happening at the expense of the other country's ties with this country, and the current geopolitical backdrop in both the White House and in the Middle East tend to suggest that this time this pattern will also turn into a self-fulfilling prophecy (Brown, 2016; Fisher 2016). In this respect, it is also important to emphasize that both the leader in Tehran and the ruler in Riyadh have been involved in a spiritual contest for the leadership over the so-called Ummah[2]

---

[2] Ummah–(الإسلام أمة) Muslim community. A fundamental concept in Islam, expressing the essential unity and theoretical equality of Muslims from diverse cultural and geographical settings. In the Quran, designates people to whom God has sent a prophet or people who are objects of a divine plan of salvation. Source: The Oxford Dictionary of Islam, Available at: <http://www.oxfordislamicstudies.com/article/opr/t125/e2427/> [Accessed on 18.04.2017, at 01:05].

that consists of 1.6 billion followers of Allah (Goldman-Eps, 2016; Ibrahim 2017).

It has to be underlined here, that it is not only about their various interpretation of the Quran that these countries are fighting. The status of bilateral relations between Iran and Saudi Arabia is undermined by their regional struggles in the greater Middle East region, as both of these influential powerhouses have contradicting interests on many different levels of their mutual interactions, starting with the fact that both Iran and Saudi Arabia fight for regional supremacy through their proxies operating in the broader region of the greater Middle East. In this respect it is worth emphasising that **Afghanistan** can also be seens as a textbook example of the escalation of the Iranian-Saudi rivalry to the territory of other Muslim countries that dates back to the aftermath of the Soviet intervention of 1979, that in turn has encouraged local Mujahedins to turn to Saudi Arabia as well as Iran for support for their pro-independence struggle. Consequently, the way this conflict has unfolded resulted in the growth of al-Qaeda there as well as the creation of less-renowned Saudi backed and Iranian backed groups that took on that fight until at least 1988. In the difficult years between the departure of the Soviets and entrance to the local theatre of war of the the US-led coalition the local Taliban government had a tendency to switch allegiances from Iranian to Saudi while the respective parties of those countries attempted to turn the country into a primary zone of their influence and landing place for their separate shady operations in the region, without facing much resistance from the central government, which was mostly nonexistent at that time. In this respect, it is worth emphasizing that Osama Bin Laden, the leader of al-Qaeda who was residing in this country at the time, had visible Saudi links, but the Saudi government eventually relinquished its ties with that group after the events of 9/11. Despite the ongoing civil war in large parts of the country, the situation in Afghanistan has significantly improved since 2002; the local government has proven to be willing to listen to various foreign influences from multiple centers of power, Tehran and Riyadh included. In this case it is worth emphasising that while previous President Hamid Karzai maintained a friendly relationship with Iran, Afghanistan's new leader Ashraf Ghani has proven to be more prone to endorsing various Saudi initiatives in the greater Middle East region such as Yemen's Houthi insurgency, which undermines Kabul-Tehran relations (Peikar, 2015; Tabatabai, 2016; Seerat, 2017).

It is essential to draw attention to the fact that we can also witness a similar situation in **Syria (2011–)** these days. In this regard, it is worth bringing to the fore that many of the parties operating in this country have a long history of working either with Tehran or Riyadh to pursue their objectives. Although the population is mostly Sunni in this country the person in power who is backed by Iran comes from an Alawite sect that is intimately connected with Shiite members of the population. It is common knowledge that it is in Tehran's best interest for President Bashar Assad's embattled regime to survive the nearly 7-year-old civil war. Therefore, Iranians do not hesitate to provide Damascus with financial, logistics, and material support. Al-Assad is also supported by Iran-backed fighters from Hezbollah from neighboring Lebanon. Meanwhile, the Saudi monarch [both former Abdullah bin Abdul-Aziz and current (ever since 2015) Salman bin Abdul-Aziz Al Saud] does everything he can to both back moderate and jihadist Sunni rebels fighting to remove al-Assad from power and exercise his diplomatic and political influence to make this goal reality. Russian military intervention of 2015 has further complicated the Saudis' chances of success in this power struggle (that was undertaken, with Tehran's silent consent, to prop up the Syrian regime).

Subsequently, Iranian and Saudi policymakers are also responsible for adding extra fuel to the fire in neighboring **Iraq (especially after 2003)** which has had an even more profound nature at least ever since the 1970s, where the lines of disagreements between both sides go even further than in Syria. Although the population is mostly Shiite, in this country, it was ruled for decades until 2003 by Sunni leader Saddam Hussein who was supported by Riyadh while Tehran encouraged the opposition to his rule. After the US-led intervention of 2003 the situation in the country has changed diametrically, as the Shiite government of Nouri al-Maliki that took over power in the country and held it until 2014, was accused of being under substantial Iranian influence, whilst Tehran has been charged with using current ISIS and al-Qaeda led turmoil in the country to make inroads among local policymakers. Still, the accusations against the government in Riyadh can be easily reciprocated as the house of Saud is very often accused of using its petrodollars to fuel various ethnic disagreements, and encourage local Sunnis who feel alienated by the Shiite government to turn to arms, even against the government of Haider al-Abadi who succeeded al-Maliki in 2014. In this respect, it is worth pointing out that some political commentators assert that there is also tangible evidence suggesting Saudi complicity in supporting various jihadist militias operating in northern and western Iraq and financing selected members of al-Nusra Front, al Qaeda, and the Islamic State, or these are groups that are entirely anti-regime operations.

Another battleground between the countries that has received very limited media attention these days (and coincidently, the media that keeps reports from Yemen away from a broader public is controlled by the people who provide the Saudis with the weapons to wage this conflict), is **the civil war in Yemen (2011/2015–present)** that accounts for the most tangible example of the power struggle for regional supremacy between the Saudi and Iranian Governments. In this instance, it is worth underlining the fact that the leaders in Riyadh decided to start a military coalition in neighboring Yemen in 2015 to prevent the Tehran-supported Houthi takeover of the central government by Abd Rabbuh Mansur Hadi. But, thus far, Saudi Arabia's intervention has been successful only to a very limited extent. The situation on the ground has been further complicated by the fact that former Yemeni President Ali Abdullah Saleh (considered to be an important factor in this regional power struggle) decided to switch his allegiances to the Houthis led by Abdul-Malik Badreddin al-Houthi, but the same Houthis decided to assassinate him on 4 December 2017[3].

---

[3] **The assassination of Ali Abdullah Saleh** had undoubtedly impacted the political backdrop of Yemen and the regional architecture of power in the Middle East for years to come. Interestingly, this influential politician was regarded as a player to be reckoned with even after he had lost power in his country in 2011. To some commentators, Ali Abdullah Saleh resembled Hosni Mubarak (President of Egypt between 1981 and 2011), as despite being regarded with contempt by his fellow citizens; like his Egyptian counterpart, President Saleh was able to exercise his power and influence in this challenging region with a relative ease for more than three decades before the outbreak of the Arab Spring in his country. During his time in office (President of Yemen between 1990 and 2012), Saleh has gained a reputation for breaking his alliances more often than British Empire used to do, at the peak of its greatness; not to mention the fact that he was also known for escaping countless assassination attempts designated to oust him from power; this includes the 2011 assassination attempt that wounded him severely and killed several of his bodyguards in his presidential compound. According to various bystanders, it could be considered a "miracle" that he managed to survive this attempt, but still, this time, Saleh had much fewer reasons to be happy about, as it turned out he had to be hospitalized in Saudi Arabia for several months that had meant that he would lose most of his power and influence in the country. That is precisely when most political commentators have just assumed that he will never be able to come back to Sana and that his political career ended in 2011. But, to everyone surprise, unlike the former President of Ukraine (2010–2014) Yanukovych who retired in Russia after the events of 2014 in Ukraine; President Saleh was not willing to settle for being a guest of the Custodian of the Two Holy Mosques, and, he decided to go back to Yemen the moment he got a chance even though the circumstances in his homeland had changed drastically in favor of his political opponents. Indeed, it was a mistake to underestimate President Saleh as he was very skillful in the art of political brinkmanship, and that was especially visible in his first political move upon his return to Yemen, when he decided to strategically recognize the transition of power to President Abdrabbuh Hadi and supposedly settled for the role of a political outsider with very little say in his successor's Government. But not many people

Timing of the U.S. President's Visit to Saudi Arabia & Israel

Undoubtedly, many political commentators would agree that President Trump's recklessness and lack of understanding of the Middle East shown during this visit is more than evident. The very fact that Trump chose to visit Saudi Arabia on the exact same day as the Iranian Presidential Election speaks louder than a million words and looks like an intentional attempt to undermine Washington-Tehran relations to secure some morally questionable reimbursement in 'petrodollars' from the Saudi leadership. Of course, to more hardnosed Republican representatives (who tend to be very skeptical about Iranian intentions in general), Trump's decision to disregard Iranian compliance with IAEA norms and regulations and efforts normalize its foreign policy initiatives will have a much more immediate dimension that might translate into very tangible results at home. Namely, the US's hostility towards Iran translates directly into the opening of a new chapter in US-Saudi relations, and results in Saudi direct investments in the US military complex, which creates jobs, and these make the Republican voter happy. After all, unfreezing relations with some parties almost always corresponds with worsening of relationships with the others, so why would US policymakers choose Iran over Saudi Arabia in this case? It is clear that choosing Saudi Arabia over Iran in this respect has been done because of a more calculated business-like opportunism combined with a utilitarian approach of outweighing the needs of the many with the requirements of few. The question, however, remains whether while prioritizing the economic interests of his country, Donald Trump took into account the global importance of sustaining worldwide peace and security. To answer this question, we will have to wait.

In Donald Trump's defence, we can emphasise that his recent rapprochement with Saudi Arabia and Israel that happened at the expense of

---

knew that it was just a very thoughtful smokescreen as the moment this old-Middle-Eastern-fox had felt that he is regaining his composure, President Saleh broke his alliance with President Hadi and the Saudis, and he had formed a coalition with the most unlikely party—namely his eternal enemy Abdul Malik al-Houthi—the leader of the Houthi rebels. This move came as a massive surprise because while he was in power, President Saleh had spent a great deal of perseverance fighting al-Houthi who was considered to be the biggest ally of Iran and Hezbollah in the region. However, the moment the Houthi-Saleh coalition was formed, the balance of power in the country has temporarily shifted in their favor. Still, this unlikely marriage of convenience of two opposite currents was not meant to last long and steadily the more profound disagreements started to emerge between these two parties. The moment his new allies-turned-foes have mistaken his shuttle diplomacy for an act of political treason, this last flirt with death has proven to be fatal to Saleh.

—In Statu Nascendi 1:1 (2018)—

US-Iran relations can be reasonably explained. As we all know, nothing happens without reason in the realm of the international affairs, and Iranian decision-makers have recently exposed a very provocative behavior in their internal response that can be seen as very hostile policy. Indeed, this country has recently tested a number of intermediate- and long-range missiles that according to many political commentators could be quickly turned into nuclear ballistic missiles, should Tehran gain nuclear weapons capacity. Not only that, when the US president and European Union leaders have warned Iran that such behaviour will not be tolerated, as it puts in question the Iranian commitment to comply with the rules and regulations of its sanction regime, President Hassan Rouhani responded with a very assertive statement suggesting that "the Iranian nation has decided to be powerful, and that these missiles are for peace and defence purposes, and the outside world should understand that whenever Iran has a need to test a missile technically, this country will do so and will not wait for anyone's permission". As expected, such behavior puts into question the very rationale of treating Teheran as a rational regional player who is committed to maintaining regional peace and stability and may inadvertently put the US decision-makers into various power-balancing strategies that will only add fuel to the fire. However, we need to emphasize that employing such a strong rhetoric is very unusual for President Rouhani who is known to be a moderate leader. It could be interpreted that this aggressiveness in his tone was expressed only in serving domestic purposes as it was uttered in the heat of the presidential campaign against hardliner Ebrahim Raisi who would have accused him of weakness. Therefore, one should not read too much into it. This being said, we need to emphasize that by using such rhetoric President Rouhani has inadvertently taken part in a hazardous game that has severely undermined his reputation as a sensible global player who is committed to fulfilling his country's 2015 obligations. The US policymaker who observes such anomalies in Iranian internal policy will have difficulty drawing a comprehensive picture of regional challenges and hurdles. Such a hesitation combined with an unnecessary confusion as to whether to treat Tehran as a threat or as a potential partner can result in choosing the first option. After all, the president who decided to believe that he can make America great again will not be willing to trust the US's enemies, either real or imaginary. There is probably not a pro-Iranian lobby in the White House these days, and both the pro-Saudi and the pro-Israeli groups of interests that surround President Trump are getting much stronger, just because their interests seem to coincide on many levels and in their common interest is to limit Iranian strategic options as far as they can.

That coincides with the fact that Donald Trump has found himself in a very positive situation where he can kill two birds with one stone, Saudi Arabia, and Israel, at the expense of Iran.

Conclusion

The current political establishment of the Islamic Republic of Iran has gone a long way to re-join the international community, and this country has gained a powerful economic incentive to maintain its efforts, in exchange for slowing down the development of its nuclear programme. The people who agreed to this deal are still in power in Iran as the Iranians have just re-elected Hassan Rouhani as their president on 19 May 2017 while Mohammad Javad Zarif, who championed this deal from the very beginning, still holds the post of Iranian foreign minister. Yet, the political situation in the US has changed dramatically since 2015 as Barack Obama, who proved to be a strong supporter of Iranian efforts to re-join the international community, has been replaced by Donald Trump, who is much more sceptical about the way the policymakers in Tehran have been behaving for the last two years. Thus far, we still don't know how the full-scale revision of US policy towards the Middle East will look like, but Trump's visit to Saudi Arabia and Israel has already given us specific indicators suggesting that the new occupant of the White House is not going to follow the in footsteps of his predecessor in respect to Iran. As we may expect for the president who once wrote *The Art of the Deal* (1987), global politics may turn into a simple calculation, and we may expect that he will not hesitate to sacrifice US relations with Tehran, if in return he will be able to improve diplomatic ties with Riyadh, Tel Aviv, and number of other Sunni countries; especially considering the fact that at the end, improving the US-Saudi relations, in particular additionally offers very quantifiable incentives. For these reasons, we need to realize that there is a delicate challenge ahead for Iranian authorities, as they need to find a way to persuade the Trump Administration to give the Iranian authorities and the nuclear deal of 2015 another chance. Otherwise, the future of this volatile region will be even more uncertain.

References

Reports & Polemics

Goldman-Eps Miriam, From 'ripping up' Iran deal to banning Muslims—what is Donald Trump's plan for the Middle East? The President-elect has contradicted himself often on policy towards Iran and the Arab world. (November 17, 2016 14:16 GMT) Available at: <http://www.ibtimes.co.uk/ripping-iran-deal-banning-muslims-what-donald-trumps-plan-middle-east-1592066/>[Accessed on 22.05.2017, at 11:23].

Fisher Max, How the Iranian-Saudi Proxy Struggle Tore Apart the Middle East, (NOV. 19, 2016) Available at: <https://www.nytimes.com/2016/11/20/world/middleeast/iran-saudi-proxy-war.html?_r=0/> [Accessed on 22.05.2017, at 22:37].

Melvin Don, 6 lesser-known facts about Iran's Foreign Minister Javad Zarif, Updated 1148 GMT (1948 HKT) (April 3, 2015) Available at: <http://edition.cnn.com/2015/04/03/middleeast/irans-foreign-minister-six-things-to-know/index.html/> [Accessed on 24.05.2017, at 18:05].

Morello Carol, DeYoung Karen, the Historic deal reached with Iran to limit nuclear program, Available at://<https://www.washingtonpost.com/world/historic-nuclear-deal-with-iran-expected-to-be-announced/2015/07/14/5f8dddb2-29ea-11e5-a5ea-cf74396e59ec_story.html/> [Accessed on 24.05.2017, at 18:05] (July 14, 2015).

Peikar Farhad, Afghanistan tries to strike a balance in escalating Iran-Saudi rivalry (22 April 2015), Available at: <https://www.theguardian.com/world/iran-blog/2015/apr/21/afghanistan-iran-saudi-arabia-yemen-conflict/> [Accessed on 27.05.2017, at 23:05].

President Obama's remarks on the impact of U.S. leadership in Iran. The Iran Deal blocks the four pathways to a nuclear weapon. Available at: <https://obamawhitehouse.archives.gov/issues/foreign-policy/iran-deal/> [Accessed on 26.05.2017, at 22:05].

Donald Trump's reset on Islam. The American president keeps quiet about human rights in the Muslim world, Middle East, and Africa, May 21st, 2017 | RIYADH, Available at: <http://www.economist.com/news/middle-east-and-africa/21722418-american-president-keeps-quiet-about-human-rights-muslim-world-donald?fsrc=scn/tw/te/bl/ed//> [Accessed on 25.05.2017, at 13:05].

Ibrahim Arwa, The Middle East, and Donald Trump: What he thinks about Israel, Iran and Syria, Available at: <http://www.middleeasteye.net/news/trump-lays-out-us-plans-middle-east-1640420644/> [Accessed on 25.05.2017, at 16:05].

M.S. Everything you want to know about the Iranian nuclear deal, Available at: <http://www.economist.com/blogs/economist-explains/2015/04/economist-explains-3/> [Accessed on 25.05.2017, at 14:05].

Seerat Rustam Ali, Iran and Saudi Arabia in Afghanistan, January 14, 2016, Available at: <http://thediplomat.com/2016/01/iran-and-saudi-arabia-in-afghanistan/> [Accessed on 27.05.2017, at 22:50].

Stephen Chris, War in Libya—the Guardian briefing, (Friday 29 August 2014 16.47 BST) Available at: <https://www.theguardian.com/world/2014/aug/29/-sp-briefing-war-in-libya/> [Accessed on 28.05.2017, at 22:09].

Tabatabai Ariane M., Saudi Arabia and Iran Face Off in Afghanistan, The Threat of a Proxy War; (October 5, 2016). Available at: <https://www.foreignaffairs.com/articles/afghanistan/2016-10-05/saudi-arabia-and-iran-face-afghanistan/> [Accessed on 25.05.2017, at 14:05].

Toone Jordan, Unintended Consequences: Gaddafi's Death and the Arab Spring, JURIST - Dateline, Oct. 29, 2011, Available at: <http://jurist.org/dateline/2011/10/jordan-toone-gaddafi-death.php/> [Accessed on 28.05.2017, at 21:27].

Policies

Joint Comprehensive Plan of Action implementation and verification and monitoring in the Islamic Republic of Iran in light of United Nations Security Council Resolution 2231 (2015), Resolution adopted by the Board of Governors on 15 December 2015, Available at: <https://www.iaea.org/sites/default/files/gov-2015-72.pdf/>[Accessed on 25.05.2017, at 18:05].

Statements

Joint Statement by EU High Representative Federica Mogherini and Iranian Foreign Minister Javad Zarif Switzerland (Bruxelles, 02/04/2015), Available at: <http://collections.internetmemory.org/haeu/content/20160313172652/http://eeas.europa.eu/statements-eeas/2015/150402_03_en.htm/> [Accessed on 25.05.2017, at 22:05].

Commentaries

Brown Hayes, This Is Why Saudi Arabia And Iran Totally Hate Each Other, (January 5, 2016, at 7:13 p.m.), Available at: <https://www.buzzfeed.com/hayesbrown/an-enumerated-list-of-why-the-saudi-iranian-split-is-hella-n?utm_term=.daKz9B50M#.qqwXdm1gy/> [Accessed on 27.05.2017, at 22:13].

President Trump Visits Israel Amid Tight Security Available at: <http://news.tamilfocus.com/usa/02/105647/> [Accessed on 24.05.2017, at 22:05].

Trump warns of Iranian nuclear threat on a visit to Israel, Available at: <http://www.bbc.com/news/world-middle-east-39973197/> [Accessed on 26.05.2017, at 07:21].

Iran will never get nuclear arms – Trump, Available at: <http://www.bbc.com/news/world/middle_east/> [Accessed on 24.05.2017, at 22:05].

Interviews

Laub Zachary, The Middle East After the Iran Nuclear Deal (Expert Roundup) The nuclear deal inked by Iran and major powers has implications not just for proliferation, but Middle Eastern security as well. Five experts weigh in on what the deal means for regional powers and conflicts, (September 03, 2015).

Interview with: Chuck Freilich, Senior Fellow at Harvard Kennedy School's Belfer Center and Former Israeli Deputy National Security Advisor.

Farideh Farhi, Affiliate Graduate Faculty, the University of Hawai'i at Manoa, on The Middle East After the Iran Nuclear Deal.

Hussein Ibish, Senior Resident Scholar, Arab Gulf States Institute in Washington.

Matthew Levitt, Former-Wexler Fellow, and Director of the Stein Program on Counterterrorism and Intelligence, Washington Institute for Near East Policy.

Sarah Birke, Staff Middle East Correspondent, The Economist. Available at: <https://www.cfr.org/expert-roundup/middle-east-after-iran-nuclear-deal/> [Accessed on 25.05.2017, at 22:33].

Hristiyana Stoyanova

The United Kingdom on the Verge of a "Constitutional Crisis":
Between the Possibility of a Second Referendum on the Membership in the European Union and a Potential Second Vote on Scottish Independence

Abstract: This piece of research was conducted in November 2016 and later complemented in March 2017. All the information was relevant at the time of writing, but the issue is continually evolving. The essay concentrates on the constitutional issues surrounding conducting a second EU referendum and a second Scottish referendum after the EU referendum results in June 2016. This study has availed itself of various journal articles, commentators' opinions and newspapers' articles, complemented with existing literature on constitutional law within the United Kingdom. The findings of the research show that the possibility to conduct a second EU vote would be undemocratic and unconstitutional regarding the current constitutional framework. Nevertheless, the paper questions the nature and methods of information and how educated voters were when making their decision. It addresses the shortcomings of each referendum, but it implies that they are political decisions, fulfilling political commitments which is take the imperative to decide on matters of constitutional change. On the other side, the research shows that the situation in Scotland is much more prone to change as the lack of particular and precise constitutional restrictions can be used by the Scottish government to act in Scotland's best interests, no matter the current constitutional arrangements. The essay also refers to how other nationalist blocs are breaking up Europe with desires for independence politics of more nationalist than EU character. Even though the research aims at showing the current constitutional scenario in the United Kingdom, the actual situation is seen as empowering other countries to seek the same outcome. The current situation is said to depend much more on the politics of the day, rather than on any written law. There are many obstacles before we can say that a second EU vote in the UK can be held, but there are less in the case of Scotland. In this scenario, it would be for the Scottish first minister and her government to try to use this momentum and pursue a different outcome for Scotland, simply because it is all about fulfilling political manifestos, rather than following a specific legal pattern.

Keywords: Scottish independence referendum, the United Kingdom European Union membership referendum, Brexit, Great Britain, Scotland, the European Union

Introduction

According to the uncodified nature of the United Kingdom's Constitution [the UK Constitution], the conducting of referendums is not a binding rule for approving constitutional reforms (Merrick 2016). It is obvious, however, that is becoming more and more common that significant constitutional questions with potential for major reforms are being referred to the people to decide. The two recent UK referendums held in the past two years are evidence that for some time now, the dynamics of British politics relies more or less on peoples' opinions on important constitutional questions in huge historical moments. After Britain voted to leave the European Union in June 2016, the uncertainty of Brexit and the strong "stay" call from Scotland led to discussions about holding a second referendum on future UK–EU relations and another independence referendum for Scotland. The assessment of these statements, within the constitutional framework of the United Kingdom, is the real core idea of this essay. Throughout the essay each critical issue which has been raised will be legally evaluated and critically assessed, having in mind that this academic work would not exhaust the matter, as it is currently subject to development.

The History of Referendums in the United Kingdom

The United Kingdom is a representative democracy. Parliamentary sovereignty, representative government and the rule of law are core principles of its constitution (Select Committee on the Constitution 2009). The parliament is the primary source of legislation, the main institution responsible for making the law of whatever kind and subject matter (Dicey, 1962, p. 39–40). During British political history, referendums have not predominantly been resorted to as a way of making political decisions. The political inconsistency in relation to their application is a reason to believe that there is no such thing as a history of referendums in the UK (Parliament Publications 2016). Those which bring about a fundamental constitutional change are even rarer (Institute for Government 2016)[1]. However, it has been widely accepted that only issues with constitutional significance deserve the right to be formulated into a question for a referendum. The referendum on EU membership and the one on Scottish independence in 2014, held within two years of each other, are regarded as being of such a significance (the repetition of them, however, depends on a lot of constitutional and political constraints, which will be examined here). These referendums also indicate that a new constitutional convention on referendums is emerging, a new political trend which places essential constitutional issues in the hands of the people to decide (Ruberto 2013). This new form of political development places the people as the third chamber of parliament.

The development of these precedents (Ruberto, 2013), poses the question about the need for relying on the people's vote for deciding constitutional questions[2], and on what basis the parliament decides that it cannot rely solely on parliamentary supremacy and resorts to a referendum instead. The Select Committee on the Constitution has proposed a number of situations of a significant constitutional nature which are regarded as "referendum-likely", or questions with a constitutional character which by all means have to be decided by the people. What is missing in their report is the explanation as to why the government and the parliament cannot act solely on these questions without resorting to a public vote.

One of the possible and most convincing answers relates to the politics of the day. In other words, when the political parties could not come to a consensus about a single political question [because of party division (Qvortrup, 2007, p. 5)] or because the government wants to exercise a political imperative in a specific direction or a mix of both, they decide that a referendum would be the most reasonable and democratic way out of the situation. The history of negotiations of referendums in the UK shows that the majority of these public votes have been initiated under the influence of party division, uncertainty about the government's own politics or political imperative (Qvortrup 2006, 61). These are the so-called facultative referendums, initiated by certain political parties (Setälä, 2006)[3].

---

[1] EEC Membership 1975, Electoral Reform 2011 and the EU Referendum 2016 are the three referendums with indisputable constitutional character, which concern the whole of the UK. Paun A, "The referendum and the British constitution: strange bedfellows?".
[2] Prof. Bogdanor calls them precedents, as they generate public expectation that major constitutional reforms remain the preserve of public sovereignty.
[3] The other ones are "constitutional".

The EU referendum is not an exception. The Conservatives have led their campaign, using the advantage of their party's popularity during their respective mandate. The intra-party division, which was leading to domestic political storms, was the initial step which convinced the Conservatives that a referendum was needed, even though they still did not have a definite idea of what the constitutional consequences might be after it (Roberts, 2016). The agreement for this referendum was achieved, and it was perfectly designed and well negotiated, but once the results came out, the political circumstances became muddy and uncertain. The outcome clearly indicated an underwhelming support for the "Leave" campaign against the "Stay" vote (The Electoral Commission 2016)[4]. The "strong, unequivocal vote" of Scotland and Northern Ireland to remain is the other issue, which brings pressure on policy-makers, threatening the integrity of the Union (BBC News 24th June 2016)[5]. Clearly, the political situation in the UK right now has not been thought through as far as these two constituencies are concerned, and the after-Brexit situation is the core reason. Regarded as the constitutional case of the century, the EU referendum is bringing a new constitutional reform for the UK, but the on-going debates about what will happen and whether it is fair for all of the UK's devolved parts is slowing politicians from moving forward and realizing a Brexit (Eeckhout, 2016). This is why calls for respective second referendums are put on the table for discussions.

Scotland's right to self-determination is one of the leading issues being raised in this regard after in 2014 they voted to remain in the United Kingdom, with the intention to remain in the European Union (The Electoral Commission 2014). Unequivocally they voted to remain again in the EU in this year's this year, this time directly asked, but there are a lot of political obstacles before Nicola Sturgeon if she wants to oppose the UK vote to leave the EU. Notwithstanding these obstacles, a draft bill on a second Scottish independence referendum has already been published, and if agreed on in Holyrood, the legal approval would be in the hands of Westminster (BBC News, 20th Oct 2016). This is the only democratic way for Scotland, no matter that the British constitution remains silent about the possibility to make this happen because the real cornerstones of today's politics depend more on the political environment and less on any statutory law.

---

[4] 51.9 % to 'Leave' against 48.1 % to 'Remain'.
[5] 62% to 'Remain' against 38% to 'Leave'.

The United Kingdom's constitution and the referendums
"The British Constitution has always been puzzling and always will be."
HM Queen Elizabeth II

The traditional nature of the constitution is that it is the highest legal document, composed of the laws and rules, which create, regulate and empower the institutions of the state and the relations between them (Political and Constitutional Reform Committee, 2015). The laws and rules it incorporates are superior and cannot be easily modified or amended by the institutions that it is intended to regulate (Ridley, 1988). The United Kingdom is a constitutional monarchy[6], but its constitution, unlike the constitutions of many other developed countries, does not appear in a single codified written document (Political and Constitutional Reform Committee, 2014). The British constitution is rather based on custom and usage, and it is quietly evolving (Bogdanor 2015). It adopts the form of constitutional conventions and understandings, and these understandings are not always understood (Low, 1904, p. 12). It follows then that the constitutional laws and rules have no special legal status, which means they cannot be superior to any other categories of law (Vick, 2002). The relative stability of the British institutions is one of the reasons for the absence of a legally-enforceable constitution.

Deriving from this, the sovereignty of the British parliament is an essential feature of the British constitution. The supremacy means that parliament can 'make and unmake any law whatever' (Ruberto, 2013). Thus, it has no restriction on the character of law it could create or abolish. The same applies as regards referendums. The politics of the day rather than any written law decides when, how and on what matters should a referendum be held. The decision to judge which issues are subject to public opinion rests in the hands of the Westminster parliament. It is the Westminster parliament who gave legal force to the EU referendum ((European Union Referendum Act 2015), but it is argued that it was more or less the initiative of the government (Conservative Party Manifesto, 2015). Notwithstanding the debate about which institution is responsible for initiating a referendum, what both the executive and the legislatures have decided is that its role should only be advisory and cannot legally bind the parliament to follow it in law (Setälä 2006)[7]. The final decision rests in the hands of Westminster, according to the recent

---

[6] This provisions, and subsequent provisions, are set out more fully in the blueprint written constitution published in the Committee's Second Report, Session 2014–15.
[7] Even though, it has been argued, that it is difficult for parliamentarians to vote against the result.

ruling of the High Court of London, overthrowing the prerogative power of the government[8]. Shortly before this ruling, the High Court of Belfast published its contrary decision in favor of the government and its prerogative power, which gives the ruling of the Supreme Court of the United Kingdom the authority of last resort to take the last word on the matter (Hunt, 2016).

As mentioned above, the result of the EU vote was not convincing and decisive, but the government accepted the results. 72% of the population decided to express their view on this public vote (The Electoral Commission 2016). The statistics are different when it comes to the knowledge and the commitment to political engagement of these people. This, arguably, is a drawback of every referendum and the focus shall not be here, but it is worth mentioning if we want to make an objective assessment of why a second referendum sounds like a reasonable option. Significantly fewer people (38%) feel knowledgeable about the EU, in contrast with their knowledge level about the UK Parliament (52%) (Audit of Political Engagement 2016), whilst only 46% of those surveyed claim to know "not very much" about the issue. This shows how the British population is hardly aware of the consequences of its vote. The education factor is an important aspect, but it is also a drawback of each referendum. It is almost impossible for the whole nation to be completely aware of the consequences of their decision and that is why the political parties are there to help and guide people in making their informed choice. The intra-party division of the United Kingdom government was the main reason for the referendum. The Labour Party's pro-European stance was the opposition which had the responsibility to give more details on the EU vote (Johnson, 2016). The popularity of the government of the day, however, is the one with the political advantage, as it gives a clear indication of what it advocates voters to do (Wratil, 2015). David Cameron's commitment to win the referendum and arguably the weak government opposition had their impacts on voters' choices. This impact was based on political commitments rather than on an objective evaluation of the circumstances.

The situation in Scotland is of a different nature. The Scottish people overwhelmingly voted to remain in the EU (The Electoral Commission, 2016). However, the question about EU membership is legally regarded as a foreign affair, and these is a matter reserved for Westminster. What this means is that the UK Parliament can legislate without seeking the consent of any of its devolved parliaments, in this case, Holyrood (Scotland Act 1998,

---

[8] The parliament has the right to trigger Art. 50, according to the recent case: R (Miller) v Secretary of State for Exiting the EU [2016] EWHC 2768.

Sch. 5). The decision to withdraw from the EU is taken as a vote of the whole UK, no matter that Scotland and Northern Ireland have expressed a different opinion. This poses the question of the democratic legitimacy of the referendum, but due to the lack of constitutional provision in this regard, the executive is free to choose what the best option for the union is. By rejecting the vote of Scotland, however, the government poses the risk of breaking up the union and dividing the UK electorate (Rampen 2016). In September 2014, David Cameron came out and recognized not only the overwhelming majority of people who wanted to stay in the UK but also those who wanted to leave the union. The result was giving more devolved powers to Holyrood (Scotland Act 2016). What Theresa May has done after the EU vote is rather undermining the "remain" call and thus undermining the vote of almost half of the population. Sturgeon's determination to act in Scotland's best interests (SNP Manifesto 2016) is evident, even if this, by some commentators, is said to be the latest blow to the devolution settlement (Harris 2016).

The democratic nature of a second referendum
"Everything which is not forbidden is allowed."
(Constitutional principle of English law)

To critically evaluate the democratic nature of a second referendum, it is essential to identify the key issues arising out of the EU referendum, which gave rise to the claims for a second vote.

The possibility to re-run a second referendum on EU membership is a contested concept and said to be an affront to democracy (Wagner, 2016). The European Union Referendum Act 2015 was the legislation which legalized and gave force to this referendum. During the negotiations, it was decided that it would not include a provision requiring a definite and overwhelming result in order for the referendum to be effective (Cockburn, 2016). Unlike most democratic countries, the UK did not introduce special requirements to secure a broader commitment on a referendum with substantial constitutional significance (Rose, 2015). Similarly, there was not a legally established threshold arrangement in the EU referendum (Ekins 2016). This and the rules governing the public vote in June urged a lot of people to sign a petition in order to hold a second EU vote, the legality of which was debated in parliament (UK Government and Parliament Petitions 2016). The petitioners were insisting on a second vote where the rules would be clarified, a threshold included and a decision only effective if a certain percent difference of the result is achieved. In theory, this may sound profound, but let us consider a few issues which this second referendum may bring.

If a considerable amount of people decide not to vote (if they are against the proposal in the referendum's question), because they know that the referendum would not become valid if the necessary turnout is not reached, then the point of having a referendum becomes meaningless (Select Committee on the Constitution 2009, 43). On the other hand, not including thresholds or a decisive difference in the result of the vote may lead to taking constitutional decisions with no overwhelming support of the electorate (as appears to be the current scenario). On what basis can legitimacy of the result be conferred – should the proposal win the support of the majority of voters, and should this group be the whole of those eligible to vote, or merely those who actually voted (Seyd 1998, p. 194)?

According to the parliament, the question of including thresholds is taken on a case-by-case basis (Select Committee on the Constitution 2009, 106). In other words, some questions require a threshold, some do not, and the parliament decides which—or once more, the political imperative takes precedence over the legal one due to the absence of a written constitution. It could be said that it was this very parliament that negotiated the terms of the EU referendum in this way, leaving people to believe that decisions for constitutional reforms can be made by a 3% difference in the vote, not overwhelming support[9], and a divided nation. A second referendum on the membership of the EU is inadmissible (Stewart and Rankin, 2016) in respect of the democratic nature of the first one, even though it would not be something new (Atikcan, 2015). What seems to be the best possible and plausible option in these circumstances is a second vote on the details of Brexit (BBC News, 28th June 2016). The only legitimate and democratic way out of the constitutional crises is to let people decide what deal for Brexit they want, but this only would happen if the government of the day makes a clear statement on its negotiating strategies and lets people make another informed vote on how exactly they are to exit the EU (Tim Farron on second EU referendum over Brexit deal, BBC News, 19th Sept 2016).

The Scottish situation, however, is much better now than it was in September 2014. The anti-nationalists believe that if Scotland holds a second

---

[9] E.g. a decisive referendum result is one which is so overwhelming, that the point of asking becomes meaningless at the first place (UK AV Referendum 2011, 67.9% voted "No" against 32.1% "Yes").

independence referendum, it would start a "neverendum" campaign until the nationalists get the result they want (Qvortrup, 2013). This might be true in theory, but the political change of circumstances for Scotland after the EU referendum gives an advantage to Nicola Sturgeon, whose position had not been so politically strong before the EU vote. Nothing in the act governing the rules of the EU referendum includes clauses or covers a possible situation of overwhelming opposition by one or two of the UK constituencies[10]. Also, unlike the first Scottish independence referendum, there was no official report from Westminster before the vote in June about what the constitutional implications would be in a situation where the UK votes to leave the European Union (Select Committee on the Constitution 2013). Similarly, there was no official publication by the government on what would a "stay" vote means for Britain. But before the Scottish referendum, such reports were published (HM Government 2014). The belief is that the electorate has been misled by the Conservatives' Euroscepticism by not presenting the full constitutional consequences of this decision before the actual EU vote (Craig, 2016, p. 2). Instead, the UK parliament and government are post–facto intense talks about who has the right to scrutinize Brexit and have the final say in triggering Article 50 (legal withdrawal from the European Union) (European Union Committee, 2016). Talks of this nature do not try to resolve the current constitutional dilemma of the union but are more or less focused on the unpredictable future after Britain leaves the EU (Gill 2016)[11].

Another argument made supporting (to an extent) Scotland's right to hold a second vote on its independence is related to the principles laid down in the Sewel Convention, which holds that the UK Parliament will not normally legislate on devolved matters or on the extent of devolved powers without the consent of the devolved legislatures. Depending on its interpretation, the wording "will not normally legislate" is a contested one—to what extent is this situation "normal"? The competences of these devolved legislatures are circumscribed by EU law, which means that when leaving the EU these features would alter the devolved competence if legislative consent is not obtained (House of Commons Library Briefing Paper 2016). As mentioned earlier in this essay, foreign affairs are a matter reserved for Westminster, and even if we accept the fact that the Sewel Convention applies, it cannot prevent the UK Parliament legislating on whatever it wishes. It would only create

---

[10] Northern Ireland also voted to remain with a majority of 55.8% against 44.2% to leave, The Electoral Commission 2016.
[11] Statements as "start cooking, recipe to follow" are becoming more and more common.

a political obstacle, which would be enough for Scotland to stand behind its electorate—the question is whether Westminster wants to create this obstacle in these circumstances? It is widely regarded that the parliament is notoriously 'executive-dominated' (Russell, 2015), so the mere assumption would be that the government is dominating the political environment until "further notice". It is more about politics than it is about law. What we came to know for sure is that "nothing is certain except the uncertainty"[12] – the constitution is uncertain, so are the referendums. Only politics is leading in a certain direction.

The Social Dimension if a Second Scottish Vote Occurs

Talking about politics and its power we should also look beyond the UK political and legal framework and see what the social dimension of a second vote would be.

Nicola Sturgeon has already declared that she will ask Westminster for permission to hold a second Scottish independence referendum, even though Theresa May announced that "this is not the right time to do so" (BBC News 2017). When the Supreme Court held that parliament's consent is needed before triggering Article 50, it also held that there is no need to obtain consent from the devolved legislatures for initiating the exit process, even if they have voted for a different outcome. However, because the Scottish electorate has voted to remain in the EU, Sturgeon is more than determined to bring the Scottish electorate the desired outcome. According to her, Scotland deserves the right to be asked on what deal to accept when it still has an alternative. She vowed to have a referendum between the autumn of 2018 and the spring of the following year. May, on the other side, is also determined not to let this happen at least in the near future.

In case a second vote occurs, and Scotland decides to leave the United Kingdom and become an independent state, it will have to re-apply for membership in the European Union and wait on the queue. Autonomous regions like Catalonia in Spain have long been denied an opportunity to hold a legal and binding referendum to leave Spain. Therefore, an opposition to a second Scottish vote from other EU states is highly likely[13]. Another possible consideration is the type of currency Scotland would use. At the moment, it is

---

[12] Professor Sir David Edward, Scotland's options for Brexit, Open lecture, The University of Aberdeen, 13 Oct 2016.

[13] It should be noted, however, that Catalonia has been promised another referendum in September 2017 (BBC News 31st Dec 2016).

tied to the pound sterling, but the fiscal politics of Scotland are not strong enough to be left on its own, and therefore it will have to continue to use the pound sterling or to establish a different currency alliance. Many other considerations would be on the table for discussions in case Scotland decides to re-apply as a sovereign state. Therefore, future collaborations with the EU would only be admissible if Scotland becomes a fully independent and autonomous country, which would take years.

To reflect upon the social dimension of a second Scottish vote, we should also see how other countries come under the spotlight of a similar scenario. An excellent point to start is to make a comparison with the situation in France and the just past presidential elections there. The French nationalist front (FN), led by Marine Le Pen had momentum before (what is now called) the most critical presidential elections since 2002 (Dale 2017). She and her party were judged to possibly win a majority as early as the first round at the elections. Even though she managed to make it to the runoff, she was beaten by the centrist candidate Emmanuel Macron. The chosen comparison is essential on a number of grounds.

Le Pen is leading a nationalist party, and like any party with a nationalist character, she is committed to more radical policy towards immigration, EU membership and what now has begun to be called "fear from Islamophobia". A nationalist party is a party directed more to domestic affairs, building-up a national economy and prosperity and less affected by external relations and unions on the international level. After the Brexit vote in June, she made her position very clear about her stance on the UK leaving the EU by congratulating the bravery of May and Boris Johnson. Madam "Frexit" (as she used to be called) promised an in-out referendum on French membership in the EU within the first six months of her presidency (if elected) (Chrisafis, 2016). This comparison is not fruitless. She wants to leave the Euro-zone, to cut the number of immigrants and to "make France great again" (there is no need to expand on this statement and reference is needless) (Vinocur, 2017). Her political commitments really resemble May's policies, even though May does not lead a nationalist bloc. Le Pen lost, but what remains is the nationalist political tendency that spreads around important EU states. Fortunately for the EU though, in France, they will be deeply frozen at least for the next few years.

In Bulgaria the "Union Patriots" became the third largest party in parliament in the recent assembly elections, replacing the Movement for Rights and Freedoms, representing the Turkish minority (The Guardian, 26th March 2017). This is another indication that nationalists around Europe are continually building up power. This also shows how prevailing the national interest becomes over the transparent and rather liberal European Union politics (with focus on the politics of immigration). Movements of national character are constantly emerging, and even though they emerge in different scenarios and circumstances, they are gaining power and popularity with time. This might create a tension in the EU establishment, and no one can predict how long movements of this nature will continue to see the EU as an obstacle to his or her respective nationalist strategies.

For the purposes of this essay, however, the UK and Scotland are in focus. The stand-off between Westminster and Holyrood will continue to be in the spotlight until the prime minister, and the first minister reach a consensus which would suit both the UK and Scotland. A second Scottish vote is currently under development, and no matter how democratic and fair this option for Scotland would be, it needs to receive Westminster's approval before any further steps are taken.

Conclusion

The framework of the United Kingdom's constitution is not legally constructed to regulate the rules and applications of referendums; it is a peremptory norm of the politics of the day, which has the imperative to do so. There are a lot of obstacles which make a second referendum on the EU membership problematic. The most important one is that the referendum in June has a legal and democratic character, there is nothing illegal in its implementation as it was negotiated, debated and passed by the parliament. Even though the electorate was not thoroughly educated on what it was voting for and lacked the necessary objective information from the government, the need to re-run it is simply democratically unacceptable. However, without a second EU vote on the terms of exiting the EU, political crises would become inevitable. The result of the EU referendum is clear, but it is only evident because the government and parliament have decided it to be so, and there is no constitution to oppose this. The Scottish vote is also evident. Moreover, even if the constitutional rules are silent about this, now Scotland deserves the right to express would be its opinion would be at a second independence referendum, and there is no constitution to oppose this either. It is in the hands of Westminster to allow this to happen, even though Theresa May might try to delay this as much as possible. Nationalist blocs within Europe are quietly evolving, and this only proves how uncertain the countries become towards the EU and its policy-making. Referendums become the tool to declare national sovereignty and independence, but this is also a tool which breaks up the EU establishment. A fair balance must be aimed at to keep both national interests and the EU alive.

This essay showed that in the UK the questions of the democratic nature of any referendum are hidden "behind the door" of the unwritten and not legally binding constitution of the United Kingdom which is used by the policy-makers to endorse their political imperatives. The referendums only publicly fulfill and legalize the current political manifestos. Moreover, if the United Kingdom's government intends to go forward with its plans, not give a "Brexit Deal" vote and disregard the Scottish electorate, the continuation of the union would be endangered.

Bibliography

Table of Legislation:

European Union Referendum Act 2015. Available at: <http://www.legislation.gov.uk/ukpga/2015/36/pdfs/ukpga_20150036_en.pdf> [Accessed 4th November 2016, at 21:13].

Scotland Act 1998, Schedule 5. Available at: <http://www.legislation.gov.uk/ukpga/1998/46/pdfs/ukpga_19980046_en.pdf>[Accessed on 10.11.2016, at. 22:55].

Scotland Act 2016. Available at: <http://www.legislation.gov.uk/ukpga/2016/11/pdfs/ukpga_20160011_en.pdf> [Accessed on 04.11. 2016, at 22:55].

Official Publications:

Audit of Political Engagement 13. 2016. Hansard Society. The 2016 Report Available at: <http://www.auditofpoliticalengagement.org/> [Accessed on 4th November 2016, at. 23:15].

Conservative Party Manifesto. 2015. Available at: <https://www.conservatives.com/manifesto/> [Accessed on 4th November 2016, at 20:55].

European Union Committee. 2016. "Scrutinising Brexit: the role of Parliament". House of Lords. 1st Report 2016–2017). Available at: <http://www.publications.parliament.uk/pa/ld201617/ldselect/ldeucom/33/33.pdf/> [Accessed on 4th November 2016].

HM Government. 2014. "What staying in the United Kingdom means for Scotland". 21 Aug 2014. Available at: <https://www.gov.uk/government/publications/what-staying-in-the-united-kingdom-means-for-scotland/what-staying-in-the-united-kingdom-means-for-scotland/> [Accessed 4th November 2016, at 21:55].

House of Commons Library Briefing Paper. 2016. "Brexit: some legal and constitutional issues and alternatives to EU membership". 28th July 2016. Available at: <http://researchbriefings.parliament.uk/ResearchBriefing/Summary/CBP-7214/> [Accessed on 4th November 2016, at 23:55].

Political and Constitutional Reform Committee. 2014. "A new Magna Carta?". House of Commons 463. 2nd Report 2014–2015. Available at: <https://www.publications.parliament.uk/pa/cm201415/cmselect/cmpolcon/463/463.pdf/> [Accessed on 4th November 2016, at 19:15].

Political and Constitutional Reform Committee. 2015. "The UK Constitution—A Summary, with options for reform". House of Commons. March 2015. Available at: <https://www.parliament.uk/documents/commons-committees/political-and-constitutional-reform/The-UK-Constitution.pdf/> [Accessed on 4th November 2016, at 12:22].

Referendums held in the UK. 2016. Parliament Publications. Available at: <http://www.parliament.uk/get-involved/elections/referendums-held-in-the-uk/> [Accessed on 4th November 2016, at 22:55].

Select Committee on the Constitution. 2010. "Government response to the report on Referendums in the United Kingdom". House of Lords 34. 4th Report, 2010–2011. Available at: <http://www.publications.parliament.uk/pa/ld201011/ldselect/ldconst/34/34.pdf/> [Accessed 4th November 2016, at 22:22].

Select Committee on the Constitution. 2009. "Referendums in the United Kingdom". House of Lords 99. 12th Report of Session 2009–10. Available at: <https://www.publications.parliament.uk/pa/ld200910/ldselect/ldconst/99/99.pdf/> [Accessed on 4th November 2016, at 22:55].

Select Committee on the Constitution. 2013. "Scottish independence: constitutional implications of the referendum". House of Lords 188. 8th Report 2013–2014.

SNP Manifesto. 2016. Available at: <http://www.snp.org/manifesto/> [Accessed 4th November 2016, at 15:30].

The Electoral Commission. 2016. EU Referendum Results. Available at: <http://www.electoralcommission.org.uk/find-information-by-subjec t/elections-and-referendums/past-elections-and-referendums/eu-refer endum/electorate-and-count-information/> [Accessed 4th November 2016, at. 22:55].

The Electoral Commission. 2014. Scottish Independence Referendum. (December 2014), Available at: <http://www.electoralcommission.or g.uk/data/assets/pdf.file/0010/179812/Scottish-independence-refere ndum-report.pdf/> [accessed 4th November 2016, at 22:55].

UK Government and Parliament Petitions. 2016. "EU Referendum Rules triggering a 2nd EU Referendum". Available at: <https://petition.parl iament.uk/petitions/131215/> [Accessed on 4th November 2016, at 20:55].

Books:
Dicey AV. 1962. Introduction to the study of the law of the constitution. London: Macmillan.
Low Sidney. 1904. The Governance of England. London: T Fisher Unwin.

Journal Articles:
Craig, Paul. 2016. "Brexit: A drama in Six Acts". European Law Review 447.

Qvortrup, Matt. 2007. "Decisions to hold referendums in the UK". The Politics of Participation. Manchester University Press.

Qvortrup, Matt. 2006. "Democracy by delegation: the decision to hold referendums in the UK", Representation. 42:1, p. 59–72. Accessed February 7, 2017. Doi: 10.1080/00344890600583792/> [Accessed on 4th November 2016].

Ridley, F F. 1988. "There is no British Constitution: A Dangerous case for the Emperor's Clothes". Parliamentary Affairs. 41:3, p. 340.

Russell, Meg; Gover, Daniel, and Wollter, Kristina. 2015. "Does the Executive Dominate the Westminster Legislative Process?: Six Reasons for Doubt". Parliamentary Affairs 69(2) p. 286–308. Available at: <https://doi.org/10.1093/pa/gsv016/> [Accessed on 4th November 2016].

Setälä, Maija. 2006. "National Referendums in European Democracies: Recent Developments". Representation. 42 (1) 13–23. Available at: <10.1080/00344890600583701/> [Accessed on 4th November 2016].

Seyd, Ben. 1998. "Regulating the referendum". Representation. 35 (4) 191–9.

Blogs:

Atikcan, Ece Ozlem. 2015. "Asking the public twice: why do voters change their minds in second referendums on EU treaties?". The London School of Economics and Political Science. Available at: <http://blogs.lse.ac.uk/europpblog/2015/10/19/asking-the-public-twice-why-do-voters-change-their-minds-in-second-referendums-on-eu-treaties/> [Accessed on 4th November 2016, at 20:55].

Bogdanor, Vernon. 2015. "The Crisis of the Constitution: The General Election and the future of the United Kingdom". The Constitutional Society. Available at: <http://www.consoc.org.uk/wpcontent/uploads/2015/02/COSJ2947_The-Crisis-of-the-Constitution_WEB_FINAL.pdf/> [Accessed on 4th November 2016 , at 18:55.

Paun, Akash. 2016. "The referendum and the British constitution: strange bedfellows?". Institute for Government. Available at: <http://www.instituteforgovernment.org.uk/blog/13867/the-referendum-and-the-british-constitution/> [Accessed on 4th November 2016, at 20:55].

Qvortrup, Matt. 2013. "The 'Neverendum'? A History of Referendums and Independence". Political Studies Association. Available at: <https://www.psa.ac.uk/politicalinsight/%E2%80%98neverendum%E2%80%99-history-referendums-and-independence/> [Accessed on 4th November 2016, at 20:55].

Wagner, Adam. 2016. "Would a second EU referendum be undemocratic?". UK Human Rights Blog. Available at: <https://ukhumanrightsblog.com/2016/06/28/would-a-second-eu-referendum-be-undemocratic/> [Accessed on 4th November 2016, at 20:55].

Wratil, Christopher. 2015. "What will drive the outcome of the UK's EU referendum?". Futurelab Europe. Available at: <http://www.futurelabeurope.eu/blog/what-will-drive-the-outcome-of-the-uks-eu-referendum/> [Accessed on 4th November 2016].

Newspapers' URL's:

Borisov's pro-EU party beats Socialists in Bulgaria's snap election. The Guardian. 26th March 2017. Available at: <https://www.theguardian.com/world/2017/mar/26/borisovs-pro-eu-party-beats-socialists-in-bulgarias-snap-election/> [Accessed on 27th March 2017, at 20:55].

Catalonia leader vows 2017 referendum on Spain independence. BBC News. 31st Dec 2016. Available at: <http://www.bbc.co.uk/news/world-europe-38477348/> [Accessed on 27th March 2017, at 16:23].

Chrisafis, Angelique. 2016. "European far-right hails Brexit vote". 24th June 2016. Available at: <https://www.theguardian.com/world/2016/jun/24/european-far-right-hails-britains-brexit-vote-marine-le-pen/> [Accessed on 23rd March 2017, at 17:55].

Cockburn, Harry. 2016. "Brexit: Government rejects second EU referendum petition signed by 4.1 million". The Independent. 9th July 2016. Available at: <http://www.independent.co.uk/news/uk/politics/brexit-government-rejects-eu-referendum-petition-latest-a7128306.html/> [Accessed on 4th November 2016, at 14:55].

Dale, Craig. 2017. "But...What if she doesn't win? UBS' Gordon on the risks of Marine Le Pen losing the French election". CNBC.com 22.03.2017. Available at: <http://www.cnbc.com/2017/03/22/french-election-marine-le-pen-loss-could-come-with-risk.html/> [Accessed on 23rd March 2017, at 11:55].

EU referendum: Scotland backs Remain as UK votes Leave. BBC News. 24th June 2016. Available at: <http://www.bbc.co.uk/news/uk-scotland-scotland-politics-36599102/> [Accessed on 4th November 2016, at. 10:55].

Harris, Tom. 2016. "Our constitution is clear: Nicola Sturgeon has absolutely no right to veto Brexit". The Telegraph. 24th October 2016. Available at: <http://www.telegraph.co.uk/news/2016/10/24/our-constitution-is-clear-nicola-sturgeon-has-absolutely-no-righ/> [Accessed on 4th November 2016, at. 20:00].

Hunt, Joanne. 2016. "A ruling in Belfast makes the high court's Brexit decision even more complicated than you think". Independent. 7th Nov 2016. Available at: <http://www.independent.co.uk/news/uk/politics/brexit-ruling-legal-challenge-article-50-northern-ireland-a7400611.html?cmpid=facebook-post /> [Accessed on 7th Nov 2016, at. 13:00].

Merrick, Rob. 2016. "UK Government agreed referendum could not be legally binding". The Independent. UK 17th October 2016. Available at: <http://www.independent.co.uk/news/uk/politics/brexit-senior-conservative-mps-seize-on-a-forgotten-government-pledge-to-letparliament-decide-the-a7366316.html/> [Accessed on 4th November 2016, at. 16:30].

New Scottish independence bill published. BBC News. 20th October 2016. Available at: <http://www.bbc.co.uk/news/uk-scotland-scotland-politics-37708545/> [Accessed on 4th November 2016].

Rampen, Julia. 2016. "Ignoring devolved nations on Brexit "risks breaking up the UK" New Statesman. 24th October 2016. Available at: <http://www.newstatesman.com/politics/staggers/2016/10/ignoring-devolved-nations-brexit-risks-breaking-uk/> [Accessed on 4th November 2016, at 15:00].

Reality Check: Could there be a second referendum?. BBC News. 28th June 2016. Available at: <http://www.bbc.co.uk/news/uk-politics-eu-referendum-36652273/> [Accessed on 4th November 2016, at 20:55].

Roberts, Richard. 2016. "The lesson of history is that Conservative divisions over Europe will get worse, not better, after the referendum". New Statesman. 22nd March 2016. Available at: <http://www.newstatesman.com/politics/staggers/2016/03/lesson-history-conservative-divisions-over-europe-will-get-worse-not/> [Accessed on 4th November 2016].

Scottish independence: Nicola Sturgeon to seek the second referendum. BBC News. 13th March 2017. Available at: <http://www.bbc.co.uk/news/uk-scotland-scotland-politics-39255181/> [Accessed on 27th March 2017].

Stewart, Heather and Rankin Jennifer. 2016. "Theresa May to tell EU's other leaders 'there will be no second referendum'". The Guardian. 20th October 2016. Available at: <https://www.theguardian.com/politics/2016/oct/20/theresa-may-to-tell-eus-other-leaders-there-will-be-no-second-referendum/> [Accessed on 4th November 2016, at 10:10].

Tim Farron on second EU referendum over Brexit deal. BBC News. 19th September 2016. Available at: <http://www.bbc.co.uk/news/uk-politics-37408662 /> [Accessed on 4th November 2016, at 19:10].

Miscellaneous URL's:

Eeckhout, Piet. 2016. "The UK Decision to Withdraw from the EU: Parliament or Government?". UK Constitutional Law Association. 15th October 2016. Available at: <https://ukconstitutionallaw.org/2016/10/15/piet-eeckhout-the-uk-decision-to-withdraw-from-the-eu-parliament-or-government/> [Accessed on 4th November 2016, at 10:10].

Ekins, Richard. 2016. "The Legitimacy of the Brexit Referendum". UK Constitutional Law Association. 29th June 2016. Available at: <https://ukconstitutionallaw.org/2016/06/29/richard-ekins-the-legitimacy-of-the-brexit-referendum/> [Accessed on 4th November 2016].

Gill, Martha. 2016. "Brexit Department 'Staffed by People of Very Low IQ' Says Yanis Varoufakis". HuffPost Politics UK. 21st Oct 2016. Available at: <http://www.huffingtonpost.co.uk/entry/brexit-department-staffed-by-people-of-very-low-iq_uk_58094e2ae4b056572d8-1ff81?ir=UK+Politics&utm_hp_ref=uk-politics/> [Accessed on 4th November 2016, at 10:10].

Johnson, Richard. 2016. "The electoral implications of Labour's EU referendum stance". The UK in a Changing Europe. 25th January 2016. Available at: <http://ukandeu.ac.uk/the-electoral-implications-of-labours-eu-referendum-stance/> [Accessed on 4th November 2016, at 22:12].

Rose, Richard. 2016. "Neglected issues in the EU Referendum Bill". The UK in a Changing Europe. 12th October 2015. Available at: <http://ukandeu.ac.uk/neglected-issues-in-the-eu-referendum-bill/> [Accessed on 4th November 2016, at 07:15].

Ruberto, Gabriele. 2013. "When does the British Constitution require a Referendum?—V. Bogdanor's opinion on the place for the referendum in the UK". The Constitution Unit. 26th February 2013. Available at: <https://constitution-unit.com/2013/02/26/when-does-the-british-constitution-require-a-referendum-v-bogdanors-opinion-on-the-place-for-the-referendum-in-the-uk/> [Accessed on 4th November 2016, at 19:10].

Vick, Douglas. 2002. "The Human Rights Act and the British Constitution". Texas International Law Journal 37. Available at: <http://www.tilj.org/content/journal/37/num2/Vick329.pdf> [Accessed on 4th November 2016, at 23:00].

Open lecture:
Professor Sir David Edward. 2016. "Scotland's options for Brexit", The University of Aberdeen. 13 Oct 2016.

Book Reviews

Piotr Pietrzak on Charles P. Webel, (2004) "Terror, Terrorism, and the Human Condition", New York: Palgrave Macmillan

"Terror, Terrorism, and the Human Condition" accounts for a fascinating position in the literature on the subject, as its author brings to the reader's attention a vibrant application of case studies, quotations, cross-references, and various examples of seemingly random acts of contemporary terrorism on non-combatants including torture, threats, murders, assassinations, kidnappings, seizure of hostages, bombings, releases of poisons and radioactive materials, the 9/11 terrorist attacks, the Hiroshima and Nagasaki nuclear bombings, and confinement at concentration camps. In this respect, Charles P. Webel shows much determination in explaining a very murky relation between terror, terrorism and unvoiced psychological traumas encountered by selected individuals targeted by groups interested in using their collective sufferings to attain concrete political goals and objectives. Furthermore, this successful academic associated with Harvard and UC-Berkeley makes it clear that despite the fact that terrorism has accompanied human development for centuries, its real nature remains profoundly mysterious, transformative and uncategorized.

Despite the fact that an influential group of contemporary pundits see the words "terrorism" and "terrorist" as politically expedient labels that can be tagged to any contemporary or historical example of political violence, the author of this sizable volume refuses to yield to popular opinion and suggests that "one person's terrorist can be considered as another person's freedom fighter". Indeed, Webel in this respect shows a reluctance to surrender to the misconstrued political correctness or self-imposed censorship and chooses to make good use of these terms by applying them to his research in a relatively unconstrained manner. That indicates that this pundit is of the opinion that the problems related to contemporary terrorism are too severe to be casually dismissed, especially having in mind that these issues are inevitably about to turn into essential security dilemmas of the age of globalization. Webel is far from being delusional about the main constraints related to the elusiveness of this term and is very vocal about terrorism's pejorative connotations, and various far-fetched conceptualizations that lead to framing most acts of contemporary political violence as acts of terrorism. Another incentive to read this book is that it is relatively short in comparison with other similar works on the market. Admittedly, this was achieved without undermining the integrity of its primary content as its author has managed to convey it in six sizable parts: an opening paragraph, four subsequent chapters, and a very informative conclusion.

The first chapter is titled "Defining the Indefinable: What are, and are not 'Terror, Terrorism, and the Human Condition'" and introduces the reader to the conceptual representation and theoretical framework of the central issue in question and makes a very smooth transition into deliberations about one of the most deadly terrorist attacks of the 21st century, the events of 11 September 2001. To one's surprise, Webel is keen to subvert a traditional paradigm that puts the whole blame for these events on non-state actors, as from his perspective even such a severe attack as the 9/11 attacks did not occur in an existential or historical vacuum. As he explains, for these reasons, they simply cannot be framed into a narrow, one-dimensional picture of the contest between weaker non-state authors and stronger actors in the traditionally state-centric global environment (Webel, 2004, p. 5–15). Indeed, the best way to explain this method is that Webel's way of understanding terrorism is far from ordinary, as he sees it as a political construct of premeditated, usually politically motivated use, or threat of use, of violence, in order to induce a state of terror in its immediate victims, often in order to influence another, less reachable audience, such as a government (Webel, 2004, p. 9).

Subsequently, this scholar goes even further by separating the notion of terrorism into two equally dangerous categories "terrorism from above" (TFA) committed by nation-states and "terrorism from below" (TFB) inflicted by individuals and groups on nation-states. Furthermore, it has to be emphasized that in this respect, according to him, TFA and TFB reinforce each other, not only in the Middle East and beyond, but also across the historical timeline and diverse political spaces. That is why Webel believes that anyone who focuses solely on such acts of terrorism as the attacks on the World Trade Centre in 1993 or 2001 may be missing the forest for the trees. Besides, by drawing one's attention to these issues, Webel inadvertently has introduced us to his central assertion that suggests that in order to get a broader insight into the matters related to contemporary terrorism one has to look at it through the prism of the experiences of its victims, their psyche and the human condition in general, defined here as the sum of total earthly experiences of the species called human. In this respect, the author is very determined to underline the fact that all of the groups that he has managed to investigate suggest that the damage inflicted during war or a random terrorist attack can be genuinely comparable as they leave on their victims a combination of intense impinging and persistent experiences that can quickly evolve into irreversible psychological wounds or traumas that are deemed to continue to reappear years or even decades after the cessation of the conflict, hostilities or an actual terrorist attack (Webel, 2004, p. 5–51).

After this clarification, in the second chapter, titled "Depicting the Indescribable: A Brief History of Terrorism", Webel directs our attention to an entirely different matter by providing us with a brief story of the genesis of terrorism in the Middle East: This journey begins just before the days of the prophet Muhammad, continues through the centuries, and concludes by depicting such developments as the creation of Hamas and the rise of Al-Qaeda. This exercise seems to have two objectives: On the one hand, it looks at the notion of terrorism through the prism of the multi-ethnic, multi-religious, and multi-linguistic features of this volatile region to uncover various clashing political issues, cultural differences and a multitude of historical and structural predispositions to terrorism and political violence in the local environment. Subsequently, by bringing to one's attention various examples of unspeakable horrors of war, torture, confinement and other forms of psychological warfare the author is hoping to de-romanticize the very notion of terrorism. It is also worth emphasizing that even in this particular instance, Webel chooses to maintain a high standard of discourse, and his objectivity and does not put any blame on any specific group or religion for any historical or contemporary radicalisation. Furthermore, he is very vocal in bolstering his argument about not making allowances for either those responsible for TFA nor the guilty of TFB, since some states have been responsible for a thousand times more victims than all actions of modern terrorist organizations taken together (Webel, 2004, p. 45–78).

Interestingly, Webel underlines the fact that he doesn't necessarily have in mind only atrocities committed by Adolf Hitler's Third Reich or Joseph Stalin's Soviet Union (however severe they may have been) but also the crimes committed by the states that are very often proud of their demo-liberal political systems and consider themselves leading examples of moral conduct in global affairs, such as the United Kingdom, France, Russia, the US, and Israel. As Webel argues, over the last few centuries, in order to attain their very often morally questionable political goals and objectives, the leaders of the above mentioned states have committed a number of indecent acts (various forms of political violence, exploitation, mass hunger, diseases, and ostensibly targeted civilians to further their political objectives) which had a massive negative impact on large groups of people in the developing world. Still, according to this academic, despite both state terrorists and non-state terrorists claiming that their deeds can be explained by the causes, in practice it is only the leaders of nation-states that can count on the privilege of vindicating their acts just because their countries are legitimate members of the family of nations. This may look like a twisted logic, but it is actually reinforced by the rhetoric of political realism, by Augustine de Hippo's doctrine of just war, Nicollo Machiavelli's assertion that the end justifies the means and Hans Morgenthau's principle of national interest that asserts that the statesman should be allowed to do virtually anything in order to protect the territorial integrity of his country (Webel, 2004, p. 43–80).

This finding brings the author of this publication to the third chapter of the book titled "Articulating the Ineffable". In "The voices of the Terrified", the author offers the reader an opportunity to try on the shoes of those who have experienced a terrorist attack. Some of them lost their relatives, and others experienced the personal tragedy of concentration camps, war, were kidnapped, were in planes that were hijacked, or were subjected to bombings or rocket attacks. In this respect, Webel clearly accentuates that to those people acts of terrorism definitely do not look like justifiable ways of achieving one's political goals and objectives, as despite the fact that most of their bodies were relatively unscratched, their minds and collective memories have been permanently inflicted with flashbacks, recollections, maladies, nightmares and panic attacks that relate to these traumatic events. Some of these people were deemed to have developed either Posttraumatic Stress Disorder (PTSD) or survivor's guilt; others will have to endure psychological therapy for their problems probably the rest of their lives (Webel, 2004, p. 45–80).

Subsequently, the following chapter attempts to look for some common denominator that could allow the victims of the terrorist attacks to be miraculously cured. In this respect Webel investigates his study group through the perspective of an individual victim's temperament, personality, character structure, gender, ethnicity, injuries, type, length and source of terror experience, and beliefs; but he is unable to elaborate practical responses to above mentioned shocking experiences. The reason has to do with the fact that it is increasingly difficult to come up with a compelling antidote to this problem, especially when one takes into consideration that the experience of political terror is profoundly sensory and often auditory, with potentially lethal assaults on one's being. What's more, this accomplished storyteller maintains that terror and terrorism are on the one hand very natural, and on the other unnatural to our human condition; its existence somehow constitutes a precondition but also presents a hurdle to our human existence in this world, and this leads him to an exciting conclusion suggesting that the above mentioned dilemmas automatically force upon humanity Sartre's vision of too-real death and disintegration, as well as the Heidegger's notion of inauthentic being-in-the-world (Webel, 2004, p. 81–110).

Finally, after discussing a wide range of fascinating matters related to political violence and terrorism, Webel refers us to Marcus Tullius Cicero's highly rhetorical question, and asks us: what can be done against force, without force? What can be done to break this vicious circle of violence that we are inadvertently left to witness on a daily basis? What is even more puzzling is that this distinctive academic leaves us with no answers to this riddle and expects us to give it proper thought (Webel, 2004, p. 106). That is why I would like to strongly recommend this book to anyone who is not afraid of a challenge and that in the meantime loves addictive page-turners and those who search for a well written, properly balanced, and logical piece of relevant scholarly literature.

The only downside I felt to this publication is that it was published more than ten years ago (for which the author cannot be blamed) and has not been updated since with more contemporary matters related to the challenges associated with the growth of Islamic State, al-Nusra Front, Boko Haram, and other more modern terrorist organizations. Having said that, I still have no hesitation in recommending this work as a textbook for readers of politics, psychology, international relations and contemporary terrorism, due to the fact that on the one hand this piece of scholarly literature is timeless and on the other due to the fact that it has been uniquely designed to explain step by step the genesis of the essential processes that have led to the creation of the insecure world we live in.

Bibliography

Bigo D, Pierre Bourdieu and International Relations: Power of Practices, Practices of Power, International Political Sociology (2011): 5.

Brannan D., Esler P. And Strindberg A. (2001), Talking to "terrorists": towards an independent analytical framework for the study of violent substrate activism', Studies in Conflict and Terrorism, 24(1).

Dershowitz A., (2002), Why Terrorism Works: Understanding the Threat Responding to the Challenge, New York: Harvard.

Carr C., 2002, The Lessons of Terror: A History of Warfare Against Civilians: Why it has Always Failed and why it will fail again, London: Random House.

Chanchal K., (2012) Challenges of Global Terrorism—Strategies, Dimensions, and Response: In Search of a Perspective, International Affairs and Global Strategy www.iiste.org ISSN 2224-574X (Paper) ISSN 2224--8951 (Online) Vol 3.

Tim Dunne, Milja Kurki and Steve Smith (eds), International Relations Theories: Discipline and Diversity (2nd Edition) 2010, New York: Oxford University Press.

Føllesdal D., The Status of Rationality Assumptions in Interpretation and in the Explanation of Action, Dialectical (1982), 36 (4).

Fournier P., (2012) "Michel Foucault's Considerable Sway on International Relations Theory," Bridges: Conversations in Global Politics: Vol. 1: Is. 1, Article 3., Available at: <http://digitalcommons.mcmaster.ca/bridges/vol1/iss1/3/> [Accessed on 05.08.2012, at 20:00].

Gerring J., What Makes a Concept Good? A Criteria Framework for Understanding Concept Formation in the Social Sciences Author(s): John Gerring Reviewed, Source: Polity, Vol. 31, No. 3 (Spring, 1999).

Guittet E. P., 'European Political Identity and Democratic Solidarity After 9/11: The Spanish Case'. Alternatives vol. 29, Winter 2004.

Falkowski M., (2008) 'Chechnya and Russia: The significance of the Chechen problem for contemporary Russia', CES studies,

Fiala, A., (2002) Terrorism and the Philosophy of History: Liberalism, Realism, and the Supreme Emergency Exemption, Essays in Philosophy: Vol. 3: Iss. 3, Article 2.

Kagan R., The September 12 Paradigm. America, the World, and George W. Bush, Foreign Affairs, September/October 2008.

Lutz J. M., Lutz B. J. (2009), How Successful Is Terrorism? The Forum on Public Policy.

Innes M., (2004), Signal crimes and signal disorders: notes on deviance and communicative action, British Journal of Sociology (55) 3.

Paletz D. L., Schmidt A. P., (eds), Terrorism and the Media. Newbury Park: Sage, 1992,

Petraeus D. H., Amos J. F., Nagl J. A., (2007) Counterinsurgency Field Manual, London: Chicago University Press.

Rupert, M., (2003). 'Globalising Common Sense: A Marxian-Gramscian Revision of the Politics of Resistance'. Review of International Studies, 29: S1.

Nacos B., (2007), Mass-Mediated Terrorism: The Central Role of the Media in Terrorism and Counterterrorism, Lanham: Rowman and Littlefield Publishers.

Jacquemet M., (1996). Credibility in Court: Communicative practices in the Camorra Trials, Cambridge: Cambridge University Press.

Taylor M., Horgan J., (2000) The Future of Terrorism, London, and Portland: Frank Cass.

Wieviorka M., (2003) The Making of Terrorism, Chicago and London: The University of Chicago Press.

Sartori G., Comparing, and Miscomputing, Journal of Theoretical Politics July 1991 vol. 3 No. 3, Available at: <http://jtp.sagepub.com/content/3/3/243.abstract/> [Accessed 05/4/2012].

Webel Ch. P., (2004) Terror, Terrorism, and the Human Condition, New York: Palgrave Macmillan.

Piotr Pietrzak on Edward Luttwak on the 2016 Turkish Coup d'État Attempt: Insights and Recommendations
[Book Review: "Coup d'État: A Practical Handbook" (1968, 1978, 2016), Article Review: "Why Turkey's Coup d'État Failed. And why Recep Tayyip Erdoğan's craven excesses made it so inevitable". Foreign Policy Magazine, July 16, 2016]

Edward Luttwak is a military strategist, political scientist, historian, senior associate at the Centre for Strategic and International Studies in Washington, D.C., and in his capacity as an expert, he has also served as an adviser to presidents, prime ministers, and CEOs of various international enterprises, corporations and selective branches of the U.S. government and military establishment. His inner circle knows him as a Machiavelli of Maryland, and similar to his Florentine predecessor, Luttwak's professional skillset is in high demand by people in authority who seek his counsel on matters related to various power maintaining mechanisms, whilst in his capacity as an author (by the way, a very successful one), he is capable of providing the broader public with very compelling descriptions of how people in power manage to preserve it, even under extremely distressing domestic circumstances (Meaney, 2015). If only **Nicolae Ceausescu** from his native Romania had more passion for reading and had come across Luttwak's publication much earlier, he might have survived the coup d'etat organized by his fellow citizens, who overthrew him from power in 1989. Indeed, in his opus magnum called "**Coup d'État: A Practical Handbook**" (First Edition 1968, Second Edition 1978, the Latest Revised Edition 2016), this distinctive scholar makes his Italian predecessor very proud by showing precisely, step by step, how an unexpected turn of events can result in overthrowing a government or a leader while also providing his reader with various readily applicable countermeasures that could be used to prevent any attempts from succeeding (Luttwak, 1979).

This book has captured the attention of his fellow scholars, policymakers, as well as at least three generations of IR students due to the fact that in order to live up to the Machiavellian tradition, Luttwak goes an extra mile to offer his reader exact, straightforward and approachable explanations that revealed various previously unknown aspects of selected successful as well as less successful coups d'etat, that have been, subsequently, compared and modeled into easily approachable case studies, and his readers have just loved it. What has proven even more useful is the fact that this author has also managed to outline the detailed conditions necessary for a preferably swift and bloodless coup to succeed, and has achieved it by dissecting various events into carefully separated stages that begin with the planning of the coup, subsequent recruitment of co-conspirators, followed by the discussions on different available methods used by the organizers of such events, up to the way they go about destabilising the situation in any given environment and taking power. Indeed, Luttwak has also asserted the necessity of seizing key strategic locations in a given context, so-called vital hubs preferably in the capital city such as railway stations, bus depots, bridges, central commands, presidential palaces where local dignitaries reside, TV stations, and of course, explained the ways one can use to capture the people in power as well as other designated individuals who otherwise might stop such an initiative at a very early stage and that could put it in more serious jeopardy. For these reasons, one should not be surprised that this publication may appeal to people in power and those who wish to replace them (Luttwak, 1979 & 2016 B).

Indeed, one also should not be surprised if one sees this publication on the bookshelves of such contemporary political figures as **General Abdel Fattah el-Sisi**, who organized 2013 Egyptian coup d'état to remove Egyptian President **Mohamed Morsi** from power (Fontevecchia 2013; Videmsek 2014). The same applies to the collection of books of **General Mohamed Oufkir**, the ringleader of a failed plot to assassinate **Moroccan King Hassan II** on 16 August 1972 (Gregory 2013; Johnson 2016; Miller 2013), and **Gen. Danilo Lim** who failed to force Filipino President **Gloria Macapagal-Arroyo** from power in 2006; both of these leaders openly admitted their fascination with Luttwak's suggestions (Laurel 2006). Naturally, the true scope of this pundit's influence may not be revealed, because it is in the best interest of those who try to put his theory into practice to stay anonymous until they manage to put their political aspirations into practice. But, there is a huge probability that **Gen. Akın Öztürk**, **Gen. Adem Huduti** and **Adil Öksüz**, and other putschists who attempted a 2016 coup d'état against President Recap Tayyip Erdoğan had come up with the idea of seizing the bridge that spans the Bosporus in Istanbul on their own, but the very fact that it is situated in the most central location in the country suggests at least a casual familiarity with Luttwak's logic of adopting warfare to constantly changing the environment. Having said that one has to admit that the way they went about their business afterward clearly suggests that they were either not fully prepared to execute their plans in full, and something may have escaped their attention or just went "terribly" wrong. Possibly, their familiarity with the actual content of Luttwak's book also was very shaky or casual (Luttwak 2016 A, Luttwak 2016 B, Luttwak 2017).

Of course, I need to emphasise in this respect that I have never visited the leader of the Justice and Development Party's (the so-called AKP) private library, and have never gone through his books, but if I was about to speculate I would not be surprised if this man might have actually kept Luttwak's "**Coup d'État**" somewhere very handy on his bookshelf and could have used it, from time to time, to gain broader understanding of the political "terrain" he has been operating on. After all, similar coup attempts had happened in this country (depending on how one counts them) between four and six times in the last 50 years, so it would only be natural for any self-respecting leader to try to pre-empt the moves of his political opponents, and protect his future and his political party from the unpredictable movements of the Turkish Army. Undoubtedly, the way the memorable evening of 15 July 2016, unfolded, suggests that even if Erdoğan himself was incapable of an adequate reaction when it came to the defence of his political career, he had definitely surrounded himself with people who had been either very familiar with Luttwak's contribution or had a very similar background, and were ideally suited to do this job. Possibly, in this respect we can also bring to the fore the fact that for the last decade or so, the entire Turkish political establishment has been under a powerful influence of an architect of the Turkish "Zero Problems with Neighbours" policy, **Ahmet Davutoğlu**[1], who is one of the most influential international relations theorists of his generation, and by default must be very familiar with most of the work of his Romanian-American counterpart. He has also elaborated a number of theories on how to protect a political leader should similar circumstances

---

[1] **Prof. Ahmet Davutoğlu** – Former Prime Minister of Turkey (28.08.2014 – 24.05.2016) Minister of Foreign Affairs of Turkey (01.05.2009 – 29.08.2014) has had a massive influence on Turkish internal and external affairs for the last decade. His Zero-Problems with Neighbors Foreign Policy Geopolitics Initiative rests on the idea of rebuilding and maintaining very close relations with former territories of the Ottoman Empire. For these reasons, it is very often believed to be closely associated with yet another flagship idea of this scholar called Neo-Ottomanism that assumes that Turkey is destined to become more than just a regional power within Europe and the Middle East and is destined to exercise a far more influential role in world politics. Despite some of Prof. Davutoğlu geopolitical ideas, especially his government's handling of the European Union refugee deal and various terror attacks by ISIS and Kurdish groups having created a massive rift between him and the country's president, it is still believed that Davutoğlu's successors Mevlüt Çavuşoğlu and Binali Yıldırım remain under very strong influence of his foreign policy ideals.

unfold (Davutoğlu 1994; Davutoğlu 1998, p. 1–17; Davutoğlu 2008; Davutoğlu 2010; Emrullah 2010; Grigoriadis 2017; Sözen 2010, p. 103–123).

So without any further ado, let us explore Luttwak's take on the way Erdoğan has managed to turn the coup d'état against his rule to his favor. According to Luttwak there were mainly two underlining reasons behind the failure of this coup: The first one, less controversial, comes down to the poor organizational skills of the putschists themselves, who, in his opinion, have undermined their positions by not securing a stronger grip on the mobile forces operating in the local environment, in the first place. In this case, the author of this article refers to the individual paramilitary units of the Turkish police that work under direct orders from the central government and a fighter jet squadron that intervened in the plot on the side of the state that proved to be much more competitive and determined that the putschists expected. Possibly, they even assumed there would be no resistance, but in fact, it was them who ended up marching in a shame the following morning. Subsequently, the second most important reason, and by any standards, one of the most controversial ones that contributed massively to the ultimate failure of this attempt, was the fact that its organizers failed to capture or kill Erdoğan. In this respect, Luttwak suggests that when you have such a strong leader who can always count on his strong popular base and by virtue of it would feel secure enough to casually dismiss any demands of the putschists, killing him seems to be the only viable option to turn this enterprise into a success, as the author of these controversial statements suggests that one has to also take into account the fact that these two reasons alone are also correlated with the timing of the events, and should have been considered as the top two priorities of the military officers who wanted to organize such a coup. Subsequently, the failure to follow these steps results typically in a leader of any given country starting the mobilisation of his support base to defend his regime, and that was precisely what happened in Turkey on 15 July 2016, as Erdoğan had not left it to chance (Al Jazeera Report 2016; Bodkin & Millward & Ensor & Rothwell 2016; Luttwak 2016 B, Tuysuz & McLaughlin 2016).

Maybe, Luttwak did not suggest it explicitly, but the way he drafted his report indicates that in his opinion had the Turkish leader missed the chance to inform his conservative base of supporters about his well-being in the crucial hours that followed the initial outbreak of the putsch, the events that unfolded later that night might have had a much happier ending for those who have secretly hoped for a more democratic, more accountable and far more European Turkey, which is not possible under Erdoğan's government.

What's more the author also allows himself a very humoristic suggestion when he maintains that it is pretty much evident where Turkey is heading when we consider that Erdoğan's main support base consists of obsessive men with moustaches who are eager to do anything to please their beloved leader, even if it means going after armed soldiers with their bare hands. From the perspective of hindsight we already know that that was precisely what happened on that memorable night: as even before the loyal brigades of police, army and secret services had managed to arrive to "liberate" captured parts of the city, masses of Erdoğan supporters had already left the rebellious soldiers without much chance when they started to disarm them and remove them from public places, squares, and governmental buildings.

Although the Turkish Government later claimed that it was a spontaneous reaction of the people of Turkey that had opposed yet another tyrannical attempt by the Turkish Army to seize power in the country from a democratically elected government, from Luttwak's perspective, there were very few women or moderate Westward thinking men who chose to stay home praying for the military officers to succeed in their attempts. To Luttwak, the paradox of this situation was even strengthened in that the same man who addressed ordinary Turks to take to the streets to face military personnel to defend his "democratically elected" government, has been instrumental in undermining the democratic procedures in this important country in the first place. For these reasons, the best way one should look at this events is not yet another example of the army that has a long history of abusing of power during similar coups in the past, but through the perspective of the military that has tried to protect the country from a very dangerous man who takes pleasure in accumulating power only to please his political ambitions. The man who depends on the audience he addresses uses religion to achieve his political goals and aspirations, or he pictures himself as the carrier of a long tradition of Kemalism, secularism, pluralism and economic freedoms who worships the forefather of Turkish nationalism with passion. Meanwhile, he is capable of criticizing the forefather of the nation for being an alcoholic, but in the meantime, he appeals to the imagination of young, educated voters in Ankara and Istanbul by promising speeding up the process of integration with the European Union (Luttwak 2016 A).

Maybe future historians will not remember Erdoğan as a role model or a champion of democracy, but until at least the middle of 2016, various Middle Eastern pundits have been trying to present Turkey under his rule as a very compelling example of a merger between demo-liberal values that the state he has inherited from its forefather Kemal Ataturk and the country that respects the religious beliefs of its citizens. Yet, ever since power has started to be accumulated in the hands of one man, Erdoğan, the simple rule separating religion from the realm of politics has been increasingly contested. The unsuccessful coup d'état of 2016, has changed the political backdrop in Turkey because the man in power took his anger on the organizers of this putsch to the uncharted territories of politically motivated revenge.

In this respect, it has to be emphasised that to anyone with at least a basic familiarity with contemporary Turkish politics it did not come as a surprise that on the following morning Erdoğan would see this putsch as a golden opportunity and lock the people responsible for killing 294 people behind bars, to strengthen his grip on power; as at the end, the Turkish leader looks like either a skilful political animal at best, and a blatant hypocrite at worst, but no one in our wildest dreams might have imagined that the man was capable of turning into a dictator in the making: Turkey's Joseph Stalin is a pseudo-sultan with neo–Ottoman ambitions in his fiefdom. Indeed, according to a 2016–2017 Amnesty International report, not only was there no mercy for the people who were directly involved in the putsch, who were threatened with death penalties, but the repercussions started affecting those who might have never been involved but had no evidence of their innocence. Due to the Turkish government launching a massive crackdown that targeted tens of thousands of university professors, doctors, teachers, judges, journalists, former long-serving and obedient members of the Turkish administration, civil servants and political opponents of the ruling party started feeling the full anger of someone who has lost any contact with reality. The sad truth is that the liberal and pro–western members of Turkish society found themselves in a situation in which suspicion alone can constitute a crime punishable by various repressions, penalties, firings from jobs or even lengthy prison sentences (Amnesty International 2016–2017).

To sum up Luttwak's ad hoc report about the events that unfolded in July 2016 in Turkey, one has to emphasize that this story has been drafted in just a few hours, as it was published on the day after the coup d'état, yet, despite the limited time and still massive uncertainty and confusion that followed these events, this distinctive scholar managed to produce an excellent piece of commentary in which he forecasted the next steps of the Turkish leader with David Copperfield-like precision. Having said that we need to remember that he did not pull out any rabbits from his hat, but has rather explained to us with surgical precision what had just happened on 15 July 2016 and offered us a plausible explanation of what will happen in Turkey in the following weeks, months, and years. For these reasons, I would recommend his work to anyone who is seriously interested in politics, international relations and the politics of the Middle East. The only disappointment about this publication is the fact that he also prematurely accused Turkish preacher Fethullah Gülen and his movement of being behind these events without providing any tangible evidence that would build the case against them. However, Luttwak's ability to explain the essence of any coup d'état has proven very handy in getting to the bottom of the issue in question, and it is my belief that we will be seeing more of his analysis in the forthcoming years, all around the world, especially in Turkey, if its leader continues to oppress its people.

Further Reading

Davutoğlu, Ahmet (1993), Alternative Paradigms: The Impact of Islamic and Western Weltanschauungs on Political Theory: University Press of America.

Davutoğlu, Ahmet (1994), Civilizational Transformation and the Muslim World. Quill.

Davutoğlu, Ahmet (2001), Stratejik derinlik: Türkiye'nin uluslararası konumu. Küre Yayınları.

Luttwak, Edward N., Why Turkey's Coup d'État Failed. And why Recep Tayyip Erdoğan's craven excesses made it so inevitable. Foreign Policy Magazine, (2016 A). Available at: <http://foreignpolicy.com/20 16/07/16/why-turkeys-coup-detat-failed-Erdoğan//> [Accessed on 17.07.2017, at 11:00].

Luttwak, Edward N., Erdoğan's Purge Is a Sectarian War, The alliance between Erdoğan and Gulen came apart because it is impossible to reconcile their rival interpretations of Islam—and Islamism. Available at: <http://foreignpolicy.com/2016/08/03/Erdoğans-purge-is-a-sect arian-war-turkey-gulen/> [Accessed on 03.06.2017, at 19:33].

Luttwak, Edward N., Post-putsch Turkish democracy still vulnerable, August 4, 2016. Available at: <http://www.demdigest.org/tag/edward -luttwak/> [Accessed on 03.06.2017, at 19:33].

Luttwak, Edward N., (1979). Coup d'État: A Practical Handbook. Cambridge, MA: Harvard University Press.

Luttwak, Edward N., (2016 B) Coup d'Éta, A Practical Handbook, Revised Edition. Available at: <http://www.hup.harvard.edu/catalog.php?i sbn=9780674737266/> [Accessed on 03.06.2017, at 19:33].

References

Al Jazeera, Turkey's failed coup attempt: All you need to know, (30 Dec 2016). Available at: <http://www.aljazeera.com/news/2016/12/turkey-failed-coup-attempt-161217032345594.html/> [Accessed on 01.04.2017, at 01:33].

Amnesty International, Turkey 2016–2017. Available at: <https://www.amnesty.org/en/countries/europe-and-central-asia/turkey/report-turkey/> [Accessed on 01.03.2017, at 01:33].

BBC Report, Turkey's coup attempt: What you need to know. Available at: <http://www.bbc.com/news/world-europe-36816045/> [Accessed on 01.04.2017, at 01:33].

Henry Bodkin David Millward Josie Ensor James Rothwell, (2016) Turkey coup attempt: World leaders warn President Erdoğan not to use uprising as an excuse for crackdown as more than 6,000 arrested. Available at: <http://www.telegraph.co.uk/news/2016/07/17/turkey-coup-plot-president-Erdoğan-rounds-up-thousands-of-soldie/> [Accessed on 01.06.2017, at 01:33].

Davutoğlu, Ahmet. (1994a) Alternative Paradigms: The Impact of Islamic and Western Weltanschauungs on Political Theory. Lanham-New York-London: University Press of America.

Davutoğlu, Ahmet. (1994b) The Civilizational Transformation and the Muslim World. Kuala Lumpur: Quill.

Davutoğlu, Ahmet. (1998) 'The Clash of Interests: An Explanation of the World (Dis)Order'. Perceptions: Journal of International Affairs. II (December 1997–February 1998).

Davutoğlu, Ahmet. (2008) 'Turkey's New Foreign Policy Vision: An Assesment of 2007'. Insight Turkey. 10 (1).

Davutoğlu, Ahmet. (2010) 'Turkey's Zero-Problems Foreign Policy'. Foreign Policy. (20.05.2010). Available at: <http://foreignpolicy.com/2010/05/20/turkeys-zero-problems-foreign-policy/> [Accessed on 01.06.2017, at 01:33].

Emrullah, Uslu, Ahmet Davutoglu: The Man behind Turkey's Assertive Foreign Policy, Eurasia Daily Monitor Volume: 6 Issue: 57, Working Paper No 8/2010. Available at: <https://jamestown.org/program/ahmet-davutoglu-the-man-behind-turkeys-assertive-foreign-policy/> [Accessed on 04.06.2017, at 01:33].

Fontevecchia, Agustino, Coup D'Etat In Egypt: Military Removes President Morsi And Suspends The Constitution. Available at: <https://www.forbes.com/sites/afontevecchia/2013/07/03/revolution-in-egypt-military-removes-president-morsi-and-suspends-the-constitution/#74c6ea116202/> [Accessed on 01.06.2017, at 02:13].

Gözaydın, İştar, Doğuş University, Ahmet Davutoğlu: Role as an Islamic Scholar. Shaping Turkey's Foreign Policy. Available at: <http://www.eisa-net.org/be-bruga/eisa/files/events/warsaw2013/Ahmet%20Davutoglu.pdf/> [Accessed on 04.06.2017, at 01:33].

Gregory, Joseph R. (July 24, 1999). Hassan II of Morocco Dies at 70; A Monarch Oriented to the West. New York Times.

Grigoriadis, Ioannis N., The Davutoğlu Doctrine and Turkish Foreign Policy, Working Paper No 8/2010, Bilkent University/Hellenic Foundation for European and Foreign Policy (ELIAMEP). Available at: <http://www.eliamep.gr/wp-content/uploads/2010/05/Grigoriadis1.pdf/> [Accessed on 04.06.2017, at 01:33].

Meaney Thomas, The Machiavelli of Maryland, (2015). Available at: <https://www.theguardian.com/world/2015/dec/09/edward-luttwak-machiavelli-of-maryland/> [Accessed on 01.06.2017, at 01:33].

Miller, Susan Gilson (2013-04-15). A History of Modern Morocco. Cambridge University Press.

Loyal Troops Seize Airfield. Chicago Tribune. Reuters. 17 August 1972. Available at: <https://www.revolvy.com/main/index.php?s=1972%20Moroccan%20coup%20attempt&item_type=topic/> [Accessed on 04.06.2017, at 02:33].

Luttwak, Edward N., Why Turkey's Coup d'État Failed. And why Recep Tayyip Erdoğan's craven excesses made it so inevitable. Foreign Policy Magazine, (2016 A). Available at: <http://foreignpolicy.com/2016/07/16/why-turkeys-coup-detat-failed-Erdoğan/> [Accessed on 17.07.2017, at 11:00].

Johnson, Peter. "General Oufkir's last interview". The Spectator. Retrieved 25 November 2016.

Laurel, Herman T (February 22, 2006). "Small setback...". The Daily Tribune. Archived from the original on September 28, 2007. Retrieved August 10, 2007.

Sözen, Ahmet. (2010) 'The Paradigm Shift in Turkish Foreign Policy: Transition and Challenges'. Turkish Studies. 11 (1).

Suspected Turkey Coup Leader General Akin Öztürk Served as Military Attaché to Israel. Available at: <http://www.haaretz.com/middle-east-news/turkey/1.731349/> [Accessed on 04.06.2017, at 01:33].

The Davutoglu effect, All change for foreign policy. Available at: <http://www.economist.com/node/17276420/> [Accessed on 04.06.2017, at 01:33].

Tuysuz, Gul & McLaughlin, Eliott C., Failed coup in Turkey: What you need to know, (18.07.2016). Available at: <http://edition.cnn.com/2016/07/18/middleeast/turkey-failed-coup-explainer/> [Accessed on 04.06.2017, at 01:30].

Videmsek Bostjan, Egypt's Military Coup d'Etat. Available at: <http://revolve.media/egypts-military-coup-detat/> [Accessed on 04.06.2017, at 22:20].

Call for Papers

Submit your *Articles, Reports, Book Reviews, Analysis, Documents, and Polemics* to the next volume of **In Statu Nascendi—Journal of Political Philosophy and International Relations**. Authors are welcome to suggest manuscripts dealing with the themes relating to the mission of the journal, which may include, but are not confined to:

- International Relations Theory: various debates between the leading classical approaches and alternative paradigms; matters related to contemporary and political theory;
- Philosophy, both Continental and Analytical traditions, Western, Eastern, Islamic, Classic, and Modern Traditions,
- Political, economic, cultural, and geographic dimensions of the contemporary decision-making process;
- Various aspects of the global pursuit of power, geopolitics, and foreign policies of the leading political powers in the modern architecture of Eurasia: US foreign policy, Sino-Russian cooperation, Japan, and the European Union;
- Issues related to rising powers and new types of Eurasian cooperation, such as the Shanghai Cooperation Organization, ASEAN, and the Turkish-Islamic Union;
- Cross-border development, inter-regional migration, demographic trends, and West-East relations,
- Contemporary issues in Religious Studies, interfaith dialogue, and threats of religious and political radicalization; conflict resolution strategies and contemporary civil wars;

Submission Instructions

Please submit an article (comprising an abstract of max. 500 words, plus a minimum of 5 keywords) including the personal information of its author(s) with full name(s), institutional affiliation(s), and contact information to *irinstatunascendi@yahoo.com*

Papers will be accepted for publication only if they meet high scholarly standards of originality, significance, and rigor in advancing an understanding of area development and policy. Authors of accepted papers will be notified by e-mail after their paper has been reviewed.

Subscription

Please contact
ibidem Press
Leuschnerstr. 40
30457 Hannover
GERMANY

Tel.: 0049 511 / 2622200
Fax: 0049 511 / 2622201
info@ibidem-verlag.de

Enquires

For any other inquiry please e-mail us at
pietrzak@alumni.manchester.ac.uk

or visit our website at

http://www.instatunascendi.com

Biographic Notes

SOPHIE GRACE CHAPPELL is Professor of Philosophy at The Open University, UK. She was educated at Magdalen College, Oxford, and the Faculty of Divinity in Edinburgh. She has taught in universities including Oxford, Manchester, UBC, and UEA. She has been a Visiting Professor in Vancouver, Oslo, Reykjavik, St Andrews, Stirling, Adelaide, and Edinburgh. Since 2000 she has been Treasurer of the Mind Association, and Associate Editor and Reviews Editor of The Philosophical Quarterly. She has published over one hundred academic articles on ethics, moral psychology, epistemology, ancient philosophy, and philosophy of religion, and her books include Understanding Human Goods (Edinburgh 2003), Reading Plato's Theaetetus (Hackett 2005), Ethics and Experience (Acumen 2009), and Knowing What To Do (OUP 2014). She has edited collections of essays including Values and Virtues (OUP 2007), The Moral Problem of Demandingness (Palgrave 2011), and Intuition, Theory, and Anti-Theory in Ethics (OUP 2015). She has published poetry, including a translation of Aeschylus' Oresteia.
Website: http://www.open.ac.uk/people/tc2973
Email: sophie-grace.chappell@open.ac.uk

KOUMPAROUDIS EVANGELOS is a PhD Candidate in Medical Philosophy at Sofia University "St. Kliment Ohridiski". Formerly, he was a host of a top-rated radio show at clipartradio.gr (one of the best radio stations in Greece). Currently, Evangelos looks after a column on Bibliotheque.gr where he frequently publishes original essays and short stories (literature). Additionally, he writes dramas and black comedies for a theatre. Professionally Evangelos' interests lie in Metaphysics, Ontology, Logic, Ethics, Aesthetics, Political Philosophy, Political Economy, Dynamic Systems and Chaos Theory. Evangelos is also the author of KAI META? (Eng: And after?) that accounts for a sizable publication on metaphilosophy (It will be translated into English in due course).
ORCID: http://orcid.org/0000-0002-1068-4376
Email: vaggelis3@yahoo.gr

JOHN DE GEUS is a PhD Candidate in Philosophy at Sofia University "St. Kliment Ohridiski". De Geus holds a Master of Science in Business Administration from Erasmus University, Rotterdam School of Management (Netherlands), where he graduated cum laude with a specialization in Global

Business and Stakeholder Management. He has also studied various interdisciplinary topics in the areas of international relations and political philosophy as a Visiting PhD Candidate at Kobe University, Graduate School of International Cooperation Studies (Japan). De Geus' current interests include globalization issues, (global) corporate governance, exterritorialy, multistakeholder deliberation, transnationalism, corporate strategy and power relations.
LINKEDIN https://www.linkedin.com/in/johndegeus/
Email: johndegeus@ff.uni-sofia.bg

CHRISTINA KORKONTZELOU is an undergraduate student at the faculty of history and archaeology of the Aristotle University of Thessaloniki, department of history, a political activist and a poet. Christina is interested in political philosophy, sociology, philosophical anthropology, social psychology and gender studies.
ORCID: http://orcid.org/0000-0002-7801-0415
Email: xkorko@gmail.com

MARYIA LAPPO is a PhD candidate in Belarusian literature at Belarusian State University (Minsk). Maryia is interested in Belarusian literature, Contemporary Art, and Contemporary Philosophy. She was also awarded an Erasmus Scholarship from the Sofia University St. Kliment Ohridiski in 2016 where she worked on the topic "Aesthetic experience as epistemological and ontological problem" supervised by Prof. Aneta Karageorgieva. During her postgraduate studies, Maryia has participated in several scientific conferences, symposiums and workshops in Minsk (Belarus), Kiev (Ukraine), Vilnius (Lithuania), and Warsaw (Poland). In her free time, she writes book reviews and articles about films and plays.
ORCID: http://orcid.org/0000-0001-5039-7219
Email: masha.lappo@gmail.com

STAVROS PANAYIOTOU is a PhD Candidate at the Sofia University "St. Kliment Ohridiski", supervised by Prof. Dimitrova preparing a thesis entitled "Levinas and Kierkegaard on Subjectivity". He graduated from University of Cyprus obtaining a BA degree in History and Archaeology in the School of Philosophy, he has undertaken an MA in Byzantine Culture, History and Religion at Cardiff University and an MA in Philosophy from the Open University of London. He is a philologist who teaches Modern Standard Arabic Language and Philosophy in the educational center of the Ministry of Education and Culture in Cyprus. His research interests cover

themes on Metaphysics, ethics and Ontology of personhood and relationalizm in Levinas' work Totality and Infinity and Otherwise than Being. Stavros has participated in several scientific conferences and symposiums concerning History, Archaeology and Philosophy in Europe such as conferences in Italy, Greece, Germany, Republic of Ireland, Bulgaria and Georgia, publishing several papers in scientific journals and conference proceedings.
ORCID: http://orcid.org/0000-0002-5584-0272
E-mail: s.panagiotou@nup.ac.cy

PIOTR PIETRZAK is a Ph.D. Candidate at the Sofia University "St. Kliment Ohridiski" (Bulgaria). He holds a Master's Degree in International Politics & International Relations from the University of Manchester (United Kingdom), and Master Degree in Politics from the University of Warmia and Mazury (Poland). Piotr was also awarded an Erasmus Scholarship from the University of Cyprus in 2007. He specializes in the politics of the Middle East, the Islamic world, and focuses his attention on theory of international relations; geopolitics, conflict resolution strategies, and international law; and primarily matters related to the First and Second World Wars, and superpower competition during the Cold War. Piotr is also interested in conflicts in Cyprus, Chechnya, the Former Yugoslavia, Afghanistan, Iraq, Georgia, Libya, Syria, Mali, Yemen, and Ukraine.
ORCID: http://orcid.org/0000-0003-0464-1991
E-mail: pietrzak_IR@hotmail.com

IVAN SIMIĆ is a Ph.D.-Research Associate at the University of Calgary. He has finished PhD studies at University College London, SSEES. His research project was fully funded by SSEES Foundation Scholarship, while he also received the prestigious FBB Trust scholarship and numerous grants. Behind him, Ivan also has a research fellowship at Yale University, and significant teaching experiences from Goldsmiths, University of London and University College London. Ivan is particularly interested in cultural and gender history of Yugoslavia, Eastern Europe, and the Soviet Union. He explores the usage of gender in global historical research and theory. Ivan currently works at the University of Calgary as a Research Assistant.
Personal blog: http://ivan-simic.info/
Email: i.simic.12@ucl.ac.uk

HRISTIYANA STOYANOVA is a Masters student in Political Science with a concentration in European Politics and External Relations at the University of Amsterdam. She completed her bachelor's degree in MA (Hons)

Legal Studies and Politics at the University of Aberdeen, United Kingdom. She is also a Junior Political Analyst at In Statu Nascendi Journal of Political Philosophy and International Relations. Hristiyana's areas of expertise are European politics, EU-Middle East relations, EU state building and conflict resolution, EU security and counter-terrorism.
ORCID: http://orcid.org/0000-0003-0108-5555
Email: h.stoyanova.13@aberdeen.ac.uk

FRANCESCO TRUPIA is a Ph.D. Candidate at the Sofia University "St. Kliment Ohridiski" (Bulgaria); he is a Political Analyst at the "Alpha-Institute of Geopolitics and Intelligence". He holds a B.A. in Political Science and International Relations from the University of Catania (Italy), and an M.A. in Political Philosophy from the Sofia University St. Kliment Ohridiski (Bulgaria). His sphere of interest is related to the policy of multiculturalism and theories of minority rights over the public realms of the former Communist Eastern Bloc.
ORCID: http://orcid.org/0000-0002-8984-7886
E-mail: trupiaf@yahoo.it

KRZYSZTOF ŻĘGOTA, Ph.D. is an Assistant Professor at University of Warmia and Mazury in Olsztyn. He is a Member of Association of Political Science in cooperation with Institute of Political Science (2003 -2005), Chief Specialist at Warmia and Mazury Regional Development Agency in Olsztyn, and a Senior Political Analyst and Russia Expert at In Statu Nascendi Journal of Political Philosophy and International Relations. His areas of expertise are Geopolitics, Russian Foreign Policy, Kaliningrad Oblast, EU-Russia Relations and the Baltic Sea Basin.
Academia.edu: https://uwm-pl.academia.edu/KrzysztofŻęgota
E-mail: krzysztof.zegota@uwm.edu.pl

MATTHEW GILL is an M.A. student in Philosophy at Sofia University and holds a B.A. in Comparative Literature from the University of North Carolina at Chapel Hill. He can be contacted regarding his proofreading and editing services at **tortuga78@yahoo.com.**

What We Stand for in Fourteen Different Languages

"To learn a language is to have one more window from which to look at the world"
Mandarin proverb

Arabic

In Statu Nascendi يوجد مجلة جديدة لاستعراض الأقران تطمح إلى أن تكون الأصلية الأكاديمية البحوث تشمل العالمي الطراز من علمية منصة نظرية ، الثقافية الدراسات ، السياسية الفلسفة لـدائرة المخصصة السياسي القرار صنع وعملية ، الخارجية السياسة ، الدولية العلاقات وفلسفي ثقافي اجتماعي نهج خلال من محددة قضايا في المجلة وتحقق الأزمات تعقيد حول المدني الوعي من جديد نوع لـرفع وأنـثروبولوجي حيوياً دوراً "الانطلاق مرحلة" تلعب حيث ، والحرب الاستقرار وعدم المعاصرة.

Bulgarian

In Statu Nascendi (Ин Стату Насенди)—е нов академичен журнал, който се стреми да бъде научна платформа от световна класа, включваща оригинални академични изследвания, посветени на политическата философия, културните изследвания, теорията на международните отношения, външната политика и политическия процес на вземане на решения. Журналът изследва конкретни проблеми чрез социално-културен, философски и антропологичен подход за издигане на нов тип гражданска осведоменост относно сложността на съвременните кризи, нестабилност и военни ситуации, където "състоянието на зараждане" (in statu nascendi) играе жизненоважна роля.

Belarusian

In Statu Nascendi—гэта новы часопіс, які рэцэнзуюць эксперты. Мэта часопіса – стаць навуковай пляцоўкай сусветнага ўзроўню. In Statu Nascendi публікуе акадэмічныя даследаванні, прысвечаныя палітычнай філасофіі, культурным пытанням, тэорыі міжнародных адносінаў, замежнай палітыцы і палітычнаму працэсу прыняцця рашэнняў. Задача публікуемых даследаванняў – спрыяць фарміраванню новага тыпу грамадзянскай свядомасці ва ўмовах сучаснага крызісу, нестабільнасці і ваенных сітуацый.

Dutch

In Statu Nascendi is een nieuw wetenschappelijk getoetst tijdschrift dat ernaar streeft een academisch platform van wereldklasse te zijn en te vormen. Het omvat origineel academisch onderzoek met een focus naar politieke filosofie, culturele studies, theorie van internationale betrekkingen, buitenlands beleid en het politieke besluitvormingsproces. Het tijdschrift onderzoekt specifieke kwesties door middel van een sociaal-culturele, filosofische en antropologische benadering om een nieuw type van burgerbewustzijn op te wekken. Aangaande de complexiteit van de hedendaagse crisis, instabiliteit en oorlogssituaties, waarbij het 'stadium van wording' een vitale rol speelt.

French

In Statu Nascendi est un nouveau journal des revues par les pairs qui aspire à devenir une plate-forme scolaire globale. Il englobe des recherches académiques dédiées aux: Philosophie politique, études culturels, théories des relations internationales, politiques étrangères et les procédés des décisions politiques. Le journal étudie des questions particulières, par une approche socio-culturelle, philosophique et anthropologique, afin d'accroître un nouveau type de sensibilisation civique concernant la crise contemporaine ; sa complexité, instabilité et situations de guerre, dont la phase de lancement joue un rôle vital.

German

In Statu Nascendi ist eine neue wissenschaftliche Zeitschrift, die Beiträge der politischen Philosophie, Kulturwissenschaften, Theorie internationaler Beziehungen, Außenpolitik und politischer Entscheidungsprozesse veröffentlicht. Die Artikel werden im Peer-Review-Verfahren geprüft und untersuchen konkrete Themen mithilfe einer soziokulturellen, philosophischen und anthropologischen Herangehensweise. Ziel ist es, zu einem neuen Bürgerbewusstsein über die Komplexität von gegenwärtigen Krisen, Instabilitäten und Kriegssituationen, bei denen die Phase der Entstehung eine wesentliche Rolle spielt, beizutragen.

Greek

Το επιστημονικό περιοδικό **In Statu Nascendi** δημοσιεύει μετά από κρίση πρωτότυπες μελέτες πάνω σε θέματα Πολιτικής Φιλοσοφίας, Κοινωνικών και Πολιτισμικών Σπουδών, Θεωρίες Διεθνών Σχέσεων, Εξωτερικής Πολιτικής, Πολιτικής Διπλωματίας και Ανθρωπολογίας. Το περιοδικό πραγματεύεται κυρίως εξειδικευμένα άρθρα που προσεγγίζουν πτυχές της κοινωνικοπολιτισμικής, φιλοσοφικής και ανθρωπολογικής επιστήμης και έρευνας με σκοπό την διαμόρφωση ορθής πολιτικής και κοινωνικής συνείδησης σχετικά με την πολυπλοκότητα της σύγχρονης 'κρίσης', την αστάθεια και τις εμπόλεμες καταστάσεις που αναδύονται στην σύγχρονη πραγματικότητα, όπου το πλαίσιο του κοινωνικο-πολιτικού γίγνεσθαι χρίζει ιδιαίτερης αναφοράς.

Italian
In Statu Nascendi–è una nuova rivista accademica che aspira a essere una internazionale piattaforma di ricerca dedicata allo studio di tematiche legate alla Filosofia Politica, gli Affari Internazionali, gli Studi Culturali e le diverse Teorie delle Relazioni Internazionali. La rivista analizza tali specificità tematiche attraverso un approccio socio-culturale, filosofico e antropologico per costruir una nuova consapevolezza civile sulle tante complessità della società odierna, della sua instabilità e conflittualità, all'interno della quale nuovi "processi-in-divenire" interagiscono tra loro in modo rilevante

Polish
In Statu Nascendi jest nowym recenzowanym czasopismem akademickim, które aspiruje do światowej klasy platformy naukowej obejmującej oryginalne badania naukowe poświęcone kręgowi zagadnień zwiazanych z filozofią polityczną, kulturoznawstwem, teorią stosunków międzynarodowych, polityką zagraniczną i złożonością współczesnego procesu decyzyjnego. To czasopismo analizuje konkretne zagadnienia za pomocą podejścia społeczno kulturowego, filozoficznego i antropologicznego, w celu podniesienia poziom świadomości obywatelskiej na temat złożoności współczesnych sytuacji kryzysowych, niestabilnosci miedzynarodowej, i wojen w których kluczową rolę odgrywa „etap stawania się".

Russian
In Statu Nascendi–это новый журнал, рецензируемый экспертами, цель которого–стать научной платформой мирового уровня. In Statu Nascendi публикует академические исследования, посвященные политической философии, культурным вопросам, теории международных отношений, зарубежной политике и политическому процессу принятия решений. Задача публикуемых исследований– способствовать формированию нового типа гражданской осознанности в условиях современного кризиса, нестабильности и военных ситуаций.

Spanish

In Statu Nascendi es una nueva revista con revisión paritaria que aspira a convertirse en una plataforma de investigación académica mundial dedicada al campo de la Filosofía Política, Estudios Culturales, teorías de las Relaciones Internacionales, Política Exterior, y procesos de toma de decisión política. Esta revista analiza asuntos de relevancia internacional a través de un enfoque socio-cultural, filosófico y antropológico. Nuestro objetivo es crear un nuevo tipo de conciencia cívica que tenga en cuenta la complejidad de las crisis coetáneas y la problemática de la inestabilidad y la guerra en las que el 'stage-of-becoming' juega un rol crucial.

Turkish

In Statu Nascendi–Siyaset Felsefesi, Kültürel Çalışmalar, Uluslararası İlişkiler Teorisi, Dış Politika ve siyasi Karar verme sürecine adanmış özgün akademik araştırmaları kapsayan dünya çapında bir akademik platform olmayı amaçlayan yeni bir hakemli dergidir. Dergi, "kriz aşamasının" hayati bir rol oynadığı çağdaş kriz, istikrarsızlık ve savaş durumlarının karmaşıklığı hakkında yeni bir sivil farkındalık yaratmak için sosyo-kültürel, felsefi ve antropolojik bir yaklaşımla belirli konuları araştırıyor.

Ukrainian

In Statu Nascendi–це новий рецензований науковий журнал метою якого стати науковою платформою на світовому рівні. Опубліковані академічні вивчення присвячені політичній філософії, культурології, міжнародним відносинам та зарубіжній політиці, і також політичному процесу прийняття питань. Вивчатимуться дослідження соціально-культурними, філософськими та антропологічними підходами та направлені на створення нового виду громадської свідомості в умовах сучасного кризису в світі, нестабільності та військових ситуацій.

Coming up next on *In Statu Nascendi*

Issue 2019:1 comprises, amongst others, the following articles:

- Reconsidering the Notion of Creative Genius in Postmodern Philosophy and Art
- The European Union Democracy Promotion in the Middle East and North Africa (MENA)
- The European Union in the Israeli-Palestinian Conflict: Normative Power Europe and its compatibility with Hamas
- Under which Circumstances can Ukraine Get the Crimean Peninsula back from the Russian Federation?
- Interview with Prof. Maria Dimitrova on Emmanuel Levinas' Philosophy
- Interview with Prof. Marcin Grabowski on the Political Situation in Asia in general and North Korea in particular

ibidem.eu